Home, School, and Community Partnerships

Larry E. Decker and Virginia A. Decker

A SCARECROWEDUCATION BOOK

The Scarecrow Press, Inc.
Lanham, Maryland, and Oxford
2003

A SCARECROWEDUCATION BOOK

Published in the United States of America
by Scarecrow Press, Inc.
A Member of the Rowman & Littlefield Publishing Group
4720 Boston Way, Lanham, Maryland 20706
www.scarecroweducation.com

PO Box 317
Oxford
OX2 9RU, UK

British Library Cataloguing in Publication Information Available

Library of Congress Cataloging-in-Publication Data

Decker, Larry E.
    Home, school, and community partnerships / Larry E. Decker and
Virginia A. Decker.
        p. cm.
"A ScarecrowEducation book."
Includes bibliographical references and index.
    ISBN 0-8108-4521-0 (alk. paper) — ISBN 0-8108-4522-9 (pbk : alk.
paper)   ISBN 978-0-8108-4522-0
    1. Home and school—United States.   2. Community and school—United
States.   I. Decker, Virginia A.   II. Title.
    LC225.3 .D435 2003
    371.19'2—dc21
                                                          2002010774

♾™ The paper used in this publication meets the minimum requirements of
American National Standard for Information Sciences—Permanence of
Paper for Printed Library Materials, ANSI/NISO Z39.48-1992.
Manufactured in the United States of America.

Contents

Preface   v

1 Family and Community Partnerships: Principles
       and Strategies   1

2 Understanding the Community and the Status of
       Families and Youth   9

3 The Essential Role of Communities   27

4 Home and School as Partners   53

5 School–Community Collaboration   99

6 School Public Relations: Bridging the Gap   147

7 Dealing with Political Realities   181

8 School Safety and Crisis Management   207

9 Planning and Evaluating a Comprehensive Home,
       School, and Community Partnership Plan   227

10 Making Friends Before You Need Them   251

Appendix A. Association and Organization
   Contact Information   261

Appendix B. Websites by Major Focus or Content Area   271

Index   279

About the Authors   285

Many Americans worry about what they see as a growing gulf between the American public and its public schools. Troubling trends seem to indicate a fraying relationship among families, schools, and communities:

- About 75 percent of households do not have school-age children and little or no contact with public schools. At the same time, public schools have received little increase in resources—financial and human—to serve a diverse mix of students whose needs are greater than any students who have come before them.
- Faith in public institutions is withering. Many people distrust government and are reluctant to pay taxes to support public institutions, including educational systems that appear to be unsuccessful.
- Growing support for alternatives to public schools, including charter schools and voucher systems, raises questions about Americans' belief in the traditional role of public schools in our democracy and the concept of public education as the glue that binds a diverse society together.

Educational reform has become the topic of many conversations, books, and articles, and it is circulated widely in the media. There is widespread agreement that schools and educational curriculums need to be *fixed,* but there is no agreement on how to do it. For example, listening to the political debate culminating in the passage of the No Child Left Behind Act of 2001, Harkavy and Blank (2002) observe that it is easy to assume that the only things that matter in education are annual testing in grades 3 to 8, having a qualified teacher in the first four years of schools, and allowing parents to move their children out of persistently failing schools. They stress that this perspective is "nonsense" since it completely ignores the fact that "research and experience confirm what common sense suggests: What happens outside the classroom is every bit as important as what happens inside."

Harkavy and Blank are concerned that several significant elements of the reauthorized Elementary and Secondary Education Act are largely ignored by federal lawmakers as well as other leaders and the public at large. These provisions offer a more comprehensive—and realistic—view of what it will take to educate all children to their highest potential. Harkavy and Blank point to the provisions that

- Place a high priority on parental involvement in education.
- Emphasize the need to coordinate and integrate school services with the support and opportunities from federal, state, and local programs serving youth and families.
- Support after-school enrichment opportunities—programs in such areas as violence prevention, service learning, family literacy, mentoring, mental health, and others; and services that go beyond a narrow focus on core academics.
- Urge an expanded role for community-based organizations that are now directly eligible for federal education funds through the 21st Century Community Learning Centers Program and are explicitly encouraged to collaborate with schools.

Despite continued evidence of the community's disenchantment with public education and having to operate in an era of high-stakes accountability, educators across the nation are implementing ideas and strategies—some simple, some complex—that are making a difference, not only in children's lives but in the health and well-being of their schools' communities. They are finding ways to keep *the public* in public education by involving families and communities in the education of children. As Schorr (1997) puts it, "The United States is rich in resources, ideas, and even goodwill. . . . Virtually all the elements that are part of the solution can be identified and described; they are a reality today, somewhere in this country."

In a *60 Minutes* segment, Stahl (2002) focused attention on the Pentagon Schools and the fact that students in schools run by the military score higher than students in civilian-run schools. These schools are succeeding in implementing many of the elements that education reformers suggest are necessary to meet the goal of academic success for all children. She asked the superintendent of these schools what the secret is and, more importantly, if it can be duplicated in the rest of the nation's schools, especially inner-city schools. He emphatically replied, "Yes, it can."

This book is intended to help educators weave together some of the best ideas for creating and sustaining family and community engagement in a comprehensive home, school, and community partnership program tailored to their own communities. It presents ideas and strategies for involving *people*—individually and in agencies, businesses, and organizations—in partnerships with schools; for creating and sustaining programs designed to help meet the diverse needs of a community; for using the varied tools of public relations to reach out to all parts of the community; and for engaging in the politics that are needed to achieve educational objectives.

We remind educators that the goal is to develop, implement, and sustain a comprehensive home, school, and community partnership plan that helps all children succeed academically so that they can live productive lives in healthy communities. This ambitious, optimistic goal has always been a part of the American dream.

REFERENCES

Harkavy, Ira, and Martin Blank (2002). *Community schools.* Retrieved April 19, 2002 from www.educationweek.org/ew/newstory.cfm?slug=31harkavy. h21.

Schorr, L. B. (1997) *Common Purpose: Strengthening Families and Neighborhoods to Rebuild America.* New York: Anchor Books, Doubleday.

Stahl, L. Pentagon Schools. Aired April 21, 2002 by CBS on *60 Minutes.*

CHAPTER 1

Family and Community Partnerships: Principles and Strategies

Educators have been blamed for falling test scores, increased school violence, rising dropout rates, a shortage of good teachers, and a lack of basic skills in too many public school graduates. This crisis in confidence, which began in the 1990s, has been more painful and prolonged than the one that followed the Soviet launch of *Sputnik* in 1957.

Almost every American agrees that the United States needs strong schools, literate and law-abiding citizens, and competitive workers for the global economy, the goal of improving public schools is as controversial as apple pie. Designing an effective curriculum is complicated by limitations on local resources and qualified personnel, and by legislative mandates. Most educational experts agree that effective responses require cooperation among the schools themselves and the communities they serve. What is needed is a comprehensive plan for a cooperative venture in which home, school, and community work together to improve public education.

MAKING THE DECISION

Historically, family and community are the pillars of public education as it has evolved in the United States. The responsibility of schools has been to transmit the knowledge that prepares children to assume places in their communities as productive workers and responsible citizens. In turn, families and communities supply the financial, moral, and practical support that enables schools to fulfill their mission. In the last decade, nevertheless, economic pressure, attention to educational concerns, increasing acceptance of the goals of lifelong learning, community involvement, and multisector cooperation have created a new environment in which to view home, school, and community partnerships.

Most educators agree that it is time to abandon adversarial relationships and accept responsibility for addressing community needs and concerns. Consequently, almost every public school system in America has developed activities and programs intended to increase home, school, and community cooperation.

Developing this cooperation has not been an easy process for many educators. Some are reluctant to share power or delegate certain responsibilities. Others focus on the loss of control that accompanies shared decision making rather than on the benefits that stem from community input and advice. Most educators realize that inviting broad-based community participation in planning and decision making and broadening the traditional role of the school in the life of the community are likely to increase conflict. They know that encouraging collaboration in order to use community resources efficiently and coordinate service delivery will raise community expectations.

Educators who are serious about improving public education must weigh possible problems against possible benefits. In an increasing number of schools and school districts, educators, administrators, and teachers have decided that the potential benefits far outweigh any potential problems. They have seen that a comprehensive home, school, and community partnership plan increases student achievement and results in greater academic accountability, better attendance rates, and improved school climate. Other important benefits include an enhanced quality of community life; greater community support, including more resources for educational programs; more positive interaction among diverse groups; and an improved atmosphere for communication within the community.

RESPONDING TO THE CHALLENGE

When the goal of creating a cooperative venture is used to guide home, school, and community partnership efforts, public schools are operated with a commitment to the idea that they belong to the community. Professional educators and staff receive training to increase their skills in enlisting family and community support. School curricula are designed to incorporate a variety of relationships and activities that involve schools, families, students, community members, businesses and industry, and local organizations and agencies.

Making the decision to create a cooperative relationship necessitates some change in the roles of school administrators and teachers. School administrators must change some practices that have become commonplace and must work conscientiously to create a productive team of staff, parents, students, and other stakeholders. Dwyer (1998) suggests that administrators

- Work side-by-side with teachers and staff in the training and development needed to make the necessary changes.
- Empower teachers by including them in designing curricula and in the decision-making process, including the allocation of financial resources.
- Maintain an open-door policy for students, teachers, and community members, including rescheduling some traditional meeting times.
- State expectations for cooperation among and between teachers and staff.
- Confront disengaged teachers and empower staff to intervene in their peers' difficulties when appropriate.
- Support teachers and staff willing to take the risks associated with change.
- Provide strong leadership in areas that emphasize community values.
- Reward efforts to increase cooperative working relationships in meaningful ways, such as providing release time, recognition, space, materials, and funds.

Dwyer also points out important changes in the teaching role that may be uncomfortable for some teachers—becoming more of a guide rather than an authority in content areas, for example, and questioning the effectiveness of their own teaching practices. He suggests that teachers

- Treat students, as well as other teachers and parents, as peers in community-building efforts.
- Enact classroom policies that reflect an understanding of children's needs and a willingness to share power.
- Design curricula that are both relevant to the lives and needs of students and meet state requirements.
- Convey to students the importance and the value of knowledge and foster joy in learning, especially if students' cultural environments promote negative attitudes toward education.

FAMILY–COMMUNITY PARTNERSHIP STRATEGIES

The ultimate goal of a comprehensive home, school, and community partnership plan is the creation of a responsive support system for collaborative action to address educational concerns, quality-of-life issues of community members, and specialized needs. The following strategies provide a framework for developing such a cooperative venture.

Strategy 1: Encourage increased use of community resources and volunteers to augment educational curricula. Every community has human, physical, and financial resources that can be used to enrich and expand traditional educational programs. Community resources such as volunteers have developed programs and expanded curricular options, including volunteer programs, field and study trips, peer tutoring, student-based enterprises, and experiential learning.

Strategy 2: Develop educational partnerships between schools and public and private service providers, business and industry, and civic and social service organizations. Complex and interrelated social and economic problems create a broad array of service needs in many communities, and meeting them effectively requires more resources than any single agency or organization can provide. This strategy encourages the development of educational partnerships that cooperate in the use of available resources, avoiding unnecessary duplication. Such partnerships might focus on child care and latchkey programs, drug education and substance abuse efforts, intensive programs to address literacy and academic competencies, assistance to at-risk youth and minorities, community economic development, internships and work-study programs, and career awareness.

Strategy 3: Use public education facilities as community service centers for meeting the educational, social, health, cultural, and recreational needs of all ages and sectors of the community. The fact that community attitudes and support affect the schools' ability to carry out their mission to educate all children necessitates that educators consider the needs and the concerns of nonparents. This strategy encourages opening school buildings on a planned, organized basis at hours beyond the regular school day. It takes advantage of the strong support community centers generally receive, as well as the economic benefits of more efficient use.

Strategy 4: Develop an environment that fosters lifelong learning. This strategy advocates the promotion of learning as a lifelong process. It recognizes that learning often takes place without formal instruction, both inside and outside the school setting. It encourages the development of lifelong educational programs to meet learning needs that change over a lifetime, including the need for acquiring new skills and knowledge. Possible programs and activities include early childhood education, extended-day and enrichment programs for school-age children, adult education, vocational training and retraining programs, leisure-time activities, and intergenerational programs.

Strategy 5: Establish community-involvement processes in educational planning and decision making. The total community has a responsibility in the mission of educating all of its members. Community members, therefore, have a right and a duty to participate in determining community needs, deciding priorities, and selecting the most appropriate allocation of resources. This cyclical process, concerned with evaluation and change as well as initial planning, takes advantage of a basic fact of human behavior: individuals who participate in planning and decision making develop feelings of ownership in the outcome. Encouraging broad-based involvement capitalizes on another principle: in general, the greater the number and diversity of people involved in planning, development, implementation, and evaluation of educational opportunities, the greater the likelihood that needs will be met and that support for education will be developed and maintained. Opportunities for involvement range from participation in ongoing community advisory councils to membership on ad hoc advisory task forces and special study committees.

Strategy 6: Provide a responsive, community-based support system for collective action among all educational and community agencies to address both community quality-of-life issues and special needs. This strategy recognizes the complexity of many problems and underscores the fact that their resolution may require cooperative use of resources. Seeking the involvement of other agencies can help schools address such social, health, educational, and economic issues as drug and substance abuse, housing, public safety and crime prevention, at-risk youth, violence and vandalism, teen pregnancy, and racial and minority concerns.

Strategy 7: Develop a system that facilitates home, school, and community communication. Research shows that schools that involve all of their publics and keep them informed have community support; those that fail to reach beyond parents do not. Effective home, school, and community communications go beyond news releases, speeches, newsletters, and open houses to include use of the media, home visitation by teachers and administrators, meet-the-community programs, school displays in the community, and programs conducted away from the school site.

These seven strategies have overlapping characteristics and functions. Taken together, they form the outline of an action plan.

CREATING A COMPREHENSIVE HOME, SCHOOL, AND COMMUNITY PARTNERSHIP PLAN

Creating a truly comprehensive perspective involves planning, experimenting, learning, communicating, revising, assessing, and trying again. In a comprehensive home, school, and community partnership plan, schools are no longer isolated providers of a single component—education for children and youth—but active collaborators in a broader effort. In a collaborative effort, the U.S. Department of Education and the Regional Educational Laboratory Network (2002) examined the role schools play in comprehensive home, school, and community partnership strategies.

> As partners, schools have increased cooperation, communication, and interaction with parents, community groups, service providers and agencies, local policymakers and other stakeholders. School staff share their knowledge and experience with the community beyond the schoolhouse walls—and return with fresh inspiration to guide policies and practices within the school.

In *Putting the Pieces Together* (U.S. Department, 2002), a guide to creating comprehensive school-linked strategies, the agencies explain that within these partnerships

- All partners begin to view children as members of families and communities, not as isolated individuals. For school staff, understanding the context in which children live helps teachers select the most appropriate methods to improve students' learning and achievement.
- By participating in preventive, capacity-building strategies, such as early childhood and family support programs, schools and their partners can play a major role in building the strength and resiliency among students, families, and communities.
- Instead of focusing only on short-term results—test scores, attendance rates, and disciplinary incidents—school staff can link with partner agencies to help families accomplish lifelong learning objectives, including adult literacy and job training.

The guide emphasizes, "As schools incorporate these ideas into their daily work, all types of staff will collaborate in developing goals, evaluating program effectiveness, representing the school as a community partner, and developing successful strategies for working with [families] and community."

The chapters that follow address various aspects of a comprehensive home, school, and community partnership plan. They present rationale for addressing particular areas; relevant research; suggested considerations, examples, and tips; and a list of references and websites for more information.

REFERENCES

Dwyer, M. D. (1998). *Strengthening community in education: A handbook for change*. Retrieved January 7, 2002, from www.newmaine.com/community/index.

U.S. Department of Education and the Regional Educational Laboratory Network. (2002). *Putting the pieces together: Comprehensive school-linked strategies for children and families*. Retrieved September 7, 2002, from www.ncrel.org/sdrs/areas/issues/envrnmnt/css/ppt/putting.htm.

CHAPTER 2

Understanding the Community and the Status of Families and Youth

What happens in a school affects the community, and what happens in the community affects the school. If teachers and school administrators expect to be successful in their primary mission of educating the community's children, they need to know a great deal about the community and the families from which the children come.

That proposition is not as simple as it sounds. For one thing, no two communities are exactly alike. For another, communities influence schools in different ways. Finally, both communities and families are constantly changing in a variety of ways, some of them highly gratifying and others thoroughly discouraging.

The urge for a quick fix is sometimes irresistible. In search of easy answers to complex problems, some school critics have been willing to overlook a single undeniable fact: educational problems reflect community and family problems in all their complexity, diversity, and intractability. Even a brief examination of the demographics of American society at the beginning of the twenty-first century shows the enormity of the challenges schools face.

A DEFINITION OF COMMUNITY

How does a school define its community? A generation ago, the answer was relatively easy. A community is "a population aggregate, inhabiting a contiguous delimitable area, and having a set of basic service institutions; it is conscious of its local unity" (Seay and Crawford, 1954). Today this definition would likely apply to only small schools in rural areas.

Neff (1999) proposes a definition and a way of looking at the characteristics of a community that may be helpful to educators. He suggests that a community does not have to be a specific geographic location and does not have to provide for the daily needs of community members. Rather, a community's "main function is to mediate between the individual and society and . . . people could relate to their societies through both geographic and nongeographic substructures or communities." Neff adds that five characteristics are necessary for a community to mediate between an individual and society:

1. *Size of Community.* It must be both small enough to give people a sense of community and large enough to help them feel they are part of the larger social structure.
2. *Focus on Institution.* It must focus on a key institutional setting and on an area of central importance to culture so that it conveys to members a sense of significant incorporation in society via membership in the organization.
3. *Stability of Community.* It must have relative stability without too much turnover and must be able to convey a sense of community or relay a community's feelings about its own significance.
4. *Social Structure.* It must have some concrete social structure, more than a community of interest, and people must be able to interact and identify with each other.
5. *Significant Interaction.* Significant primary (face-to-face) and secondary (mass media) communication must be intertwined in the community, and there must be feelings of congeniality and an opportunity for community members to participate in social processes.

In *Strengthening Community in Education*, Dwyer (1998) defines community as "a group of people who are socially independent, who participate together in discussion and decision making, and who share certain practices that both define community and are nurtured by it." He points out that within a community there are "generally accepted rules and social norms that protect, respect and please members of the community" and that a "true community requires its participants to engage in the working of a society consensually." Dwyer points out that membership within a community is about meeting basic needs; each need is intertwined with the purpose of the community.

THE SCHOOL COMMUNITY

Just as educators need to understand the community from which students come, they must also examine the community that exists within a school. As Belenardo (2001) emphasizes:

> It is often forgotten that student effort—as well as teacher and parent effort—may depend greatly on the underlying climate and culture of the school. When parents, teachers, and students all feel surrounded by a caring and supportive school environment, they are more likely to respond favorably to schoolwide challenges such as the pressure for students to perform well on tests.

Belenardo also points out that even in much of the rhetoric on the importance of a sense of community in schools, a clear understanding of the organizational elements that contribute to its existence does not exist. She gathers research to help define elements that indicate whether a sense of community is present or absent in a school. She identified the following six elements, which provide a comprehensive framework for measuring the presence and strength of community in schools. The combination and integration of the elements defines the strength of a school's sense of community.

Shared values. A cohesive, reinforcing school program is built on a core of common beliefs and expectations. These shared values underlie the school's vision and provide uniform direction for the development of the instructional program and behavioral expectations. Indicators of shared values include agreements on instructional expectations and practices, the enforcement of schoolwide discipline standards, high academic standards for all students, and explicit achievement goals.

Commitment. Commitment is evidenced by a willingness to go beyond the expected participation. The commitment level of members is demonstrated by behaviors and actions that support the group's shared values and beliefs.

A feeling of belonging. There is a shared emotional connection that provides participants with a sense of being part of something that has a past, present, and future. This feeling of belonging is created by school programs that recognize the positive performance and contributions of individual members; that hold a common agenda of activities and similar experiences that link students, families, teachers, and administrators to the school's traditions; and that accept all members into the group regardless of their individual differences.

Caring. Caring connects members of the group and results in mutual respect, support, and interest. A feeling of cooperation, rather than competition, is demonstrated through the willingness of adults—educators, families, and community members—to help each other as well as students.

Interdependence. A recognized interrelationship exists among individuals, as well as an understanding that all actions occur in relation to others rather than in isolation. Cooperative interaction results in ongoing, mutually beneficial skill development and contributes to the collegiality of the school.

Regular contact. Importance is placed on providing opportunities for all members to meet and communicate. There are regularly scheduled activities that provide ample opportunities for members to interact with one another, develop relationships, and celebrate their membership in the organization. Established procedures ensure that all members are kept informed of school programs and activities.

To be effective, educators must develop an understanding of the demographic and socioeconomic conditions that exist in the communities in which they work. They also need to examine the strength of the sense of community within the school. Only then can they define their own roles in building the kind of healthy community—in the school and in the larger community—in which learning is valued by all.

HEALTHY COMMUNITIES

What is a healthy community? Dwyer suggests that examining the way a community provides for individuals' basic needs can give an understanding of what constitutes a healthy community. In an ideal community, basic needs are purposefully and assertively met; this contributes to the functionality of the community itself. Dwyer acknowledges disagreement over what constitutes basic needs but suggests general agreement on most of the following:

Security. The essence of security lies in building networks of trust through honest and sustained relationships. A community can establish shared values and social norms that resist actions and circumstances that might harm its members. It can provide security through the very basic assurance of support; individual members notice others' needs and provide assistance when possible.

Adventure. The need for adventure manifests itself in a desire for new experiences, drama in one's life, and a sense of anticipation and hope for the future. A healthy community allows new ideas, encourages exploration of interests, allows members to make changes in the course of their lives, and nurtures the need for adventure as a way to create a stronger sense of self-confidence and optimism.

Freedom. The need for freedom involves having and making choices and being in control of one's own destiny. A healthy community shares ideals and principles but does not demand uniformity of experiences, interpretations, and choices. The community is, by design, willing to change in response to innovation and the beliefs of its members.

Exchange. The need for exchange is the desire to share information, love, concern, praise, encouragement, and ideas between caring parties. A healthy community encourages cooperation and respect and policies that support exchange.

Power. This need involves *power to*, not *power over*. A healthy community provides its members with a real sense that their actions and decisions affect the common good; the community as a whole is authentically reliant on the contributions of individuals.

Expansion/creation. This is the need to build, add, create, and grow. A healthy community provides a supportive atmosphere in which individuals have room to shape their lives and the direction of the community and are, in turn, strengthened by the skills and achievements of community members.

Acceptance. The need for acceptance has as much to do with accepting others and our own changing circumstances as it does with the need to belong. A healthy community offers an atmosphere that promotes empathy, forgiveness, understanding, tolerance, and encouragement among its residents.

Expression. Individuals need to have their presence and their contributions seen, heard, and felt by others. A healthy community encourages various forms of articulation and provides forums that encourage and accept expression.

Why are some communities more effective than others in dealing with their problems? Mathews (Decker and Boo, 2001), president of the Charles F. Kettering Foundation, says that Foundation studies have identified *shared knowledge* as the key to effective communities. Effective communities are well educated as a whole, meaning they are good at educating the entire community about their collective business. An effective community appears to have more than just facts: it knows what the facts mean in the lives of the people who make up the community. What an effective community knows is not just personal knowledge, it is shared knowledge, and it also makes a distinction between "government officials" and "public leaders." Mathews believes that one of the most important things leadership organizations can do to increase the effectiveness of their communities is develop leadership that is truly public and representative of the total community.

Another approach to examining the health of a community is measuring its competence. Rotenberg (1986) says that a competent community

- Collaborates on identifying problems and needs.
- Actively seeks diverse input.
- Establishes consensus on goals and priorities.
- Agrees on strategies for meeting agreed-upon goals.

- Has strong psychological identification.
- Allows individuals to play significant roles.
- Has a record of positive results.
- Has members with effective communication skills.
- Uses outside expertise effectively while retaining community control and direction.

To determine whether a community is healthy or not requires an understanding of the various parts of the community that make up the whole. According to Decker and Decker (2001), educators need the following types of information about a community in order to work effectively within it:

- Population data and characteristics
- Customs and traditions
- Characteristics and organization of the political system and the power brokers (both formal and informal)
- Communication channels
- Significant community groups and organizations
- Economic conditions
- Patterns of employment and unemployment
- Social structures, tensions, and problems that affect the learner and the school
- Community resources and services
- School–community relationships
- Geographic strengths and weaknesses

DEMOGRAPHICS AND SOCIOECONOMIC VARIABLES

One way to begin to understand a community is to look at the trends and the issues that will have an impact on it over time. For example

- What do *majority* and *minority* mean? This is a socioeconomic as well as a racial question.
- Approximately one-third of all children in the United States are economically disadvantaged.

- The support base for education is eroding:
  - Less than 25 percent of U.S. households have school-aged children.
  - American society is aging—the first baby boomers are now over the age of sixty.
- Educational systems must make proactive efforts to connect community with school.
- Potential exists for intergenerational conflict:
  - In 1940 there were seventeen workers for every Social Security recipient.
  - In 1990 there were three workers for every Social Security recipient.
  - In 2000 there were two workers for every Social Security recipient.
- More coordinated social services are needed, and schools are being expected to fill voids.
- Growing numbers of working women mean a growing need for comprehensive child-care services.
- Acknowledgment that public education is a right and a responsibility of all citizens requires a broad definition of education.

Hodgkinson (1992) examines these and other trends and issues and poses thought-provoking questions:

- In 2010, four states (New York, Texas, California, and Florida) will have about one-third of the nation's youth; more than *half* will be minority. The real minority will be non-Hispanic, white youth in these key states. What will we call minorities when they constitute more than half the population? How will these states interact with Maine, which will have only 3 percent minority youth in 2010?
- In the 1960s, housing moved to the suburbs. In the 1980s, so did everything else: jobs, churches, colleges, movies, and shopping. How will cities survive if success is defined as moving to a suburb? What will bring middle-income people back to the cities? Many urban problems, such as crime, drugs, poverty, and violence, will continue to spread to the suburbs. What is the best way to govern a metro area that includes both cities and their now-dominant suburbs?

- About 82 percent of all children have working mothers. Business and government must respond to the rapidly increasing demand for child care.
- About 60 percent of all children will spend some time with a single parent before reaching age eighteen, making the single-parent family the new "typical" American family.
- The U.S. population is aging rapidly. There will be 65 million people over the age of sixty-five by 2020. Many will have one year of retirement for every year of work. Children under age eighteen (34 percent of our total population in 1970) were 25 percent of the population in 2000. Yet, even as children become increasingly scarce, as many as 30 percent are at serious risk of failure in school and in life.
- As more African Americans, Hispanics, and Asians move into the middle class, many formerly racial problems become issues of race and class. The single factor that holds most children back is poverty, regardless of race.
- The U.S. population increased 10 percent between 1980 and 1990; the prison population by 139 percent. Prisoners cost taxpayers more than $20,000 per individual annually; 80 percent of prisoners are high school dropouts. The United States now leads the world in the percentage of its population behind bars. One prisoner consumes about the same amount of public money as six children in Head Start programs.
- The middle of our society is declining, while the numbers of rich and poor are increasing. We are creating two workforces: one in minimum-wage jobs; the other in well-paying jobs. For every new job created for a computer programmer, eight new jobs are created for food-service workers. This is leading to an information-rich and information-poor split in our society.
- Instead of worrying about the test scores of U.S. students compared to those of Asian students, we should be concerned about the scores of U.S. inner-city students compared to those of suburban students.

THE STATUS OF CHILDREN AND FAMILIES IN AMERICA

By one estimate, less than 6 percent of U.S. families fit the traditional image of working father, homemaker mother, and two children. Alarming statistics go along with this change in the U.S. family:

- In 1990, there were 6.6 million single-parent households headed by a female, an increase of 21.2 percent from 1980. There were about 1.2 million single-parent households headed by a male, an increase of 87.2 percent from 1980 (U.S. Census Bureau, 1991).
- In 1990, 75 percent of mothers in the labor force had children aged 6 to 17; 60 percent had children under 6 (Children's Defense Fund, 2001).
- From 1975 to 1996, single-parent families increased from 17 percent to 29 percent of all families (Annie E. Casey Foundation, 1997).
- The number of children living with relatives with no parent in the home grew 75 percent in the first half of the 1990s. The number of children living with grandparents and without a parent increased 66 percent in the same period (Children's Defense Fund, 1997).
- Among children who live in single-parent families, 63 percent who have unmarried mothers live in poverty; 34 percent with a divorced mother live in poverty. About 11 percent of children who live with both parents are in poverty (*U.S. News & World Report*, 1992).
- Children in single-parent families are more likely to be suspended or expelled from school (17 percent with unmarried mothers, 11 percent with divorced mothers, and 5 percent with both parents); repeat a grade in school (33 percent with unmarried mothers, 23 percent with divorced mothers, and 13 percent with both parents); and be on welfare for more than 10 years (39 percent with unmarried mothers and 14 percent with divorced mothers) (*U.S. News & World Report*, 1992).
- Of children in juvenile correctional facilities, 56 percent had lived with one parent, 28 percent with both parents (*U.S. News & World Report*, 1992).
- About 25 percent of children younger than six live in poverty; the rate rises to 27 percent for children younger than three (Children's Defense Fund, 1994).
- Some estimates place the number of children born in the U.S. each year with fetal alcohol syndrome at 12,000 (Institute of Medicine, 1995).

In *Years of Promise*, the Carnegie Corporation (1996) reported:

- One in five American children (14.7 million) lives in poverty.
- During 1995, fewer than half of all three- to five-year-olds with annual family incomes of $40,000 or less were enrolled in preschool, compared to 82 percent from families with incomes of more than $75,000.
- Fewer than half of eligible low-income three- and four-year-olds receive Head Start services. No more than one in six three- to five-year-olds of all income levels attends a child care center that can be considered high quality.

In their 2001 report, *State of America's Children Yearbook,* Children's Defense Fund (CDF)* reported these sobering facts about children in America:

1 in 2 will live with a single parent at some point in childhood
1 in 3 is born to unmarried parents
1 in 3 will be poor at some point in their childhood
1 in 3 is behind a year or more in school
1 in 4 lives with only one parent
2 in 5 never complete a single year of college
1 in 5 is born poor
1 in 5 is born to a mother who did not graduate from high school
1 in 5 has a foreign-born mother
3 in 5 preschoolers have their mothers in the labor force
1 in 6 is poor now
1 in 6 is born to a mother who did not receive prenatal care in the first three months of pregnancy
1 in 7 has no health insurance
1 in 7 has a worker in the family but is still poor
1 in 8 lives in a family receiving food stamps
1 in 8 is born to a teen mother
1 in 8 never graduates from high school
1 in 12 has a disability
1 in 13 was born with low birth weight

*CDF updates the website data for national, state, and key facts on an annual basis. *See* www.childrensdefense.org.

1 in 15 lives at less than half the poverty level
1 in 24 lives with neither parent
1 in 26 is born to a mother who received late or no prenatal care
1 in 60 sees his parents divorce in any given year
1 in 139 will die before his first birthday
1 in 1,056 will be killed by a gun before age 20

In their 2001 report, *Every Day in America,* Children's Defense Fund translated many of these same statistics into a profile. Every day in America, CDF says:

3 young people under age twenty-five die from HIV infection
6 children and youth under twenty commit suicide
10 children and youth under twenty are homicide victims
10 children and youth under twenty die from firearms
34 children and youth under twenty die from accidents
78 babies die
156 babies are born at very low birth weight (less than three pounds, four ounces)
186 children are arrested for violent crimes
410 babies are born to mothers who had late or no prenatal care
817 babies are born at low birth weight (less than five pounds, eight ounces)
1,310 babies are born without health insurance
1,354 babies are born to teen mothers
1,951 babies are born into poverty
2,324 babies are born to mothers who are not high school graduates
2,911 high school students drop out.*
3,544 babies are born to unmarried mothers.
4,342 children are arrested.
17,297 students are suspended from school.*

Each year since 1990, the Annie E. Casey Foundation has presented in its *Kids Count Data Book* a broad array of data intended to illuminate the status of America's children and assess their well-

*Based on calculations per school day (180 days of seven hours each).

being. *Kids Count* provides ongoing benchmarks against which to evaluate efforts to improve the lives of children. As the Foundation explains, the ten measures used do not capture the full range of conditions that shape children's lives, but do reflect a wide range of factors that affect their well-being and experiences across a range of developmental stages from birth through early adulthood. Since the data are consistent across states and over time, legitimate comparisons are possible.

In addition, each year the *Kids Count Overview* focuses on a particular topic and the implications of the relevant data. The 1993 report from the Annie E. Casey Foundation featured a "Vulnerable Family Index," identifying the three factors that put children at risk from birth: (1) the mother was under twenty when she had her first baby, (2) the mother had not completed high school when her first child was born, and (3) the parents of the first baby were not married.

The 1995 *Kids Count Overview*, "Fathers and Families," showed that in 1994, 24 percent of American children lived in mother-only families; factoring in the divorce rate, researchers estimated that before they grow up, more than half of today's children are likely to spend some of their childhood in a single-parent home. The report outlined the implications of these numbers. Children in father-absent families are five times more likely to be poor and about ten times more likely to be extremely poor. By definition, they are likely to have less parental time and supervision. Children of single mothers are twice as likely to drop out of high school and significantly more likely to end up in foster or group care and in juvenile justice facilities. Girls from single-parent families have a threefold greater risk of bearing children as unwed teenagers. Boys whose fathers are absent face a much higher probability of growing up unemployed, incarcerated, and uninvolved with their own children. The report also noted the growing body of research emphasizing the important role father involvement can play in the positive cognitive, emotional, and social development of both sons and daughters.

The 1996 report, "Child Poverty and the Working Poor," stated:

Although many factors put children at risk, nothing predicts bad outcomes for a kid more powerfully than growing up poor. . . . Today fully one-quarter of the nation's population under age 6 lives in poverty. Taken together, these numbers add up to a U.S. child poverty rate that is among the highest in the developed world—a distinction that threatens not only the future for many of our kids, but also the future competitiveness of our nation in a global economy.

The 1997 *Kids Count Overview* focused on success in school. It indicated that improving the odds for children in low-income communities requires greater employment opportunities for parents, higher-quality health care, formal and informal networks of adults who can assist in times of crisis, vibrant religious and social institutions, organized recreation, and safer streets. It also emphasized that "of all the community institutions that help children become capable adults, perhaps none is more important than school." The report continued:

Specifically, we can point to four ideas that have demonstrated that they can positively contribute to kids' success in school and overall development:

- preschool experiences that prepare children to learn;
- schools that are small enough to engage every child;
- high standards in curriculum, instruction, and assessment; and
- strong, meaningful family participation; making education part of a larger community commitment to healthy youth and family development.

The 1999 report focused on the number of youth that are growing up "outside the continuing economic boom, hampered by extraordinarily difficult family conditions that are likely to rob them of their chances of success as adults."

The futures of 9.2 million American children—one in seven—are at serious risk due to a combination of four or more chronic family conditions. These factors include growing up in a single parent home, having parents with low educational attainment, living in poverty, having parents who are not in the work force, being dependent on welfare, and lacking health insurance.

The Casey Foundation uses a threshold of four or more family risk factors to locate the children who are at the highest risk of failure. Some of the 1999 *Kids Count* report key findings are:

- Some 26 percent of kids with four or more family risk factors were high school dropouts in 1998, compared to only 1 percent of kids with none of the risks.
- 16 percent of high-risk females ages fifteen to nineteen were teenage mothers, compared to only one-tenth of 1 percent of those with none of the risks. Nationally, 25 percent of high-risk kids are in rural areas, 44 percent in central cities, and 31 percent in suburbs.
- About one-third of identifiable high-risk kids, or about 3 million, live in poor central-city neighborhoods.
- Nearly 30 percent of all Black children and nearly 25 percent of all Hispanic children are in the high-risk category, compared to only 6 percent of white children.

The 1999 report emphasizes that of the many complex variables that shape children's futures, none is more important in determining a child's chances in life than the contribution parents are able to make. The report adds, "combined disadvantages tend to be mutually reinforcing" and "community conditions can also be powerful subverters of family strength. . . . High levels of crime and violence and concentrated poverty severely undermine family life and make it all the more difficult to change circumstances."

The press release for the 2001 *Kids Count* report had the headline, "Promising Progress Yet Troubling Trends Face Kids in the New Millennium." Findings show that over the last decade, the well-being of kids improved on seven of ten key *Kids Count* measures. Among the improvements were decreases in the infant mortality rate, the child and teen death rates, and the high school dropout rate. The child poverty rate fell to 16.9 percent in 2000 from a decade high of 22.7 percent in 1993. There has also been a steady decline in the rate of teenage births—a drop from 37 per 1,000 teens in 1990 to 30 per 1,000 teens in 1998. However, there were increases in the rate of low-weight births and the percentage of children living in single-parent families. Statistics also showed that more than 16 million children have parents who, despite being employed all year, fall into the category of working-poor families who continue to be trapped in a cycle of hardship.

The 2001 *Kids Count* report called attention to the dramatic growth in the number of children under age eighteen (up to more than 72 million), due in large part to immigration. Focusing on the progress and prospects for the nation's young people, the press release quoted Nelson, president of the Annie E. Casey Foundation:

> Based on the nation's experience with the baby boom of the 1950s, it's clear that this recent rise in America's under-18 population will put heavy new demands on our already struggling public education, child care, and family support systems. If we are going to sustain the recent progress we've seen in conditions affecting kids in the U.S., we will have to do far more to keep pace with the needs of this larger and more diverse generation of American children. . . . The first decade of this millennium will be pivotal. Our policy and investment decisions for families in the next few years will determine whether we'll build on the progress of the nineties or see important gains eroded.

THE POTENTIAL

Research shows that all children are born ready and willing to learn. The Carnegie Corporation (1996) poignantly describes the potential of children:

> By age three or four, children have the ability to make daring cognitive leaps, to negotiate the slippery slopes of peer relationships, and to manage the emotional ups and downs that are part of everyday life. If all of us could see their agile minds as easily as we observe their physical agility, perhaps more Americans would believe that every one of these children can learn to levels that surpass any expectations that we might have for them. If we as a nation commit ourselves to their success, if we keep their promise, these children will astonish us.

The sobering reality is that we, as a nation, are not keeping their promise. Children's Defense Fund (2002) points out:

> Equal educational opportunity is a myth in millennial America. The richest school districts spend 56 percent more per student than do the poorest. While expenditures are not the sole determinant of educational success, this gaping chasm effectively denies a Head Start to millions of children who happen to live in lower-income school districts. Overall, America's children are not being educated to the high levels they have a right to expect.

The challenge to educators is not to divide up responsibilities, but reconceptualize the role of schools and their relationship to home, community, and the larger society. The key to building an effective relationship is mutual respect. Developing respect may take work on all sides.

REFERENCES

Annie E. Casey Foundation. (1993). *Kids count data book.* Washington, D.C.: Center for the Study of Social Policy.

Annie E. Casey Foundation. (1995). *Kids count data book.* Washington, D.C.: Center for the Study of Social Policy.

Annie E. Casey Foundation. (1996). *Kids count data book.* Washington, D.C.: Center for the Study of Social Policy.

Annie E. Casey Foundation. (1997). *Kids count data book.* Washington, D.C.: Center for the Study of Social Policy.

Annie E. Casey Foundation. (1999). *Kids count data book.* Washington, D.C.: Center for the Study of Social Policy.

Annie E. Casey Foundation. (2001). *Kids count data book.* Washington, D.C.: Center for the Study of Social Policy.

Annie E. Casey Foundation. (2001). Promising progress yet troubling trends face kids in the new millennium. Retrieved January 7, 2002, from www.aecf.org/kidscount/kc2001/kc2001_press.

Belenardo, S. J. (2001). Practices and conditions that lead to a sense of community in middle schools, *National Association of Secondary School Principals Bulletin,* 85, 627.

Carnegie Corporation. (1996). *Years of promise.* New York: Carnegie Corporation.

Children's Defense Fund. (1992). *Falling by the wayside: Children in rural America.* Washington, D.C.

Children's Defense Fund. (1994). *Wasting America's future: Cost of child poverty.* Washington, D.C.

Children's Defense Fund. (1997). *Poverty Matters: The cost of poverty in America.* Washington, D.C.

Children's Defense Fund. (2001). *Every day in America.* Retrieved September 7, 2002, from www.childrensdefense.org/everyday.htm.

Children's Defense Fund. (2001). *The state of America's children yearbook 2001.* Retrieved September 7, 2002, from www.childrensdefense.org/keyfacts.htm.

Children's Defense Fund. (2002). *Key facts about education.* Retrieved September 7, 2002, from www.childrensdefense.org/keyfacts_education.htm.

Decker, L. E., and Boo, M. R. (2000). *Community schools: serving children, families and communities*. Fairfax, Va.: National Community Education Association.

Decker, L. E., and Decker, V. A. (2001). *Engaging families and communities: Pathways to educational success*. Fairfax, Va.: National Community Education Association.

Dwyer, M. D. (1998). *Strengthening community in education: A handbook for change*. Retrieved January 7, 2002, from www.newmaine.com/community/index.

Hodgkinson, H. (1992). *A demographic look at tomorrow*. Washington, D.C.: Institute for Educational Leadership.

Institute of Medicine, Study Committee. (1995). *Fetal alcohol syndrome: Diagnosis, epidemiology report*. Washington, D.C.: Institute of Medicine.

Mathews, D. (2001). In Decker, L. E., and Boo, M. R., *Community schools: Serving children, families, and communities*. Fairfax, Va.: National Community Education Association.

Neff, M. (1999). *Community*. Retrieved March 5, 2000, from www.coe.ufl.edu/courses/EdTech/Vault/Folk/Rubin.htm.

Rotenberg, R. L. (1986). Community analysis techniques: An anthropologist's perspective. In J. J. Lane (Ed.), *Marketing techniques for school districts*. Reston, Va.: Association of School Business Officials International.

Seay, M. F., and Crawford, F. N. (1954). *The community school and community self-improvement*. Lansing, Mich.: Department of Public Instruction.

U.S. Census Bureau. (1991). *Current population survey: Household and family characteristics*. Washington, D.C.: U.S. Government Printing Office.

U.S. News & World Report. (1992). The war over family values. (June 8).

WEBSITES FOR MORE INFORMATION AND LINKS TO OTHER RELEVANT SITES

Annie E. Casey Foundation, www.aecf.org

Carnegie Corporation, www.carnegie.org

Child Trends, www.childtrends.org

Children's Defense Fund, www.childrensdefense.org

Children, Youth and Family Consortium, www.cyfc.umn.edu

Education Week on the Web, www.edweek.org

Kids Count Data Online, www.aecf.org/kidscount

National Center for Education Statistics, NCES.ed.gov

The State of the States, www.edweek.org/reports/qc97

U.S. Department of Education, Research and Statistics, www.ed.gov/stats

CHAPTER 3

The Essential Role of Communities

Since the 1983 publication of the landmark assessment of American schools, *A Nation at Risk* (National Commission on Excellence in Education), public attention has focused as never before on our public school system. As the public has come to believe that the system is deficient and getting worse, blame is often placed on teachers and administrators. Increasingly, however, both professional educators and the public are realizing that children who come from families and communities that have overwhelming social problems present severe challenges to educators' ability to teach.

Historically, the importance of the community has been recognized in a number of educational improvement efforts. Educators have launched many initiatives to bring the community into the school, take school programs and activities into the community, and create communities of learning within the school itself. What many have failed to do is include the community in the planning and implementation of academic improvement efforts. A potential problem is that while the community's cooperation and collaboration are needed, they may not be easy to get.

REPAIRING THE BOND

That communities must accept responsibility for children's education and be willing to help schools prepare students to be educated has become a common theme in many education reform efforts. Reporting on a series of Kettering Foundation research projects on the public and its relationship to public education, Mathews (1996) pointed out:

> A healthy public life is essential to good schools. . . . Strong communities, with people banded and pulling together, are our last line of defense against the breakdown of families and society. And they are also an essential source of "social capital," a necessary form of reinforcement from outside the school that encourages students to learn.

But the Kettering studies also led to a disconcerting conclusion: the public and public schools are, in fact, moving apart (Mathews, 1996). Not only must schools be improved, but also the relationship between schools and the community must be repaired. Mathews suggests several steps for "putting the public back into public education."

Step 1. Reconstitute publics. Public relationships emerge when people see a connection between what is happening to them and what is valuable to them. They form together around a sense of common fate, interdependence, and overlapping purposes. They come alive in a willingness to talk together, act together, and judge results together.

Step 2. Reaffirm educational imperatives. If people believe—as they say they do—that education is important to solving many of society's ills, from eliminating racism to strengthening the economy, to safeguarding the environment, then providing that education should become a community strategy, not a school strategy.

Step 3. Reconnect the public to its schools. One of the first responsibilities of a democratic citizenry is to make decisions about public purposes and, with respect to education, set the mission for schools within the context of public objectives.

BUILDING COMMUNITIES FROM THE INSIDE OUT

Economic and social issues—in suburban and rural areas as well as in cities—have caused problems for defining a specific community and delineating ways to improve it. Kretzmann and McKnight (1993) examined ways to build a healthy community using the traditional needs-driven approach and an alternative capacity-focused approach. Although the traditional approach is used the most and commands the greatest financial and human resources, the authors pointed out that it creates mental images of a needy, problematic community populated by deficient people. The result is that problems are addressed through deficiency-oriented programs, and community members begin to think of themselves as incapable of taking charge of their lives and their community's future. Other negative consequences of the traditional approach to building a healthy community include a fragmented approach to solving intertwined problems, policies more oriented to maintenance and survival than to development, and a deepening cycle of dependence on outside resources.

An alternative capacity-focused approach begins with a commitment to identify a community's assets and leads to the development of policies and activities based on the capacities, skills, and resources of people and their community. In addition to the problems associated with the traditional approach, two other factors argue for the alternative approach. One is the evidence that significant community development takes place only when community people are committed to the effort. The second is that the hope of getting significant outside help to develop a community's internal assets is dim.

Kretzmann and McKnight presented a guide to building communities from the inside out, outlining the asset-based approach to community development and providing examples of successful community-building initiatives. They also answered the most frequently asked questions on the potential and the limits of using the building-inside-out approach:

Will these internally focused strategies really work? The obvious necessity is for citizens to use every resource at local command to create the future. There is clear evidence in developing societies that domination by outside plans and resources that overwhelm local initiatives and associations cause massive social and economic disasters. The same lesson can be learned about development efforts in the United States in which the designs of outsiders have been imposed on local communities.

Is there a danger that local communities and groups will not be inclusive? Are there parochialism and discrimination problems in

many local groups and associations? Yes. The effort to create open
communities has been, and will be, a never-ending struggle.

*Are there some communities in which there is not much associational
life among local citizens? What do you do then?* Communities
vary greatly in both the number and the formality of local
associations. In some, local citizens may not have had time to create them. In others, there are so many institutions to manage and
serve the local residents that associational life may have atrophied
for lack of function. Nevertheless, some informal associations
may be doing critical community work, even if they do not have a
name or officers. Community organizers must find, honor, and
enhance the associational relationships already at work.

In mid-1995, the Annie E. Casey Foundation, the Rockefeller Foundation, and the U.S. Department of Housing and Urban Development
jointly funded a project to broaden public understanding of community
building and its implications. In the resulting monograph, *Community
Building Coming of Age,* Kingsley, McNeely, and Gibson (1997) stated:

> Community building cannot provide all of the jobs or other opportuni-
> ties that will be needed to diminish poverty and social isolation in this
> country. But there are many case experiences showing that community
> building initiatives can make an important difference in people's lives;
> that they can enhance opportunities for those now impoverished and,
> probably more important, equip them much more powerfully to take ad-
> vantage of opportunities that become available to them.

The researchers identified seven types of community-building
efforts:

*Type 1. Efforts focused on specific improvement initiatives in a manner
that reinforces values and builds social capital.* Community builders
spend most of their time working with their neighbors on productive
activities. However, they emphasize such broader objectives as
building the friendships, trust, institutions, and capacity that form
the social capital that is, in turn, essential to fundamentally strengthening the lives of families and individual human beings.

Type 2. Community-driven efforts with broad resident involvement. Community participation is not enough. The community must play the central role in devising and implementing strategies for its own improvement. This does not mean that outside facilitators cannot help or that community members cannot form partnerships with outside agencies to achieve specific goals. It means that neighborhood residents must feel that they *own* the improvement process.

Type 3. Comprehensive, strategic, and entrepreneurial efforts. Successful community building often starts with an assessment of community assets and a brief planning phase, but it does not wait too long to move into action. It works entrepreneurially to identify and tackle one or two high-priority issues and produce some quick results because results build confidence and capacity. But as it does so, successful community building is rethinking and fleshing out a broader, long-term vision and strategy, reassessing priorities and opportunities, and laying the groundwork for other linked initiatives that will create a comprehensive agenda over time.

Type 4. Asset-based efforts. Even distressed neighborhoods have a substantial number of assets. Identifying those assets and developing plans to build on them is a powerful community-organizing device that, by evidencing opportunities to change things, motivates collaboration and commitment to action.

Type 5. Efforts tailored to neighborhood scale and conditions. The core unit for community building should be a neighborhood. There are two reasons for this: First, the natural face-to-face interactions that support friendships and mutual trust among most residents do not work much beyond the neighborhood scale. Second, even in the concentrated impoverished areas of inner cities, neighborhood conditions vary substantially; planning only for larger areas is likely to miss nuances that may be critical to developing effective strategies.

Type 6. Efforts collaboratively linked to the broader society to strengthen community institutions and enhance outside opportunities for residents. Community builders proactively look to end the devastating isolation of inner-city neighborhoods. They mount initiatives to prepare residents for work and link them to outside jobs, while at the same time trying to stimulate new business formation in the neighborhood. They look for opportunities to partner with outside institutions in ways that will serve neighborhood interests and strengthen internal institutions while helping outside institutions change their practices so that they become stronger partners, more sensitive to community interests.

Type 7. Efforts to consciously change institutional barriers and racism. Community building is not simply a matter of strengthening the connection between mainstream economic, political, and social institutions and those neighborhoods that have become isolated; it also requires institutions to give up business as usual. Commitment to the product draws participants beyond conventional barriers. The coming together may not be without conflict. Regardless, community-building efforts bring the best skills of organization development and conflict resolution to bear so that solutions, rather than blame, are the focus, and, in their differences, parties see assets they can contribute to the common endeavor.

The *Search Institute* (n.d.) undertook the challenge of identifying the key factors in community building that enhance the health and well-being of young people. The institute contends:

> We have research to suggest that the [developmental] assets make a difference. If our society would invest more in the positive things young people need, then we could expect high yields (in terms of healthier youth) as young people become healthy, contributing members of families, communities, workplaces, and society.

The Search Institute researchers (n.d.) identified critical influences on young people's growth and development and designated them as external or internal assets. The four categories of external assets focus on positive experiences provided to young people by individuals and institutions:

1. Support: Young people need to experience support, care, and love from their families, neighbors, and many others. They need

organizations and institutions that provide positive, supportive environments.

2. Empowerment: Young people need to be valued by their community and have opportunities to contribute. For this to occur, they must be safe and feel secure.

3. Boundaries and expectations: Young people need to know what is expected of them and whether activities and behaviors are inbounds or out-of-bounds.

4. Constructive use of time: Young people need constructive, enriching opportunities for growth through creative activities, youth programs, congregational involvement, and quality time at home.

The Search Institute's report also stresses the importance of internal assets:

There needs to be a similar commitment to nurturing the internalized qualities that guide choices and create a sense of centeredness, purpose, and focus. Indeed, shaping internal dispositions that encourage wise, responsible, and compassionate judgments is particularly important in a society that prizes individualism.

The institute identifies four categories of internal assets:

1. Commitment to learning: Young people need to develop a life-long commitment to education and learning.

2. Positive values: Youths need to develop strong values that guide their choices.

3. Social competencies: Young people need skills and competencies that equip them to make positive choices, build relationships, and succeed in life.

4. Positive identity: Young people need a strong sense of their own power, purpose, worth, and promise.

One of the outcomes of the Presidents' Summit for America's Future in April 1997 was the formation of America's Promise—The Alliance for Youth, a national organization headed by General Colin Powell.

The organization is dedicated to mobilizing the nation to ensure that children and youth have access to the fundamental resources they need to become successful adults. The Alliance identifies five functions of those fundamental resources (America's Promise, 2001):

1. Mentor: Establish an ongoing relationship with a caring adult— parent, mentor, tutor, or coach.
2. Protect: Create safe places and structured activities during non- school hours.
3. Nurture: Ensure a healthy start.
4. Prepare: Ensure a marketable skill through effective education.
5. Serve: Provide an opportunity to give back through community service.

America's Promise is intended to serve as a national catalyst, urging states, counties, cities, and municipalities as well as public, private, and nonprofit organizations to focus their combined talents and resources on improving the lives of youth. Organizations—States of Promise, Communities of Promise, and Schools of Promise—have been formed. Members are committed to bringing the goals of the Presidents' Summit to state, community, and school levels. A Community of Promise commits to (America's Promise, 2001):

• Engage a diverse community team to ensure that the needs of all its young people are known, that community resources are fully tapped, and that these resources are effectively and broadly delivered.
• Take responsibility for reaching a targeted number of young people at risk (the goal is to have communities target 10 percent).
• Secure commitments from all sectors in the community in order to provide the five fundamental resources to young people.
• Establish a point of contact to report local events, plans, commit- ments, and progress to America's Promise.
• Monitor progress in the community using standard measurement tools provided by America's Promise.

A School of Promise is a school-based, school–community collabo- rative. Local stakeholders in partnership with school officials commit to fulfilling all five basic promises to young people either directly or indirectly through existing school facilities. Criteria for being designated a School of Promise include (America's Promise, 2001):

- Fulfilling any of the five basic resource functions that are lacking in the lives of many of its young people.
- Setting specific, measurable goals for fulfilling the five functions within the school.
- Designating a full-time responsible Promise Coordinator to be located at the school site to oversee the delivery of resources to young people in a coordinated, personal, and accountable manner.
- Organizing a site team (to work closely with the Promise Coordinator) that includes representation from parents, the school, young people, social service agencies, local businesses, and other local community organizations for the purpose of providing a focal point for planning, coordination, and accountability.
- Seeking resources to support the activities through local commitments to include corporate, university, and foundation partners.
- Tracking the generation and delivery of local commitments and providing summary information to representatives of America's Promise.

Is this kind of a multilevel approach enhancing the health and well-being of America's youth? A follow-up report, *Why the Five Fundamental Resources Matter: A Reassessment of the Evidence* (Benson and Walker, 1999), states:

New research shows that developmental strengths and resources such as those captured in the five fundamental resources have an additive power. That is, the more the better. Access to three of the resources, for example, is better than having access to one. And access to all five is particularly powerful. This line of reasoning is supported by a new study of 99,000 public school 6th–12th grade students across the United States. As the number of developmental assets (or resources) increases in a young person's life, two important trends are seen. First, multiple forms of health-compromising behavior decrease dramatically, including alcohol, tobacco, and other drug use, violence, anti-social behavior, attempted suicide, and driving and drinking. And, as the number of assets or resources increases, multiple forms of thriving increase, including school success, affirmation of diversity, and optimism for the future. These relationships between positive developmental experiences and youth outcomes hold across many demographic variables, including race/ethnicity, age, gender, geography, and community size. The point: the more developmental resources, the better.

A SCHOOL SYSTEM FOR THE NEW MILLENNIUM

Actualizing the proposition that a community must take responsibility for its schools is a challenge that Timpane, former vice president of the Carnegie Foundation for the Advancement of Teaching, thinks educators should accept: "School leadership must be at the head of this parade. No one else can speak with as much legitimacy and effect in every community in the land" (as cited in Decker and Boo, 2001).

The American Association of School Administrators (AASA) has taken the lead in trying to stimulate a discussion that will result in reconceptualizing the role of schools in relation to their communities. In a year-long project, the Association's Council of 21 took a look ahead at the kind of school system the nation will need in the future. The resulting report (Withrow, 1999) is designed to stimulate debate in communities about the characteristics of schools and school systems capable of preparing students for the global information age. Houston, the association's executive director, explains that AASA does not see the study and its conclusions as the last word, but rather as "a bridge from what our schools and school systems are to what they need to become" (as cited in Withrow, 1999).

The Council of 21, composed of leaders in business, government, education, and other areas, identified sixteen characteristics that schools and school systems should have in order to prepare students for the global information age (Withrow 1999). (The council noted that the characteristics are not listed in order of priority because all are important.)

The definitions of school, teacher, and learner are reshaped by the digital world. The term "school" must take on an expanded meaning beyond the physical structure and become more encompassing, embracing communities of knowledge and learning that are interest-wide, community-wide, and worldwide. While there may always be a school building, a school is likely to resemble a nerve center that connects teachers, students, and the community to the wealth of knowledge that exists in the world. "Teachers" must become orchestrators of learning, moderators and facilitators as well as purveyors of knowledge and subject matter, so that they can help students turn information into knowledge and knowledge into wisdom. "Learner" needs to be thought of in terms of preparing students for life in the real world. Out of both necessity and curiosity, lifelong learning must become a reality in people's lives.

All students have equal opportunity for an outstanding education, with adequate funding, no matter where they live. An equal opportunity philosophy must drive everything from funding to the expectations we have for our students. It must apply to individuals with disabilities, the disadvantaged, and the legions of children just recently arrived from other countries.

Educators are driven by high expectations and clear, challenging standards that are widely understood by students, families, and communities. Standards and expectations must be high but realistic, and schools, teachers, students, families, and other community members must be part of the process of developing those standards and expectations.

A project-based "curriculum for life" engages students in addressing real-world problems, issues important to humanity, and questions that matter. Students must be able to connect what they are learning with what is happening or may happen in the real world. They need to be prepared for responsible citizenship in a democracy. Teachers will be challenged to help students make connections and understand why what they are learning has value.

Teachers and administrators are effectively prepared for the global information age. All teachers and administrators must be prepared to make the best possible use of technology, both for student learning and for school and school-district efficiency. Ultimately, teachers and administrators must move beyond managing time and space to managing for results.

Students, schools, school systems, and communities are connected around the clock with each other and with the world through information-rich, interactive technology. With a concern for equal opportunity, schools and school districts will use technology and electronic networks to get families and the community on the education team.

School systems conduct, consider, and apply significant research in designing programs that lead to constantly improving student achievement. Schools and school systems must do more research focused on improving student achievement and must use that research as part of the decision-making process. Teachers must take a more active role in research, assisted by training that will help them interpret and apply significant research in the classroom.

Students learn to think, reason, and make sound decisions and demonstrate values inherent in a democracy. Critical thinking, higher-level thinking, and decision-making skills are basic to a sound education, and those skills must penetrate every area of the curriculum. Schools as well as communities have a responsibility to help students become more civil; understand the importance of being honest, respectful, trustworthy, and caring; understand and become participants in a free and democratic society; understand the consequences of their own actions and how their actions affect others; and understand the need for a code of ethics. Students need to understand rights and exercise responsibilities basic to maintaining those rights.

School facilities provide a safe, secure, stimulating, joyous learning environment that contributes to a lifelong passion for learning and high student achievement. The school should be in touch with the rest of the community and the world. The buildings themselves should be up-to-date, clean, and appropriately lighted, with proper temperature and air-quality controls. They should be places where students want to be.

Leadership is collaborative, and governance is focused on broad issues that affect student learning. Rather than making major decisions in isolation, administrators must ask the opinions of teachers, families, and others on the staff and in the community; one of the challenges they will face is the management of expectations. However, teachers and principals must have enough flexibility and control to run their schools and classrooms effectively. What is needed ultimately is communities in which citizens and schools are both willing and able to say, "We're in this together."

Students learn about other cultures, respect and honor diversity, and see the world as an extended neighborhood. Educators and communities must help students understand and appreciate the beauty of other cultures and respect all people. Students must have a solid grounding in the principles of human rights. They must try to understand people who hold different values and learn to accept dissent and individual differences. Schools must embody the principles of a democratic society and model democratic principles and respect for diversity in the way they are run.

Schools promote creativity and teamwork at all levels, and teachers help students turn information into knowledge and knowledge into wisdom. We need both individual initiative and the synergy that comes from collaboration. Teamwork involving students, staff, and community must become commonplace, with teams working together, face-to-face and electronically. The teacher's role will change dramatically from dispensing information to working alongside students, helping them transform information into knowledge and, eventually, wisdom.

Assessment of student progress is performance-based, taking into account students' individual talents, abilities, and aspirations. Flexibility is needed in standards and assessments.

A student-centered, collaboratively developed vision provides power and focus for education community-wide. Educational leaders must develop a vision for education in their communities, and must bring educators, families, and others together to help them do it. School systems and their leaders need to know—through surveys, advisory groups, and just plain listening—what constituents know, what they do not know, and what they need to know to give schools their support. Administrators must be open to what staff and community can teach them and must become masters of collaboration while ensuring the intellectual and moral integrity of the school and school system.

Continuous improvement is a driving force in every school and school system. Planning must be a continuous process, and educators must apply the principles of quality management.

Schools are the crossroads and central convening point of the community. Schools must be around-the-clock hubs for lifelong learning, the connecting point for education and achievement for all who live and work in the community. They also should be centers for health care, housing assistance, social services, and other community services and agencies. School systems must become ever more creative at getting people involved so that everyone in the community is on the education team.

A TESTED METHOD FOR BUILDING COMMUNITY

One proven process for building communities and involving families in the education of their children is community education, usually implemented through community schools. Dryfoos (2002) compiled evaluation data from a number of organizations including the Academy for Educational Development, the Stanford Research Institute, and the Chapin Hall Centers for Children that demonstrate the positive impact on student learning, healthy youth development, family well-being, and community life.

For more than six decades, community educators have worked to build exceptionally strong ties between public schools and their communities, usually by developing community schools, transforming traditional 9-A.M.-to-3-P.M. schools into extended-day learning, recreation, and social centers for community residents of all ages and needs (Decker and Boo, 2001). In these multipurpose community schools, local residents and professional educators work together to address community problems in partnership with other community agencies and institutions.

Community education offers local residents and community agencies and institutions the opportunity to become active partners in providing educational opportunities and addressing community concerns. It is based on the following principles (Decker and Boo, 2001):

Lifelong learning. Education is viewed as a birth-to-death process and everyone in the community—individuals, businesses, public and private agencies—shares responsibility for educating all members of the community and providing learning opportunities for residents of all ages, backgrounds, and needs.

Self-determination. Local people have a right and a responsibility to be involved in determining community needs and identifying community resources that can be used to address those needs.

Self-help. People are best served when their capacity to help themselves is acknowledged and developed. When people assume responsibility for their own well-being, they build independence and become part of the solution.

Leadership development. The training of local leaders in such skills as problem solving, decision making, and group process is an essential component of successful self-help and improvement efforts.

Institutional responsiveness. Public institutions exist to serve the public and are obligated to develop programs and services that address continuously changing public needs and interests.

Maximum use of resources. The physical, financial, and human resources in every community should be interconnected and used to their fullest to meet the diverse needs and interests of community members.

Integrated delivery of services. Organizations and agencies that operate for the public good can better meet their own goals and serve the public by collaborating with organizations and agencies with similar goals.

Decentralization. Services, programs, and other community involvement opportunities that are close to people's homes have the greatest potential for high levels of public participation. Whenever possible, these activities should be available in locations with easy public access.

Inclusiveness. Community services, programs, and other community involvement opportunities should be designed to involve the broadest possible cross section of community members and eliminate the segregation or isolation of people by age, income, sex, race, ethnicity, religion, or other factors that impede participation.

Access to public information. Public information is shared across agency and organizational lines. Community members know more than just the facts; they know what the facts mean in the lives of the diverse people who make up the community.

Using the community education process to design and implement a comprehensive plan for educational and community improvement takes time and the ongoing effort of committed people. But experiences in countless communities across the nation show benefits that are clearly worth the effort (Edwards and Biocchi, 1996; Dryfoos, 2002). Three examples of systems based on the principles of community education are community schools, full-service schools, and 21st Century Community Learning Centers.

As the Annie E. Casey Foundation (1999) points out:

These and other models represent a move away from education controlled by school boards and central offices toward greater influence (and responsibility) by parents and school-based educators. These approaches can be thought of as "systems of community schools"—systems in which each school has its own staff, mission, and approach to instruction but all are working to improve education and other outcomes for children, parents, and neighborhoods.

COMMUNITY SCHOOLS

A community school is not just another program being imposed on a school. As Harkavy and Blank (2002) emphasize:

It is a way of thinking and acting that recognized the historic central role of schools in our communities—and the power of working together for a common good. Educating our children, yes, but also strengthening our families and communities, so that they, in turn, can help make schools even stronger and children more successful. . . . Educators are major partners, but not always in the lead role. A capable partner organization—a child- and family-services agency, for example, or a youth-development organization, a college, or a family support center—can serve as the linchpin for the community school, mobilizing and integrating the resources of the community, so that principals and teachers can focus on teaching and learning. In some communities, schools themselves will be best equipped to provide the necessary leadership and coordination.

Community schools extend the concept of public education beyond the traditional K–12 program. They are not limited by traditional school schedules and roles, focusing instead on current community needs. Community schools are open schools, available for use before and after school for academic, extracurricular, recreation, health, social service, and workforce-preparation programs for people of all ages. They involve a broad range of community members, businesses, public and private organizations, and local, state, and federal agencies. They become places where people gather to learn, enjoy themselves, and become involved in community problem solving.

Designing schools as community schools is a win-win proposition for educators and community members. From a problem-solving viewpoint, a school can be a support center for a whole network of agencies and institutions committed to addressing community needs and expanding learning opportunities for all community members. Community schools are practical and cost-effective because:

- School buildings are located in most neighborhoods and are usually easy to reach.
- Schools belong to the public and represent a large public investment.
- Schools have good resources and professional staffs.
- Traditional school hours leave plenty of time for other uses.

Community school programs work because they provide places and programs in which community members can educate themselves. They involve families and other community members in efforts to improve academic achievement and school climate. They develop public knowledge about the diverse interests and interrelationships characteristic of a community. They provide a setting for community members to meet, talk through issues, and work together to address problems. They provide opportunities to discover and nurture the public leadership needed to sustain a healthy, vibrant community.

From an educator's viewpoint, community schools are a way to meet the challenges faced by public education. The sweeping changes that have occurred in families, schools, and communities require educators to collaborate with families and communities if they are to be successful in their primary mission of educating children.

FULL-SERVICE SCHOOLS

The full-service school meets the need for a community-wide, multiagency approach to providing for the diverse needs of children and families. As Flaxman (2001) explains:

> [It is] a way to coordinate services through new institutional arrangements in a comprehensive, collaborative, and coherent system for changing youth, families, and the social environment shared by educators; community and business leaders; and health, social services, and mental health practitioners. The school becomes a mechanism for coordinating services that are fragmented among several bureaucracies, training teachers to take a new role in the development of their students, and working cooperatively with families.

A full-service school deals with the educational needs of the children who attend and also provides a full range of additional services for the children and their families. As Dryfoos (2002) explains, in full-service schools:

> The primary responsibility for high-quality education rests with the school authorities, while the primary responsibility for "everything else" rests with the outside agencies. The school system pays for education; the other services are supported by an array of non-school sources of funding. It is important to make this distinction clear because some have misinterpreted these community school concepts to mean that the school is asked to provide and to pay for added health and social services or extended hours or parenting education. Quite the contrary, the idea is to divide up the responsibility among a number of agencies, with one set of services devoted to helping children learn and another devoted to helping children and families gain access to the supports they need. The goal is to take some of the burden of rearing and nourishing children off the school system. . . . The services that fall under "everything else" are broadly construed. Experience is showing that almost anything can be provided in a school as long as it meets the needs of the school/community and as long as resources can be identified to bring it in. The most frequently mentioned supports are health, mental health, and social services . . . before- and after-school programs are almost always included along with mentoring and

tutoring. . . . New thinking about old problems can also be worked into the design.

This approach is identified by several characteristics (Dryfoos, 2002):

- Services are provided to children and their families through a collaboration among schools, health care providers, and social services agencies.
- The schools are among the central participants in planning and governing the collaborative effort.
- The services are provided at a school or are coordinated by personnel located at a school or at a site near the school.
- The role of school personnel is to identify children and families who need services and link them to the services that are available.

21ST CENTURY COMMUNITY LEARNING CENTERS

The U.S. Department of Education's 21st Century Community Learning Centers initiative is a federal response to the growing challenges facing schools and communities. Former President Clinton (1996) explained the rationale for the initiative:

Increasingly, our schools are critical to bringing our communities together. We want them to serve the public not just during school hours but after hours; to function as vital community centers; places for recreation and learning; positive places where children can be when they can't be at home and school is no longer going on; gathering places for young people and adults alike. Bringing our schools into the twenty-first century is a national challenge that deserves a national commitment.

The 21st Century Community Learning Centers Program was established by Congress in 1997. The authorizing legislation states (U.S. Department of Education, 1997):

[Schools] should collaborate with other public and nonprofit agencies and organizations, local businesses, educational entities (such as vocational and adult education programs, school-to-work program, community colleges, and universities), recreation, cultural, and other community and human service entities, for the purpose of meeting the needs of, and expanding the opportunities available to, the residents of the communities served by such schools.

The grants awarded under this program may be used to plan, implement, or expand community learning centers. The program defines a "community learning center" as

An entity within a public elementary, middle or secondary school building that (1) provides educational, recreational, health, and social service programs for residents of all ages within a local community, and (2) is operated by a local educational agency in conjunction with local governmental agencies, businesses, vocational education programs, institutions of higher education, community colleges, and cultural, recreational, and other community and human service entities.

In 1997, the Charles Stewart Mott Foundation and the U.S. Department of Education entered a multiyear public–private partnership in support of the 21st Century Community Learning Centers (21stCCLCs), an initiative designed to enable school districts to fund public schools as community learning centers that provide additional academic support to children who need it, expanded learning opportunities that complement the school day, mentoring for young people by caring adults in their communities, lifelong learning opportunities for community members, and a safe place to support these activities. Under the terms of the partnership (C. S. Mott Foundation), the U.S. Department of Education would administer the 21stCCLCs program and supply funds to local communities through a competitive proposal process. The C. S. Mott Foundation would underwrite training and technical assistance to 21stCCLCs grantees for implementing and sustaining high-quality programs and provide training for potential applicants on how to create high-quality applications.

In 1998, the U.S. Department of Education's Office of Educational Research and Improvement administered the first national competition for the grants in a competition that proved to be one of the most competitive in the history of the department. More than five thousand people attended a series of regional "bidders conferences" cosponsored by the U.S. Department of Education and the C. S. Mott Foundation. Nearly two thousand grant applications were received.

The first ninety-nine grants totaled $40 million. The federal commitment to the 21stCCLCs initiative has risen from $40 million in 1998 to $200 million in 1999, $453 million in 2000, and $846 million in 2001. The C. S. Mott Foundation committed $100 million over a multiyear period.

The 21st Century Community Learning Centers Program has been reauthorized as Title IV, Part B, of the *No Child Left Behind Act*, which President Bush signed into law on January 8, 2002. Of the $1 billion appropriated to fund the 21stCCLC Program, approximately $325 million will be available for new grants. The $325 million will be awarded to state agencies and state departments of education making each state responsible for the administration of the grants (U.S. Department of Education, 2002).

The U.S. Department of Education's After-School initiative falls under this program. It encourages schools to stay open longer, providing a safe place for homework centers, mentoring, drug and violence prevention counseling, college preparation courses, enrichment in core academic subjects and the arts, and recreational activities.

A publication of the Partnership for Family Involvement in Education (1998) (a joint effort of U.S. Departments of Education and Justice), *Safe and Smart—Making After-School Hours Work for Kids,* describes research on the effects of high-quality after-school programs and identifies the characteristics of high-quality programs:

- Clear goal setting and strong management
- Quality after-school staffing
- Attention to safety, health, and nutrition issues
- Strong involvement of families
- Effective partnerships with community-based organizations, juvenile justice agencies, law enforcement, and youth groups
- Coordination of learning with the regular school program
- Linkages between school-day teachers and after-school personnel
- Evaluation of program progress and effectiveness

An updated version of the *Safe and Smart* publication entitled *Working for Families and Children: Safe and Smart After-School Programs* (U.S. Departments of Education and Justice, 2000) is available. It contains more information about the evidence of the success of after-school activities, key components of high-quality programs and effective program practices, and how communities are meeting their local needs for after-school activities. The U.S. Department of Education (2000) has also released a new report, *21st Century Community Learning Centers: Providing Quality Afterschool Learning Opportunities for America's Families.*

A SOLEMN CONCLUSION AND A WARNING

In March 1997 the nation's governors met at the National Education Summit and reaffirmed their commitment to school reform. They invited voters to hold them accountable and called for "an external independent, nongovernmental effort to measure and report each state's annual progress" (*Education Week* on the Web, 1998). *Education Week*, with the support of the Pew Charitable Trusts, undertook the task, publishing the *State of the States* report, which contains a solemn conclusion and a warning:

> Public education systems in the 50 states are riddled with excellence but rife with mediocrity. Despite 15 years of earnest efforts to improve public schools and raise student achievement, states haven't made much progress. As the millennium approaches, there is growing concern that if public education doesn't soon improve, one of two outcomes is almost inevitable:
>
> - Our democratic system and our economic strength, both of which depend on an educated citizenry, will steadily erode; or,
> - Alternative forms of education will emerge to replace public schools as we have known them.
>
> This will not happen next year or perhaps even in the next 10 years. But in time, if our education systems remain mediocre, we will see one of those two results. Either would be a sad loss for America.

The Carnegie Foundation for the Advancement of Teaching reached much the same conclusion. Its former vice president, Timpane, offered the following advice:

Our schools need new ways to think about and foster parental and community involvement in education. . . . We must develop a new perspective, and it must rest on three challenging propositions:

- Schools cannot succeed nowadays (or, to put it more strongly, schools will fail) without the collaboration of parents and communities.
- Families need unprecedentedly strong support to become and remain functional.
- Communities must take charge of all the developmental needs of their children. (As cited in Decker and Boo, 2001)

REFERENCES

Annie E. Casey Foundation. (1999). *Improving community school connections.* Baltimore, Md.: Annie E. Casey Foundation.

America's Promise. (2001). Retrieved September 7, 2002, from www. americaspromise.org

Benson, P. L., and Walker, G. (1999). *Why the five fundamental resources matter: A reassessment of the evidence.* Alexandria, Va.: America's Promise.

Charles Stewart Mott Foundation. (n.d). *21st century schools.* Retrieved January 17, 2001, from www.mott.org/21.asp.

Clinton, W. J. (1996). Rose Garden Speech, July 11.

Decker, L. E., and Boo, M. R. (2001). *Community schools: Serving children, families and communities.* Fairfax, Va.: National Community Education Association.

Dryfoos, J. G. (2002). Full-service community schools: Creating new institutions. *Phi Delta Kappan, 83,* 5.

Education Week on the Web. (1998). *Quality counts 97: The state of the states.* Retrieved January 10, 2002, from www.edweek.org.

Edwards, P., and Biocchi, K. (1996). *Community schools across America.* Flint, Mich.: National Center for Community Education.

Flaxman, E. (2001). The promise of urban community schooling. *ERIC Review, 8,* 2.

Harkavy, I., and Blank, M. (2002). *Community schools.* Retrieved April 19, 2002, from www.educationweek.org/ew/newstory.cfm?slug=31harkavy.h21.

Kingsley, G. T., McNeely, J. B., and Gibson, J. O. (1997). *Community building coming of age.* Washington, D.C.: Development Training Institute, Inc., and Urban Institute.

Kretzmann, J. P., and McKnight, J. L. (1993). *Building communities from the inside out: A path toward finding and mobilizing a community's assets.* Evanston, Ill.: Center for Urban Affairs and Policy Research, Northwestern University.

Mathews, D. (1996). *Is there a public for public schools?* Dayton, Ohio: Kettering Foundation Press.

National Commission on Excellence in Education. (1983). *A nation at risk: The imperative for educational reform.* Washington, D.C.: U.S. Government Printing Office.

Partnership for Family Involvement in Education, U.S. Departments of Education and Justice. (1998). *Safe and smart—Making after-school hours work for kids.* Washington, D.C.: U.S. Government Printing Office.

Search Institute. (n.d.). *Developmental assets: An overview.* Retrieved January 18, 2002, from www.search-institute.org/assets.

Search Institute. (1998). *Developmental assets: An investment in youth.* Minneapolis, Minn.

Withrow, F. (with Long, H., and Marx, G). (1999). *Preparing schools and school systems for the 21st century.* Arlington, Va.: American Association of School Administrators.

U.S. Department of Education. (1997). *21st century community learning centers program.* Retrieved January 30, 2000, from www.ed.gov./offices/OERI/21stcclc.htm.

U.S. Department of Education. (2000). *21st century community learning centers: Providing quality afterschool learning opportunities for America's families.* Washington, D.C.: U.S. Government Printing Office.

U.S. Department of Education. (2002). *No child left behind: Reauthorization of the elementary and secondary education act.* Retrieved January 23, 2002, from www.ed.gov/offices/esea.htm.

U.S. Departments of Education and Justice. (2000). *Working for families and children: Safe and smart after-school programs.* Washington, D.C.: U.S. Government Printing Office.

WEBSITES FOR MORE INFORMATION AND LINKS TO OTHER RELEVANT SITES

America's Promise, www.americaspromise.org
Civic Practices Network, www.cpn.org
Education Week on the Web, www.edweek.org
Charles F. Kettering Foundation, www.kettering.org

Charles Stewart Mott Foundation, www.mott.org
National Center for Community Education, www.nccenet.org
Search Institute, www.search-institute.org
U. S. Department of Education, www.ed.gov
21st Century Community Learning Centers, www.ed.gov/21stcclc

CHAPTER 4

Home and School as Partners

Parent and family involvement has become a major component of almost every plan to restructure schools. Parental roles have taken on heightened importance in the school effectiveness movement, the implementation of site-based management, and the issue of school choice. The growing body of research continues to demonstrate that parent involvement has a significant impact on student achievement. Public opinion agrees with the research findings.

The American Association of School Administrators (AASA) recently conducted a national poll to determine what the public believes are the best indicators that schools are providing a high quality education. Reporting on the results of this poll conducted by professional pollsters, Houston (2001), AASA Executive Director, points out that:

> The American public believes that "high parental involvement" is the best indicator that a school is providing a high quality education. "Children who are happy and like school" was the second best indicator. "High scores on statewide tests" was selected as the best indicator by only 18.8 percent.
>
> These findings don't come as a surprise; they are consistent with AASA polls conducted over the past three years. In October 1999, AASA conducted a nationwide survey to determine what were the most important factors for deciding whether a school is good. "Children who are happy and like school" appeared as the No. 1 choice while "high parental involvement" ranked as No. 4.

An agenda for education reform adopted by President George Bush and the nation's governors in 1990, America 2000: An Education Strategy, created a national impetus to increase parent and family involvement in school reform and restructuring. The America 2000 strategy was expanded under the Clinton administration and given a new name, Goals 2000. Two goals were added to the 1990 agenda (Decker and Decker, 2001):

- All teachers will have the opportunity to acquire the knowledge and skills needed to prepare U.S. students for the next century.
- Every school will promote partnerships that will increase parental involvement and participation in promoting the social, emotional, and academic growth of children.

On January 8, 2002, President Bush signed his new education plan, No Child Shall Be Left Behind, into law (U.S. Department of Education, 2002). In response to the emphasis on standards and accountability, the reauthorization of the Elementary and Secondary Education Act contained some sweeping changes for public schools. States are now required to test all students annually from third to eighth grade in the basic subjects of reading and math as well as launch a federally guided drive for universal literacy among schoolchildren.

There is reason for concern among educators about what the emphasis on accountability and high-stakes testing will mean for other elements of school restructuring and reform efforts, particularly in schools serving low-income and minority children. As Harkavy and Blank (2002) observe:

Listening to the recent political debate culminating in the passage the "No Child Left Behind" Act of 2001, it would be easy to assume that the only things that matter in education are annual testing in grades 3–8, having a qualified teacher in the first four years of schooling, and allowing parents to move their children out of persistently failing schools.

The National Center for Fair and Open Testing (2002) points out:

There is an important role for good assessment of student learning. The public deserves to know how well schools are doing, schools need to use information about student learning to improve teaching, and there should be intervention in schools which are unable to improve even when they have been provided the resources and tools to do so. None of this requires heavy reliance on results from state or commercial standardized tests.

A large percentage of the American public also seems to question the assumption that high test scores correlate to the goal of achieving academic success for all children. In the 1999 AASA poll, "high test scores" was ranked thirteenth out of seventeen possible choices. In a 2000 AASA poll of registered voters, 63 percent of the public disagreed that a student's progress for one school year can be accurately summarized by a single standardized test.

The thirty-third annual Phi Delta Kappa/Gallup Poll (Rose and Gallup, 2001) on the public's attitudes toward public schools reinforces the validity of the AASA findings. That poll found that 66 percent of the public believes that standardized tests should be used to guide instruction; only 30 percent believe such tests should be used to measure student learning. Additionally, 65 percent believe student achievement should be measured by classroom work and homework; only 31 percent would rely on testing.

Many educational experts hope that emphasis will remain on the significant link between student achievement and parent involvement. Education Week on the Web (2001) cited one analysis of national test results that found that three factors over which parents have enormous control—student absenteeism, variety of reading material in the home, and the amount of television watched—accounted for nearly 90 percent of the differences in student test scores. However, the article also pointed out that

> If parents have a central role in influencing their children's progress in school, research has shown that schools in turn have an important part to play in determining levels of parent involvement. Research indicates . . . that for parent involvement to flourish, it must be meaningfully integrated with the school's programs and community.

BENEFITS OF FAMILY INVOLVEMENT

The most comprehensive survey of the research on parent and family involvement in children's education is a series of publications developed by Henderson and Berla: *The Evidence Grows* (1981); *The Evidence*

Continues to Grow (1987); and *a New Generation of Evidence: The Family Is Critical to Student Achievement* (1994). More than eighty-five studies are cited that document the benefits for students, families, and schools when parents and family members are involved in children's education. This involvement has positive effects on student success as well as school quality and program design.

Effects on Student Success

- When parents are involved, students achieve more, regardless of socioeconomic status, ethnic/racial background, or parents' education level.
- The more extensive the family involvement, the higher the student achievement.
- Students whose families are involved have higher grades and test scores, have better attendance records, and complete their homework more consistently.
- When parents and families are involved, students display more positive attitudes and behavior.
- Students whose families are involved have higher graduation rates and higher enrollment rates in postsecondary education.
- Different involvement levels produce different gains. To produce long-lasting gains for students, the parent and family involvement activities must be well-planned, inclusive, and comprehensive.
- Educators have higher expectations of students whose parents and families collaborate with teachers. They also have higher opinions of those parents and families.
- In programs designed to involve parents and families in full partnerships, the achievement of disadvantaged children improves, sometimes dramatically, with the children farthest behind making the greatest gains.
- Children from diverse cultural backgrounds tend to do better when families and professionals collaborate to bridge the gap between the home culture and the school culture.
- Antisocial student behaviors, such as alcohol use and violence, decrease as family involvement increases.

- The benefits of involving parents and families are significant at all ages and grade levels. Middle and high school students whose parents and families remain involved make better transitions, maintain the quality of their work, develop realistic plans for the future, and are less likely to drop out.
- The most accurate predictor of a student's success in school is not income or social status, but the extent to which the student's family is able to (1) create a home environment that encourages learning; (2) communicate high, yet reasonable, expectations for achievement and future careers; and (3) become involved in their children's education at school and in the community.

Effects on School Quality

- Schools that work well with families have better teacher morale and higher ratings of teachers by parents.
- Schools in which families are involved have more support from families and better reputations in the community.
- School programs that involve parents and families outperform identical programs without such involvement.
- Schools in which children are failing improve dramatically when parents and families are enabled to become partners with teachers.
- Schools' efforts to inform and involve parents and families are stronger determinants of whether inner-city parents will be involved in their children's education than are the level of parent education, family size, marital status, or student grade level.

Effects on Program Design

- The more the relationship between parents and educators approaches a comprehensive, well-planned partnership, the higher the student achievement.
- For low-income families, programs offering home visits are more successful in involving parents and families than programs requiring parents to visit the school.
- When families receive frequent and effective communication from the school or program, their involvement increases, their overall

evaluation of educators is higher, and their attitudes toward the program are more positive.

- Parents and families are much more likely to become involved when educators encourage and assist them in helping their children with schoolwork.
- When parents and families are treated as partners and given relevant information by people with whom they are comfortable, they put into practice the involvement strategies they already know are effective but have been hesitant to use.
- Collaboration with families is an essential component of a reform strategy, but it is not a substitute for high-quality educational programs or comprehensive school improvement.

Moles and D'Angelo (1993) and Wherry (1999) report on other teacher, administrator, school, and community benefits of successful home–school involvement. When parent involvement is a goal, teachers receive in-service training on how to work with families from diverse backgrounds, get more support from principals for their work with families, have more respect for and better appreciation of parents' time and ability to reinforce learning, and maximize time and resources by sharing knowledge, skills, and resources cooperatively. Administrators benefit from better communication between school and home, fewer family complaints about inconsistent and inappropriate course content and homework, and improved school climate as children see parents and teachers as partners. Schools and communities benefit from improved teacher morale, higher ratings of teachers by families, decreased teacher turnover, more school support from families and community members, and improved school climate and reputation.

STANDARDS AND MODELS OF PARENT INVOLVEMENT

There are many models for involving parents in the education of their children. Two models often cited in the literature were developed by Joyce Epstein (1992) of Johns Hopkins University in Baltimore and Susan Swap (1993) of Wheelock College in Boston.

The National PTA (1998) developed the National Standards for Parent/Family Involvement Programs in cooperation with education and parent-involvement professionals through the National Coalition for Parent Involvement in Education. The standards closely follow the Epstein model. There are six standards, each with quality indicators. The first five relate to parent and family involvement, the sixth to collaboration with the community at large. The National PTA (n.d.) explains that "these standards, together with their corresponding quality indicators, were created to be used in conjunction with other national standards and reform initiatives in support of children's learning and success." The following are the National Standards for Parent/Family Involvement Programs (National PTA, 1998):

Standard I. Communicating

Communication between home and school is regular, two-way, and meaningful. When families and educators communicate effectively, positive relationships develop, problems are more easily solved, and students make greater progress.

Quality Indicators. Effective programs:

- Use a variety of communication tools on a regular basis, seeking to facilitate two-way interaction through each one.
- Establish opportunities for families and educators to share pertinent information such as student strengths and learning preferences.
- Provide clear information regarding course expectations and offerings, student placement, school activities, student services, and optional programs.
- Mail report cards and regular progress reports to parents. Provide support services and follow-up conferences as needed.
- Disseminate information on school reforms, policies, disciplinary procedures, assessment tools, and school goals, and include parents in related decision making.

- Conduct conferences with parents or another family member at least twice a year, with follow-up as needed. The conferences accommodate the varied schedules of parents, language barriers, and the need for child care.
- Communicate with parents regarding positive student behavior and achievement as well as misbehavior or failure.
- Encourage immediate contact between home and teachers when concerns arise.
- Distribute student work for parental comment, and review it on a regular basis.
- Translate communications to assist limited-English- and non-English-speaking families.
- Provide opportunities for parents and family members to communicate with principals and other administrative staff.
- Promote informal activities at which families, staff, and community members may interact.
- Provide staff development regarding effective communication techniques and the importance of regular two-way communication between school and family.

Standard II. Parenting

Parenting skills are promoted and supported. School staff recognize parent roles and responsibilities, ask families what supports they need, and work to find ways to meet those needs.

Quality Indicators. Effective programs:

- Communicate the importance of a positive relationship between parents and children.
- Link parents and families to supportive programs and resources within the community.
- Reach out to all families, not just those who attend parent meetings.
- Establish policies that support and respect family responsibilities, recognizing the variety of parenting traditions and practices within the community's cultural and religious diversity.

- Provide an accessible parent/family information and resource center to support parents and families with training, resources, and other services.
- Encourage staff members to demonstrate respect for families and their primary role in rearing children to become responsible adults.

Standard III. Student Learning

Parents and families play an integral role in assisting student learning. Enlisting families' involvement provides educators and administrators with a valuable support system, creating a team that is working for each child's success.

Quality Indicators. Effective programs:

- Seek and encourage parental participation in making decisions that affect students.
- Inform families of expectations for students in each subject at each grade level.
- Provide information about how to foster learning at home, give appropriate assistance, monitor homework, and give feedback to teachers.
- Regularly assign interactive homework that requires students to discuss with their parents or other family members what they are learning in class.
- Sponsor workshops or distribute information to assist families in understanding how students can improve skills, get help when needed, meet classroom expectations, and perform well on tests or other assessments.
- Involve families in setting annual student goals and planning for postsecondary education and careers. Encourage the development of a personalized education plan for each student, with families as full planning partners.
- Provide opportunities for staff members to learn and share successful approaches to engaging families in children's education.

Standard IV. Volunteering

Families are welcome in the school, and their support and assistance are sought. In order for parents and family members to feel appreciated and welcome, volunteer work must be meaningful and valuable. Capitalizing on the expertise and skills of parents and family members provides much-needed support to educators and administrators in their attempts to meet academic goals and student needs.

Quality Indicators. Effective programs:

- Ensure that greetings by office staff, signs near entrances, and other interactions with families create a climate in which parents and family members feel valued and welcome.
- Survey families regarding their interests, talents, and availability, and coordinate these resources with those that exist within the school.
- Ensure that family members who are unable to volunteer in the school building are given options for helping in other ways, at home or in their places of employment.
- Organize an easy, accessible program for using volunteers, providing ample training on procedures and school protocol.
- Develop a system for contacting all families for assistance as the year progresses.
- Design opportunities for those with limited time and resources to participate by addressing child-care, transportation, work schedule, needs, and so on.
- Show appreciation for families' participation, and value their diverse contributions.
- Educate and assist staff members in creating an inviting climate and using volunteer resources effectively.
- Ensure that volunteer activities are meaningful and built on volunteer interests and abilities.

Standard V. School Decision Making and Advocacy

Families are full partners in the decisions that affect children and families as individuals and as representatives of others. Families and educators depend on shared authority in decision-making systems to foster family trust, public confidence, and mutual support of each other's efforts in helping students succeed.

Quality Indicators. Effective programs:

- Provide an understandable, accessible, and well-publicized process for influencing decisions, raising issues or concerns, appealing decisions, and resolving problems.
- Encourage the formation of PTAs or other parent groups to identify and respond to issues of interest to families.
- Include family members on all decision-making and advisory committees, and ensure adequate training in such areas as policy, curriculum, budget, reform, safety, and personnel. Where site governance bodies exist, give equal representation to parents or other family members.
- Provide families with current information regarding school policies, practices, and both student and school performance data.
- Enable families to participate as partners when setting school goals, developing or evaluating programs and policies, and responding to performance data.
- Encourage and facilitate active family participation in decisions that affect students, such as student placement, course selection, and individual personalized education plans.
- Treat family concerns with respect and demonstrate genuine interest in developing solutions.
- Promote family participation on school district, state, and national committees.
- Provide training for staff and families on collaborative partnering and shared decision making.

Swap (1993) studies home–school involvement from a slightly different perspective, examining involvement in terms of the mutuality of interaction between home and school (see Table 4.1). She identifies four models reflecting a continuum of increasing involvement: protective, school-to-home transmission, curriculum enrichment, and partnership. For each model, she discusses the goal, the assumptions on which the model is based, and the model's advantages and disadvantages.

Table 4.1. Swap's Home–School Involvement Model

Protective Model

Goal is to reduce conflict between parents and educators, primarily through the separation of parents' and educators' functions, and to protect the school from interference by parents.

Assumptions:
- Parents delegate to the school the responsibility for educating their children.
- Parents hold school personnel accountable for results.
- Educators accept this delegation of responsibility.

Advantage:
- Generally effective at achieving its goal of protecting the school against parental intrusion.

Disadvantages:
- Exacerbates many conflicts between home and school by failing to create structures or predictable opportunities for preventive problem solving.
- Ignores the potential of home-school collaboration for improving school achievement.
- Rejects important resources for enrichment and school support that could be available to the school from families and other members of the community.

School-to-Home Transmission Model

Goal is to enlist parents in supporting objectives of the school.

Assumptions:
- Children's achievement is fostered by continuity of expectations and values between home and school.
- School personnel should identify the values and practices outside the school that contribute to student success.
- Parents should endorse the importance of schooling, reinforce school expectations at home, provide conditions at home that nurture development and support school success, and ensure that the child meets minimum academic and social requirements.

Advantages:
- Programs based on this model have increased children's school success.
- Parents receive clear direction from the school about the social and academic skills needed for children's success and about the parents' role in supporting the development of those skills.
- Parents welcome clear transmission of information, particularly when they have not had access to the social mainstream and seek such access for their children.

Disadvantages:
- Programs built on this model often contain components that reflect an unwillingness to consider parents as equal partners with important strengths.
- Some conditions such as dangerous housing, poor health, or stringent employment demands may limit some parents' ability to devote time and energy to parent-involvement activities.
- Schools may find it difficult to draft clear boundaries between the roles of school and home in formal education.

(continued)

- There is a danger of demeaning the value and importance of the family's culture in an effort to transmit the values and goals of the school.
- Differences in class or educational background can make teachers and parents uncomfortable; turf concerns may have to be addressed and negotiated.

Curriculum Enrichment Model

Goal is to expand and extend school's curriculum by incorporating families' contributions.

Assumptions:

- Continuity of learning between home and school is critically important to children's learning.
- The values and cultural histories of many children are omitted from the standard curriculum, leading to a discontinuity of culture between home and school, and often to reduced motivation, status, and achievement.
- The omission of cultural values distorts the curriculum, leading to a less accurate and less comprehensive understanding of events and achievements, and to a perpetuation of damaging beliefs and attitudes about minorities.
- Parents and educators should work together to enrich curriculum objectives and content.

Advantages:

- Model offers an attractive approach for incorporating parent involvement into children's learning.
- Drawing on the knowledge and expertise of parents increases the resources available to the school and provides rich opportunities for adults to learn from each other.
- The contributions of minorities who have not traditionally participated in schools are especially welcomed.

Disadvantages:

- Creating continuity between home and school demands a significant investment of parents' and educators' time and resources.
- The number of different cultures represented in some classrooms may make curriculum adaption very complex.
- Debate still rages about what the school's mission should be in educating children from diverse backgrounds. Should a "majority" culture be taught to all, or should curriculum reflect the diversity of the children?
- Differences in class or educational background can make teachers and parents uncomfortable; turf concerns must be addressed and negotiated.

(continued)

Table 4.1. Swap's Home–School Involvement Model *(continued)*

	• Relationships between home and school are based on mutual respect, and both parents and teachers are seen as experts and resources in the process of discovery.
Partnership Model Goal is for parents and educators to work together to accomplish a common mission, generally, for all children in school to achieve success.	*Assumptions:* • Accomplishing the joint mission requires a revisioning of the school environment and the discovery of new policies, practices, structures, roles, relationships, and attitudes in order to realize the vision. • Accomplishing the joint mission demands collaboration among parents, community representatives, and educators. Because the task is highly challenging and requires many resources, no single group acting alone can accomplish it. *Advantage:* • A true partnership requires a transforming vision of school culture based on collegiality, experimentation, mutual support, and joint problem solving. *Disadvantages:* • This model is difficult to implement. • It requires exchanging the traditional solitary role of the educator for a collaborative role and the development of new patterns of scheduling and interaction to support this new role.

WHY ARE THERE SO FEW COMPREHENSIVE PROGRAMS?

Summarizing almost three decades of research, Henderson and Berla (1994) conclude:

> The evidence is now beyond dispute. When schools work together with families to support learning, children tend to succeed not just in school, but throughout life. The form of parent involvement chosen is not as critical to the success of children as the fact that it be reasonably well planned, comprehensive, and long lasting.

Why, in the face of this evidence, have so few schools implemented comprehensive family involvement programs? Swap (1993) states the paradox:

> Given the widespread recognition that parent involvement in schools is important, that it is unequivocally related to improvements in children's achievement, and that improvement in children's achievement is urgently needed, it is paradoxical that most schools do not have comprehensive parent involvement programs.

Representatives of more than forty organizations and institutions involved in school reform, parent involvement, education, youth development, and research met in Del Mar, California, in 1997 to examine three closely related problems (Lewis and Henderson 1997):

> Overall, gains in student achievement are meager and far too slow. The gap between our most and least advantaged students, which had been narrowing, is again beginning to widen.
>
> Schools serving the lowest income areas, in general, have the fewest resources, the least qualified teachers, the lowest parent and community support and the worst student achievement. In many of these schools, the majority of students are scoring not just below average, but in the bottom quartile.
>
> Despite persuasive research showing a close connection between parent involvement and improved student achievement, few school reform efforts are making serious attempts to include low-income families.

Part of the explanation for the lack of programs is simple. Many educators—teachers and administrators—receive little or no training in how to involve families. The Harvard Family Research Project (National PTA, 1997) analyzed the certification requirements of all fifty states and found that only a minority specifically mention parent involvement. Most of the states that did list parent involvement training as a requirement "used vague terminology, such as working with parents, with no additional elaboration." Furthermore, the majority of school systems offer no formal training in parent involvement.

The Del Mar conference participants candidly acknowledged that in many low-income schools, "the most formidable barrier to parent involvement is racism. Racism in personal attitudes and in public policy must be out on the table" (Lewis and Henderson). The report noted that parents interviewed for a Title I study of parent involvement often defined what they wanted from school in one word: respect.

Another explanation for the lack of parent involvement programs is the changing definition of family. Moore (1993) observes:

> The United States is expanding its definition of "family." Gone are the days when "family" consisted of Mom, Dad, Dick, Jane, Puff, and Spot. "Family" now includes single mothers and children, single fathers and children, grandparents raising children, single unrelated adults living together and, increasingly, single adults living alone who claim other "family" members living elsewhere.

Moore might also have included foster parents, foster grandparents, and older siblings among the kinds of child-care arrangements. Educators need to change the way they think about children's support systems and devise ways to work with all families, however defined.

Finally, part of the explanation for the lack of programs resides with staff priorities. Researchers Funkhouser and Gonzales (1997) suggest what schools might do:

> Above all, schools, under the leadership of principals, possess the primary responsibility for initiating school-family partnerships. Schools can invest heavily in professional development that supports family involvement, create time for staff to work with parents, supply necessary resources, design innovative strategies to meet the needs of diverse fam-

ilies, and provide useful information to families on how they can contribute to their children's learning.

Funkhouser and Gonzales conclude: "Once schools initiate the dialogue and bring parents in as full partners, families are typically ready and willing to assume an equal responsibility for the success of their children."

CHARACTERISTICS OF SUCCESSFUL PARTNERSHIPS

There is no blueprint for a partnership school—a school that collaborates effectively with families. Because schools are so different, there is no single model, no single set of practices to which people can point and say, "That is the definitive partnership school." In recognition of this diversity, the U.S. Department of Education published *Family Involvement in Children's Education—Successful Local Approaches: An Idea Book* (Funkhouser and Gonzales, 1997), which reports on selected local approaches. The U.S. Department of Education's Office of Educational Research and Improvement published a condensed version of the publication in 2001.

Researchers found that schools that are successful in involving large numbers of parents and other family members use a team approach in which each partner assumes responsibility for the success of the partnership. They concluded that, although the most appropriate strategies for a particular community depend on local interests, needs, resources, successful approaches share an emphasis on innovation and flexibility.

The experiences of local schools and districts suggest the following guidelines (U.S. Department of Education, Office of Educational Research and Improvement, 2001):

There is no one-size-fits-all approach to partnership. Build on what works well locally. Begin the school–family partnership by identifying, with families, the strengths, interests, and needs of families, students, and school staff, and design strategies that respond to identified strengths, interests, and needs.

Training and staff development is an essential investment. Strengthen the school–family partnership with professional development and training for all school staff, as well as for parents and other family members. Both school staff and families need the knowledge and skills that will enable them to work with one another and with the larger community to support children's learning.

Communication is the foundation of effective partnerships. Plan strategies that accommodate the varied language and cultural needs, lifestyles, and work schedules of school staff and families. Even the best-planned school–family partnerships will fail if the participants cannot communicate effectively.

Flexibility and diversity are key. Recognize that effective parent involvement takes many forms that may not necessarily require parents' or other family members' presence at a workshop, meeting, or the school. The emphasis should be on families helping children learn, and this can happen in schools, homes, or elsewhere in the community.

Projects need to take advantage of the training, assistance, and funding offered by sources external to schools. These may include school districts, community organizations and public agencies, local colleges and universities, state education agencies, and regional assistance centers.

Change takes time. Recognize that developing a successful school–family partnership requires continued effort over time and that solving one problem often creates new challenges. Furthermore, a successful partnership requires the involvement of many stakeholders, not just a few.

Projects need to regularly assess the effects of the partnership using multiple indicators. This may include indicators of family, staff, and community participation in, and satisfaction with, school-related activities. They may also include measures of the quality of school-family interactions and varied indicators of student progress.

Swap (1993) identified four elements that families and educators should consciously incorporate into a partnership:

Two-way communication. Families and educators both have vital information to share. Educators share information with parents about children's progress in school; their expectations and hopes for the school and the children; and their curriculum, policies, and programs. Families share information with educators about each child's needs, strengths, and background and their expectations and hopes for the school and the child.

Enhanced learning at home and at school. Families contribute to children's learning by having high expectations, providing a setting that allows concentrated work, supporting and nurturing learning that occurs in school and elsewhere, and offering love. Educators develop curriculum and instructional practices and strong relationships with children that create conditions for optimal learning. Families and educators develop an array of ways in which parents and family members can be involved in and out of the classroom to enrich children's learning.

Mutual support. Educators support families by offering them educational programs that are responsive to their interests and needs. Families support educators in many ways, such as volunteering in school, organizing and planning activities, raising money, and attending school functions. Educators and families build trusting relationships and arrange occasions to acknowledge and celebrate each other's contributions to children's growth. Increasingly, the school becomes the critical institution in the community for linking families with useful health, education, and social services.

Joint decision making. Families and educators work together to improve the school through participation on councils, committees, and planning and management teams. They are involved in joint problem solving at the level of the individual child, the classroom, the school, and the district.

The National Coalition for Parent Involvement in Education (NCPIE) (2001) stresses that in order to create and *sustain* comprehensive home–school partnership programs, educators need to develop written policies that support them. NCPIE emphasizes that the policies should be developed in collaboration with teachers, administrators, families, students, businesses, community-based organizations, and other key stakeholders, and should address:

- Opportunities for all families to become involved in making decisions about how involvement programs will be designed, implemented, assessed, and strengthened.
- Involvement of families of all children at all ages and all grade levels.
- Recognition of diverse family structures (including nonbiological caregivers) and differing circumstances and responsibilities that may impede involvement.
- Outreach efforts that facilitate the participation of families who have low-level literacy skills or for whom English is not their primary language.
- Frequent provision of information to families about educational programs' objectives and their child's participation and progress in the programs.
- Professional development opportunities for teachers and staff to enhance their effectiveness in working with families.
- Linkages with service agencies and community groups that address key family issues.
- Opportunities for families to share in decision making regarding school policies and procedures that affect their children.

NCPIE also points out that the development of written policies is not enough. Implementation strategies must be designed to put the policies into practice. Implementation strategies should include:

- Assessing family's needs and interests about ways of working with the schools.
- Setting clear and measurable objectives based on parent and community input to help foster a sense of cooperation and communication between families, communities, and schools.
- Hiring (or designating) and training a parent/family liaison to directly contact parents and coordinate family activities. The liaison should be sensitive to the needs of families and the community, including the non-English-speaking community.
- Developing multiple outreach mechanisms to inform families, businesses, and the community about involvement policies and programs.

- Recognizing the importance of a community's historic, ethnic, linguistic, and cultural resources in generating interest in involvement.
- Using creative forms of communication between educators and families that are personal, goal-oriented, and make optimal use of new communication technologies.
- Mobilizing parents and family members as volunteers in the school assisting with instructional tasks and tutoring, support services, and administrative office functions.
- Providing staff development for teachers and administrators to enable them to work effectively with families and with each other as partners in the educational process.
- Ensuring access to information about nutrition, health care, services for individuals with disabilities, and support provided by schools or community agencies.
- Scheduling programs and activities flexibly to reach diverse families.
- Evaluating the effectiveness of the involvement programs and activities on a regular basis.

The National PTA (2000) recommends that schools use action teams representative of all concerned parties to help develop formal policies and action plans and monitor and evaluate the implementation process. These action teams are a way to harness the enthusiasm and energy necessary to create and sustain a system for making real and lasting changes.

GETTING STARTED

Three familiar family-involvement programs—parent conferences, home visits, and family resource centers—can become vehicles for launching a comprehensive home–school partnership initiative.

Parent–Teacher Conferences

A parent–teacher conference is one occasion when the expectations of the teacher and the family member should be the same: each speaking and listening to the other, each asking questions. These conferences should be a welcomed opportunity for both teachers and families, but frequently the opposite is true. Family members may have only their own experiences as a student—good or bad—as preparation for the conference. They may be apprehensive, burdened by a perception that the teacher knows it all, the teacher is in control, or the teacher doesn't really know my child. Teachers may have their own apprehensions based on their own experience—or lack of it—in working with families.

Schools can do much to make the parent–teacher conference successful for both teachers and families. In-service training sessions can be developed, and veteran teachers can give role-playing demonstrations of what to expect and how to react.

In scheduling conferences, schools must be sensitive to family demographics and cultural diversity. Scheduling must be flexible, often including time before school, before or after a family member's job, and on weekends. It may also be appropriate to include the student in the conference.

Teachers can do a number of things that will help make parent-teacher conferences a positive experience for both families and themselves:

- Begin on a positive note and listen closely and sympathetically for things that will be helpful in dealing with the child.
- Sit at a small table or a student desk so that the teacher's desk does not become a barrier between the teacher and the family member.
- Be prepared. Bring records such as grade sheets, papers, and other examples of student work, test results, notes, and so on.
- Make notes on the main points you want to get across to family members. Be specific, using simple language and avoiding jargon.
- Ask family members for their opinions and advice and show respect for their contributions.
- Give family members ample opportunity to discuss their concerns. When appropriate, invite them to visit the classroom during the regular school day.
- Focus on solutions arrived at jointly, concentrating on one or two areas, if possible.

The school can also help families prepare for conferences. Newsletters, PTA meetings, local newspaper features, and television and radio programs can provide tips on how to prepare for a productive meeting, including suggesting questions to ask the teacher.

Translators should be provided if language barriers are expected. Some schools recruit volunteers to check on the progress and well-being of students whose parents are either unable or unwilling to come to school.

Home Visits

Home visits are a family involvement strategy with several purposes. They may be used to welcome new families to the school community, survey families for their views on school policies and programs, report on student progress, demonstrate home-learning activities, help find solutions to specific problems, and so on. They may be conducted by the principal, teachers, community aides, or trained volunteers.

Teacher home visits can be especially beneficial. By visiting a student's home, teachers have an opportunity to gain insights and parental support that may help them work with students. Parents have an opportunity to communicate from the security of their own homes, both receiving and giving information about their children. In addition, students may enjoy welcoming teachers into their homes and seeing them in a new, more personal setting. Preparation for home visits should follow most of the same steps as preparation for a parent-teacher conference.

A major constraint historically has limited home visits. Most teachers have little training in establishing relationships with parents in any setting, although many have developed competence by working with parents in events held at the school. However, home visits require a somewhat different approach, and lack of specific training may be a formidable barrier. In considering whether to make a home visit, a teacher should keep several principles in mind. The home visit should have a clearly communicated purpose. At all times the teacher must be sensitive to cultural differences and set a tone for mutual respect. Regardless of personal feelings or opinions about the family or the household, the teacher must realize that there can be no viable relationship without mutual, demonstrated respect.

The reality is that a home visit may be refused by a parent or other family member. That person's rights must be respected. Another reality is that some neighborhoods are not safe to visit. In either case, consideration should be given to holding visits in the meeting rooms of housing projects or in other religious and community facilities.

Family Resource Centers

Family resource centers located within a school are often developed based on the growing belief that schools can be the linkage point for a variety of services often available to students and their families, but located in disparate sites around the community. In these centers, sometimes called parent education centers, schools can offer families a wealth of resources, including written and audiovisual materials in several languages that address a wide range of concerns. Topics may include school issues such as homework and child development issues such as discipline, communication, self-esteem, and stress management. Information may also be provided on community resources that families can draw on. Family resource centers may also provide speakers for community groups on specific topics.

Family resource centers are an effective way for schools to more proactively reach out to families. In addition to providing support services, the centers can offer parents information and training on the raising and educating of children. Nicoll (2002) cites research on parenting styles, which would appear to advocate for schools to provide parent-education services because parenting style and children's academic achievement are related.

> Across all ethnic groups, education levels, and family structures, the researchers consistently found that of the three parenting styles [authoritative, permissive, and authoritarian], authoritarian parenting was associated with the lowest grades, permissive parenting with the next lowest, and authoritative with the highest grades (mean GPA 3.2). In addition, inconsistent parenting or a frequent switching from an authoritarian to a permissive style was found to be strongly associated with the worst academic outcomes (1.8 GPA). These researchers concluded that parenting style is a more powerful predictor of student achievement than parent education, ethnicity or family structure.

Nicoll emphasizes that while various parenting styles are found across all income and educational levels, several studies have indicated a tendency for certain parenting styles to appear more frequently among different socioeconomic populations. He points out that family resource centers can offer parenting information and classes as part of a preventive/intervention program. "Formal parent education programs consistent with the authoritative parenting model can be offered . . . to train parents in effective child rearing practices."

Other kinds of family resource centers are not directly connected to a school. Parent Information Resource Centers, an outcome of Goals 2000, are in every state. The Individual with Disabilities Education Act also provides for parent resource centers, called Parent Training Information Centers, in every state.

TITLE I AS A TOOL FOR PARENT INVOLVEMENT

The Center for Law and Education (n.d.) recommends using Title I as a tool for building parents' capacity for school involvement. Under Title I, schools are required to provide assistance to parents to help them understand the National Education Goals, the standards and assessment that will be used to determine children's progress, and how family members may help. Every school district, except the smallest, is required to spend at least 1 percent of its Title I funds on training and education programs for parents, and parents must be involved in decisions about how this money is spent.

The local education agency (LEA) must have a parent-involvement policy that is jointly developed with parents (Center for Law and Education, n.d.). This policy must outline how the LEA will:

- Involve parents in the development of the local Title I plan.
- Build parents' capacity for involvement in decisions regarding their children's education.
- Coordinate strategies with parents in other programs, such as Even Start and Head Start.
- Conduct annual evaluations of the effectiveness of the parent involvement effort.
- Use the results of the annual evaluations to design strategies for school improvement and revise policy as needed.

In addition, every school that receives Title I funds must have a parent-involvement policy as part of its Title I plan. This policy must be developed jointly with, approved by, and distributed to, parents and must include a description of how the school will:

- Convene an initial annual meeting for parents to explain Title I.
- Offer flexible meetings for parents. Such meetings should include time to share experiences, brainstorm about creative programs to involve parents, and participate in decisions about the education of their children.
- Involve parents in planning, review, and improvement of the program.
- Give parents timely information about the program, including a description of the school curriculum and the assessments used to measure student progress.
- Implement a school-parent compact.
- Build capacity to ensure the effective involvement of parents. Schools and school districts are to provide training and materials and must coordinate with other programs, such as literacy training programs, in order to help parents help their children at home. Schools must also help teachers, principals, and other staff work well with parents.

The required school-parent compact must be jointly developed with parents and must outline how the school and parents will work together to help Title I students achieve the high content and performance standards set by the state for all students. The compact must:

- Describe the school's responsibility to provide high-quality curriculum and instruction in a supportive and effective environment that will enable students to meet the state standards.
- Describe how parents will be responsible for supporting their child's learning. (Examples given are monitoring whether children have finished their homework and how much television children are allowed to watch.)
- Address the importance of communication between teachers and parents. The school is required to provide at least (1) parent–teacher

conferences in elementary schools, at least once a year, when parents and teacher will discuss the compact as it relates to an individual child's achievement; (2) frequent reports to parents on the children's progress; and (3) reasonable access to staff and to classrooms to observe activities.

BARRIERS TO FAMILY INVOLVEMENT

One barrier to establishing a school–family partnership may be the community's perception of the school and its staff. From 1973 to 1993, the proportion of Americans who expressed confidence in educational institutions dropped from 27 to 22 percent, while the proportion of those expressing little confidence rose from 8 to 18 percent (National Opinion Research Center, 1993). In a report reviewing almost thirty years of polling, Phi Delta Kappa International (1999) maintains that the most obvious conclusion is that the closer people are to the public schools, the higher their regard for them: "The relationship between proximity and regard should make it clear that educators need to be diligent in their efforts to get more people into public schools."

An earlier study by Phi Delta Kappa Foundation (1988) examines the factors that most influenced the gain or loss of community confidence in a local school. The top three factors ranked as sources of gaining confidence were, in order, teacher attitudes, administrator attitudes, and student attitudes. The top three factors resulting in a loss in confidence were teacher attitudes, the decision-making process, and administrator attitudes. Obviously, the attitudes of teachers and administrators toward family involvement affect the ways in which they reach out to students and families, determining whether the school environment is welcoming.

Sarason (1991) points out that students have a great deal of influence on the public's confidence in schools. Students are the most important constituency of any school, but they are often left out of decisions:

We often act as though students are the products of school, when, in fact, kids must be the workers in order to learn. They must want to come to school, and they must be willing to work, even when no one is hanging over them. If we can't achieve this, no kind of school reform, however ambitious, will improve student learning and public education. So it's hard to explain why we don't routinely ask kids—especially kids in trouble—about how to improve schools.

Finders and Lewis (n.d.) examined some of issues affecting how families—particularly minority and low-income families—view schools. They point out that in many schools, "the institutional perspective holds that children who do not succeed in school have parents who do not get involved in school activities or support school goals at home." The institutional view of nonparticipating parents is based on a deficit model, frequently expressed in terms of "Those who *need* to come, don't come." In many instances, this view also ignores the reality of the enormous changes in family structures, employing family-involvement efforts based on a two-parent, economically self-sufficient nuclear family.

Parent-involvement studies find that most parents very much want to help their children succeed in school. The most commonly cited barriers to parental involvement are lack of time, uncertainty about what to do, cultural differences, and lack of a supportive environment (White-Clark and Decker, 1996).

The feeling of having nothing to contribute is a common barrier for minority parents and those of a lower socioeconomic status. A similar barrier to involvement is the feeling of powerlessness—the conviction that what one person does or does not do will make no difference. Sarason (1991) sums up the effect of this feeling on an individual's willingness to become involved: "When one has no stake in the way things are, when one's needs or opinions are provided no forum, when one sees oneself as the object of unilateral actions, it takes no particular wisdom to suggest that one would rather be elsewhere." If educators—teachers and administrators—truly want families' involvement in school and in the education of children, they will have to find ways to empower families and share some of their power in making decisions about their children's education. Encouragement and support must be offered to each group; each group must be made to feel wanted and needed.

OVERCOMING BARRIERS

Funkhouser and Gonzales offer practical suggestions and strategies for overcoming other common barriers to family involvement in schools.

Overcoming Time and Resource Constraints

Families and school staff need time to get to know each other, learn from one another, and plan how to work together. Strategies for helping teachers include (1) assigning parent coordinators or home–school liaisons to help teachers make and maintain contact with families through home visits or by covering classes so teachers can meet with family members; (2) providing time during the school day for teachers to meet with parents or visit them at their homes; (3) providing stipends or compensatory time off for teachers who meet with families after school hours; and (4) freeing teachers from such routine duties as lunchroom supervision so that they can meet with family members. Schools can also provide teachers easier access to telephones and voice mail, provide information hot lines, and use technology in other ways to make communication easier and more efficient.

Schools can demonstrate sensitivity to families' time and safety concerns by scheduling meetings to accommodate families' working schedules and holding them at places other than the school when advisable. Schools can also help by (1) providing early notices about meetings and activities to allow families to adjust their schedules; (2) offering the same event more than once; (3) providing information to families who could not attend a meeting; and (4) establishing homework hotlines and voice-mail systems within the school so families can stay in touch from their homes. Schools can address families' resource constraints by providing transportation and child-care services, holding school-sponsored events in nonschool facilities convenient to families' homes, and making home visits.

Dispelling Misconceptions

Effective training for teachers and other school staff can play a key role in dispelling some of the misconceptions and stereotypes that are barriers to effective partnerships. Schools can provide school staff with information and strategies on how to reach out to families and work effectively with them. Some schools have found that using parent coordinators or parent volunteers to train school staff not only builds parents' leadership skills but also gives staff the opportunity to learn about families from a family member's perspective.

Schools can use a variety of ways to inform and involve parents. Newsletters and school information hot lines can help families keep up-to-date with school issues and events. Posting fliers in places where families congregate, developing parent handbooks, and making telephone calls (especially to share positive information) can channel information to families. Holding periodic parenting workshops can help families learn about child development. Schools can offer workshops, hands-on training, and home visits to help parents learn how to support children's learning at home. Other programs can help family members capitalize on their skills and expertise and learn how to assist school staff and students as volunteers. Family resource centers, as discussed earlier, can provide a wide variety of information and support services.

Bridging Differences

Differences in language, culture, and educational attainment can make communication between families and school staff difficult, and may adversely affect family participation in school activities. In addition, some immigrant families have different views of schools and their own role in their children's education. Schools must be sensitive to the needs of families who may not easily understand the written communications sent to them or may see themselves as unprepared to help with homework or school work. Family members' bad memories of their own school experiences may also deter involvement. Solutions to overcoming this barrier include designing ways for nonreaders or those with limited English proficiency to work with children to promote literacy. Schools can give family members an opportunity to experience what their children are learning in an environment that is pleasant and nonthreatening, thus allaying doubts about the family members' ability to help their children. Schools can provide translation services (written and oral), workshops, and classes in the families' first language. Home–school liaisons can also play an important role in reaching out to parents of different backgrounds, building trust between home and school. Schools can provide training to school staff specifically targeted to bridging cultural differences between home and school.

Tapping External Supports

Schools rarely have funds, staff, or space for all the family-involvement activities they want or need to offer. However, they can forge partnerships with local businesses, agencies, colleges, and universities to provide such supports as educational programming and homework hot lines, health and social services, conferences and workshops, adult education, school refurbishing, transportation, and nonschool meeting space. District and state supports for family involvement initiatives may include funding, training, and resource centers.

Funkhouser and Gonzales stress that schools that succeed in involving large numbers of parents and other family members are investing in finding solutions, not making excuses. Haugen (2001) suggests that administrators and teachers who are serious about eliminating roadblocks to parent involvement begin by:

- Building teacher/parent relations to develop trust.
- Building and valuing parent strengths, knowledge, and skills.
- Collaborating to set clear goals and objectives for all involved, along with gathering feedback.
- Researching and collaborating with colleagues, administration, and community to resolve issues.

Involving Hard-to-Reach Parents

As White-Clark and Decker (1996) point out, the terms "at-risk" and "hard-to-reach" have become clichés—verbal dumping grounds for a variety of conditions, some of them educational, others personal or societal. The student population labeled "at-risk" is usually poor and often from a minority culture, and "hard-to-reach" parents are often assumed to be minorities, with low socioeconomic status, an inner-city residence, and little formal education. Another label for such parents is "disadvantaged."

Educators often perceive Hispanic families as hard-to-reach. Inger (1992) points out that there is a reason for this misperception:

In Hispanics' countries of origin, the roles of parents and schools were sharply divided. Many low-income Hispanic parents view the U.S.

school system as "a bureaucracy governed by educated non-Hispanics whom they have no right to question." . . . Many school administrators and teachers misread the reserve, the non-confrontational manners, and the non-involvement of Hispanic parents to mean that they are uncaring about the children's education—and this misperception has led to a cycle of mutual mistrust and suspicion between poor Hispanic parents and school personnel.

Inger (1992) and Manning and Baruth (2000) contend that many educators do not understand the important role of the extended family in some cultures. The role of the extended family remains very important in Hispanic families, but it does not extend to involvement in school. As Inger explains, "At home, Hispanic children are usually nurtured with great care by a large number of relatives. Often, however, family members don't extend their caregiving role into their children's schools; they are reluctant to become involved in either their children's education or in school activities."

Inger is emphatic that ways must be found to increase the involvement of Hispanic families in schools:

There is considerable evidence that parent involvement leads to improved student achievement, better school attendance, and reduced dropout rates, and that these improvements occur regardless of the economic, racial, or cultural background of the family. . . . Thus, given that 40 percent of Hispanic children [1992 statistic that is greater today] are living in poverty, that Hispanics are the most under-educated major segment of the U.S. population, and that many Hispanic children enter kindergarten seriously lacking in language development and facility, regardless of whether they are bilingual, speak only English, or speak only Spanish, the need to increase the involvement of Hispanic parents in their children's schools is crucial.

Inger outlines a number of lessons that have been learned from the efforts of educators and community groups to improve the involvement of Hispanic parents:

- Programs that increase and retain the involvement of Hispanic parents follow a simple, basic rule: they make it easy for parents to participate. For example, programs and materials are bilingual, child care is provided, there are no fees, times and locations of meetings are arranged for the convenience of the parents, and transportation is provided.

- Outreach efforts require extra staff. They take considerable time and cannot be handled by a regular staff person with an already full job description. Also, successful outreach is organized by people who have volunteered, not by people who have been assigned to the job.
- Hispanic parents need to be allowed to become involved with the school community at their own pace. Often, before they join existing parent organizations, Hispanic parents want to acquire the skills and confidence to contribute as equals.
- The hardest part of building a partnership with low-income Hispanic parents is getting parents to the first meeting. Impersonal efforts— letters, flyers, announcements at church services or on local radio or television—were largely ineffective, even when these efforts were in Spanish. The only successful approach is personal: face-to-face conversations with parents in their primary language in their homes. Home visits not only personalize the invitations but help school staff to understand and deal with parent's concerns.
- Since many low-income Hispanic parents feel uncomfortable in schools, successful projects hold the first meetings outside of the school, preferably at sites that are familiar to the parents. Successful first meetings are primarily social events; unsuccessful ones are formal events at school, with information aimed "at" the parents.
- To retain the involvement of low-income Hispanic parents, every meeting has to respond to some needs or concerns of the parents. Programs that consult with parents regarding agendas and meeting formats and begin with the parents' agenda eventually cover issues that the school considers vital; those that stick exclusively to the school's agenda lose the parents.

"Many schools have unconsciously erected barriers to Hispanic parents, adopting a paternalistic or condescending attitude toward them" (Inger, 1992).

Also, educators often perceive fathers as hard-to-reach. As the National Center for Educational Statistics (1997) reports, school programs traditionally have been heavily dominated by mothers who are more likely than fathers to attend a school event. School programs also tend to focus on mothers' involvement because the overwhelming majority of children in single-parent households live with their mother. Nicoll contends that schools need to increase their efforts to involve fathers in their children's education. "While the research on father influences on children's adjustment is still somewhat limited and inconsistent in design, the importance of the father's role must be recognized and father involvement fostered." In support for his contention, he cites the National Center for Educational Statistics report that says that one plausible conclusion from the existing body of research is that maternal involvement is beneficial for the children's social and emotional adjustment to school, but paternal involvement may be most important for academic achievement.

The 1995 *Kids Count,* "Fathers and Families" (Annie E. Casey Foundation), reported on the negative effect of the absence of fathers in many children's lives, particularly children from minority and low-income families. In October 1999, the U.S. Departments of Education and Health and Human Services held a live, interactive teleconference for educators and family service providers on strategies for engaging fathers in children's learning. The rationale for the teleconference was based on research showing that when fathers are involved, children learn more, perform better in school, and exhibit healthier behavior. It was emphasized that even when fathers do not share a home with their children, their active involvement can have a lasting, positive impact. A two-hour national satellite event, "Fathers Matter!", offered strategies and tools for teachers, school principals, child-care providers, and others to involve fathers in children's learning, including readiness. Hosted by the Secretary of Education and the Secretary of Health and Human Services, the teleconference suggested ways to make schools more welcoming to parents, develop family-friendly policies in workplaces, encourage support for fathers' roles in education, and provide professional development for those who work with children and families (Partnership for Family Involvement in Education, 1999).

The truth is that any parent can be hard to reach. Professional parents who work long hours or parents who lack child care may be just as "hard-to-reach" as parents who fit the common stereotypes of poor and minority.

White-Clark and Decker acknowledge that there are often barriers to overcome in involving parents and families in children's education, and that no one approach will work with all families at all times. They agree that schools should be family-friendly and that every effort should be made to bridge language gaps and cultural differences, but they contend that fewer families would be labeled "hard-to-reach" if educators took a more optimistic approach to them. They suggest that educators should:

- Believe family involvement is important and that educational programs are incomplete without it.
- Embody an ethic of caring, making a sincere effort to understand the life situations of families who are not involved in the school and, when possible, helping them overcome barriers to involvement.
- Disregard "hard-to-reach" stereotypes, facing up to their own misperceptions.
- Develop high expectations for all families, seeking realistic rather than maximum involvement.
- Conceptualize the roles of parents in their individual situations when designing opportunities for involvement.
- Be willing to address personal concerns, including any of their own experiences that may impede the implementation of activities for family involvement.
- Study the framework of family-involvement programs in order to develop a clear understanding of their purpose and function.
- Be willing to work to improve family involvement, including getting out of the school building and into the community when it is beneficial to do so.

PREPARING EDUCATORS FOR FAMILY INVOLVEMENT

The Harvard Family Research Project has been looking into the relative lack of teacher certification requirements in the area of family involvement since 1992. As recently as 1997, researchers (Shartrand, Weiss, Kreider, and Lopez) found the same lack and noted that the training offered was often limited in both content and method.

A recent ERIC Digest (Hiatt-Michael, n.d.) cited research confirming that training teachers to work with families is still lacking. One study found a significant increase during the late 1990s in the number of states with some administrative or credential statement requiring teachers to possess some knowledge and skills related to family and community involvement. The author reported that the results of this and other studies were similar to additional studies reported by Epstein (1992). She noted that within university preparation and in school practice, early childhood and special education focus a disproportionate amount of attention on family involvement, and that "although classroom teachers assert that working with families is important to the child's positive school outcomes, they receive little formal training and, thus, possess minimal knowledge and skills to work with parents."

Although the Harvard Family Research Project's publication *New Skills for New Schools: Preparing Teachers in Family Involvement* (Shartrand et al., 1997) focuses on teacher training, the research findings are of interest to all educators who seek to involve families in the education of children. In addition to identifying the skills, knowledge, and attitudes necessary to prepare for family involvement, the research confirmed three needs:

1. More direct experience with families and communities.
2. Support in making school conditions conducive to family involvement.
3. Opportunities to share successful experiences and outcomes with colleagues.

The publication focuses on developing mutual partnerships involving all families while recognizing a range of types of family involvement. It places training needs in a framework of content areas:

- general family involvement
- general family knowledge
- home–school communication
- family involvement in learning activities
- families supporting schools
- schools supporting families
- families as change agents

Each of the content areas is divided into four approaches (see Table 4.2): a functional approach, based on the work of Epstein; parent

Table 4.2. Training Needs by Type of Family Involvement

General Family Involvement

Functional Approach	Parent Empowerment	Cultural Competence	Social Capital
• Attitude that all teachers should learn skills and sensitivity in dealing with parents.	• Attitude that all parents want what is best for their children and want to be good parents.	• Knowledge that minority and low socioeconomic status students benefit academically from family involvement.	• Knowledge of the idea of social capital and parental investment in their children's learning.
• Knowledge about the goals and benefits of family involvement and the barriers to it.	• Attitude that parents are children's first and most important teachers.	• Skills in using culturally appropriate themes in the curriculum.	
• Skills in involving parents of all backgrounds in school.	• Attitude of respect for the family's role in children's nurturance and education.		
• Knowledge of the role of school administration in promoting or preventing family involvement.	• Attitude that the most useful knowledge about rearing children can be found within the community.		

General Family Knowledge

Functional Approach	Parent Empowerment	Cultural Competence	Social Capital
• Knowledge of different cultural beliefs, lifestyles, childrearing practices, family structures, and living environments.	• Attitude of support toward parents, focused on strengths rather than deficits.	• Knowledge about cultural influences on discipline, learning, and childrearing practices.	• Knowledge that schools and homes have different norms and values, and that such differences influence partnerships between home and school.
• Attitude of respect for different backgrounds and lifestyles.	• Knowledge of power differences among groups in society.	• Knowledge of personal assumptions, belief systems, and prejudices that can affect relationships with family and community.	• Knowledge of common values that span different cultures and institutions.
• Knowledge of the functions of families.	• Knowledge of the history of disenfranchised groups.	• Skills in understanding and reversing negative stereotypes of parents, families, and community members.	• Skills in conflict negotiation and consensus building.
	• Knowledge of the effects of a family's disadvantaged status on its interactions with teachers or other professionals.		
	• Knowledge of how families interact with schools and similar institutions.		

(continued)

Table 4.2. Training Needs by Type of Family Involvement *(continued)*

Home-to-School Communication

Functional Approach

- Skills in effective interpersonal communication.
- Communication skills to deal with defensive behaviors, distrust, hostility, and frustration.
- Skills in using active listening and effective communication to understand families and build trust and cooperation.

Parent Empowerment

- Skills in effective interpersonal communication.
- Skills in treating parents as equal partners.
- Knowledge of the importance of positive communication with parents, even when a child is having problems.
- Attitude that parents should not be controlled, but rather that their views and needs should be understood.

Cultural Competence

- Knowledge of the importance of logistics of obtaining translators for families who do not read or speak English.
- Knowledge of the styles of communication of different cultural groups.

Social Capital

- Skills in communication expectations and values to build a sense of trust among members in the community.
- Skills in communicating with parents in a way that models how values will be transmitted between other members of society.
- Skills in being attentive, persistent, dependable, and showing caring over time in relationships with families.

Family Involvement in Learning

Functional Approach

- Skills in involving parents in their children's learning outside of the classroom.
- Skills in sharing teaching skills with parents.

Parent Empowerment

- Skills in developing activities that build parents' confidence and facility in conducting home learning activities.
- Skills in providing constructive feedback.

Cultural Competence

- Skills to incorporate family "funds of knowledge" into homework projects so that families and communities can contribute to children's learning.

Social Capital

- Skills in motivating family involvement in home-learning activities.
- Skills in home visiting.
- Skills in fostering community participation in educational activities.

(continued)

Families Supporting Schools

Functional Approach
- Skills in involving parents in the school and in the classroom.

Parent Empowerment
- Skills in making parents feel valued by inviting them to contribute their expertise in the classroom and in the school.

Cultural Competence
- Knowledge of the financial and time constraints of parents.
- Skills in creating opportunities for parental and family-member involvement in school.
- Skills in discovering different potential contributions of families.

Social Capital
- Skills in fostering families' investment in school by volunteering, attending events, and fundraising.
- Skills in utilizing resources of other community groups.
- Skills in building reciprocal exchanges between school and home.

Schools Supporting Families

Functional Approach
- Knowledge of how schools can support families' social and educational needs.
- Knowledge about processes of consultation and communication.
- Knowledge of the roles of various specialists and interprofessional collaboration.
- Skills in referral procedures.

Parent Empowerment
- Knowledge of and skills in promoting parent empowerment through adult education and parenting courses.
- Knowledge of and skills in ameliorating families' basic needs as a first step to helping them help their children academically.
- Skills in incorporating families' self-identified needs in parent programs and school activities.

Cultural Competence
- Knowledge of resources for cultural minorities.
- Skills in creating opportunities for families with different backgrounds to learn from one another.
- Sensitive attitude toward different groups' perceptions of school "help" and reciprocity.
- Skills in incorporating family preferences into parent programs.

Social Capital
- Skills in identifying the expectations and goals of families.
- Knowledge of how school events can create social capital.
- Skills in building reciprocal exchanges between school and home.

(continued)

Table 4.2.   Training Needs by Type of Family Involvement *(continued)*

Families as Change Agents

Functional Approach	Parent Empowerment	Cultural Competence	Social Capital

• Skills in supporting and involving families as decision makers, action researchers, advocates, and parent and teacher trainers.
• Skills in sharing information to help families make decisions.
• Skills in sharing leadership and transferring it to parents.
• Skills in interacting with parents on an equal footing.
	• Skills in promoting political empowerment for families through:
	  – Advocating shared decision making in schools.
	  – Informing families of governance roles in the school.
	  – Recruiting family members to sit on boards and councils.
	  – Preventing families' voices from being overridden in meetings.
		• Skills in encouraging parents or other family members to run for seats on school councils.
		• Knowledge of importance of providing translators at school council meetings.
		• Knowledge of importance of having teachers from various cultures be present on councils to make all families feel welcome.
			• Attitude that shared decision making is an essential ingredient to establishing and maintaining a common set of core values.
			• Skills in negotiating differences and conflicting opinions.
			• Skills in involving families in the design of curriculum that represents shared values.
			• Skills in co-development of mission statement that represents shared values.

empowerment, based on the work of Cochran; cultural competence, based on the work of Moll; and social capital, based on the work of Coleman (Shartrand et al., 1997).

TRAINING MATERIALS

As part of its continuing effort to increase family involvement, the U.S. Department of Education's Partnership for Family Involvement in Education held a video teleconference on preparing teachers to work with families using the Harvard Family Research Center's *New Skills for New Schools* as a base. After the event, it produced *Partners for Learning: Preparing Teachers to Involve Families* (Partnership for Family Involvement in Education, 1999) which contains a guide on how to use it for in-service and pre-service training.

The Individuals with Disabilities Education Act (IDEA) emphasizes the importance of family participation in educational decision making. The U.S. Department of Education's Office of Special Education Programs (1999) prepared training materials designed to provide parents and schools with a first tool to ensure that IDEA is consistently and properly implemented throughout the country. Although its focus is on disability programs and policies, the training materials are broadly useful, particularly the section on parent and student participation in decision making. The National Information Center for Children and Youth with Disabilities (www.nichcy.org), a national information and referral center, has the *IDEA 97 Training Package* posted online.

Two national centers focus specifically on involving fathers in children's lives and offer resources and training materials useful to educators and community organizations. The National Center for Fathering (NCF) was founded in 1990 in response to the dramatic trend toward fatherlessness in America. NCF conducts research on fathers and fathering and develops practical resources for fathers in a variety of fathering situations (www.fathers.com). The National Center for Strategic Nonprofit Planning and Community Leadership (NPCL) focuses on the special needs of fathers in *fragile families*—those with low-income parents who never married. NPCL offers a full range of services, including needs assessment, evaluation, conference planning, professional development, financial management, and program development (www.npcl.org).

REFERENCES

Annie E. Casey Foundation. (1995). *Kids count data book*. Washington, D.C.: Center for the Study of Social Policy.

Center for Law and Education. (n.d.). Title I as a tool for parent involvement. In *CLE issue/project areas*. Retrieved January 23, 2002, from www.cleweb .org/title1/tool.

Decker, L. E., and Decker, V. A. (2001). *Engaging families and communities: Pathways to educational success*. Fairfax, Va.: National Community Education Association.

Education Week on the Web. (2001). Parent involvement. Retrieved January 7, 2002, from www.edweek.org/context/topics/issuespage.cfm?id=12.

Epstein, J. (1992). School and family partnerships. In *Encyclopedia of educational research*. New York: Macmillian.

Finders, M., and Lewis, C. (n.d.). Why some parents don't come to school. Retrieved January 23, 2002, from www.ascd.org/readingroom/edlead/9405/ finders.htm.

Funkhouser, J. E., and Gonzales, M. R. (1997). *Family involvement in children's education—Successful local approaches: An idea book*. Washington, D.C.: Government Printing Office.

Harkavy, I., and Blank, M. (2002). *Community schools*. Retrieved April 19, 2002, from www.educationweek.org/ew/newstory-cfm?slug=slharkavy.h21

Haugen, J. (2001). Who wants to eliminate roadblocks to parent involvement? Retrieved January 23, 2002, from www.ascd.org/readingroom/classlead/ 0108/clhaugen7.htm.

Hiatt-Michael, D. (n.d.). Preparing teachers to work with parents (Digest: 2001-02). Retrieved September 7, 2002, from www.ericsp.org/pages/ digests/Teachers-Parents.html.

Henderson, A. T., and Berla, N. (1994). *A new generation of evidence: The family is critical to student achievement*. Washington, D.C.: National Committee for Citizens in Education.

Houston, P. (2001). E-Mail letter to American Association of School Administration members. (August 31).

Inger, M. (1992). Increasing the school involvement of Hispanic parents. *Clearinghouse on Urban Education Digest*, 80. Retrieved April 3, 2002, from eric-web.tc.columbia.edu.

Lewis, A. C., and Henderson, A. T. (1997). *Urgent message: Families crucial to school reform*. Washington, D.C.: Center for Law and Education.

Manning, M. L., and Baruth, L. G. (2000). *Multicultural education of children and adolescents*. Boston, Mass.: Allyn and Bacon.

Moles, O. D., and D'Angelo. D. (Eds.). (1993). *Building school-family partnerships for learning: Workshops for urban educators.* Washington, D.C.: Office of Educational Research and Development, U.S. Office of Education.

Moore, L. (1993). Re-defining; re-inventing, and re-establishing community. In S. Thompson (Ed.), *Whole child whole community.* Boston, Mass.: Institute for Responsive Education.

National Center for Education Statistics. (1997). *Fathers' involvement in their children's schools.* Washington, D.C.: U.S. Department of Education, Office of Educational Research and Improvement.

National Center for Fair and Open Testing. (2002). Will more testing improve schools? *FairTest.* Retrieved January 24, 2002, from www.fairtest.org/facts/Will%20More%20Testing%20Improve%20Schools.html

National Coalition for Parent Involvement in Education. (2001). *Developing family/school partnerships: Guidelines for schools and school districts.* www.ncpie.org

National Opinion Research Center. (1993). Public opinion and demographic report: Confidence in institutions. *American Enterprise,* 4.

National PTA. (1993). *School is what we make it! A parent involvement planning kit.* Chicago: National PTA.

National PTA. (1997). *Teacher's guide to parent and family involvement.* Chicago: National PTA.

National PTA. (1998). *National standards for parent/family involvement programs.* Chicago: National PTA.

National PTA. (2000). *Building successful partnerships: A guide for developing parent and family involvement programs.* Bloomington, Ind.: National Educational Service.

National PTA. (n.d.). Foreword. *National standards for parent/family involvement programs.* Retrieved September 7, 2002, from www.pta.org/parentinvolvement/standards/pfistand.asp.

Nicoll, W. G. (2002). *The case for family involvement programs: A look at the research evidence.* Paper presented at the Academic Achievement and Best Practices Leadership Conference of the Florida Department of Education's Office of Family Involvement. Safety Harbor, Fla., April 9, 2002.

Partnership for Family Involvement in Education. (1999). *Partners for learning: Preparing teachers to involve families.* Retrieved March 4, 2002, from pfie.ed.gov.

Phi Delta Kappa Foundation. (1988). *Handbook for developing public confidence in school.* Bloomington, Ind.: Phi Delta Kappa.

Phi Delta Kappa International. (1999). *Fast facts PDK/Gallup poll: Local schools supported but more outreach needed.* Retrieved March 5, 2002, from www.pdkintl.org/whatis/ff4poll.htm.

Rose, L. C., and Gallup, A. M. (2001). The 33rd annual Phi Delta Kappa/ Gallup Poll of the public's attitudes toward the public schools. *Phi Delta Kappan*, 83, 1.

Sarason, S. B. (1991). *The predictable failure of educational reform.* San Francisco: Jossey-Bass.

Shartrand, A. M., Weiss, H. B., Kreider, H. M., and Lopez, M. E. (1997). *New skills for new schools: Preparing teachers in family involvement.* Cambridge, Mass.: Harvard Family Research Project.

Swap, S. M. (1993). *Developing home-school partnerships: From concepts to practice.* New York: Teachers College Press.

U.S. Department of Education. (2002). *No child left behind: Reauthorization of the elementary and secondary education act.* Retrieved January 23, 2002, from www.ed.gov/offices/OESE/esea/index.htm.

U.S. Department of Education, Office of Educational Research and Improvement. (2001). *Family involvement in children's education: Successful local approaches—An idea book.* Washington, D.C.: U.S. Department of Education.

U.S. Department of Education, Office of Special Education Programs. (1999). IDEA 97 training package. Retrieved March 4, 2002, from www.nichcy.org/ Trainpkg/toc.htm.

Wherry, J. H. (1999). Selected parent involvement research. The Parent Institute. Retrieved February 3, 2001, from www.par-inst.com.

White-Clark, R., and Decker, L. E. (1996). The hard-to-reach parent: Old challenges, new insights. Fairfax, Va.: National Community Education Association.

WEBSITES FOR MORE INFORMATION AND LINKS TO OTHER RELEVANT SITES

Association for Supervision and Curriculum Development, www.ascd.org

Center for Law and Education, www.cleweb.org

Colorado Parent Information and Resource Center, www.cpirc.org

Harvard Family Research Project, gseweb.harvard.edu/~hfrp

Middle Web Index, www.middleweb.com

National Center for Fathering, www.fathers.com

National Center for Strategic Nonprofit Planning and Community Leadership, www.npcl.org

National Center for Parent Involvement in Education, www.ncpie.org

National Education Association, www.nea.org

National Information Center for Children and Youth with Disabilities, www .nichcy.org

National Parent Information Network, npin.org

National PTA, www.pta.org

National Standards for Parent/Family Involvement Programs, www.pta.org/ programs/

Teachers Guide to Parent and Family Involvement, www.pta.org/programs/

North Central Regional Educational Lab, www.ncrel.org

Parent Institute, www.par-inst.com

Partnership for Family Involvement in Education, www.pfie.ed.gov

Phi Delta Kappa International, www.pdkintl.org

U.S. Department of Education, Urgent Message: Families Crucial to School Reform, www.ed.gov/pubs/parents

CHAPTER 5

School–Community Collaboration

School consumes a surprisingly small portion of children's lives in America. Young people who diligently attend school six hours a day, 180 days a year, from kindergarten through the twelfth grade, will, upon their eighteenth birthday, have spent just 9 percent of their time since birth in school. This fact raises two critical questions: (1) What leverage does the other 91 percent of a child's time have on achieving the goal of academic success for all children? and (2) In what ways can educators ameliorate the negative effects and build on the positive ones from that 91 percent portion?

These are not new questions. In 1913, Joseph K. Hart pondered basically the same considerations in his examination of the educational resources of villages and rural communities.

> No child can escape his community. He may not like his parents, or the neighbors, or the ways of the world. He may drown under the processes of living, and wish he were dead. But he goes on living, and he goes on living in the community. The life of the community flows about him, foul or pure; he swims in it, drinks it, goes to sleep in it, and wakes to the new day to find it still about him. He belongs to it; it nourishes him, or starves him, or poisons him; it gives him the substance of his life. And in the long run it takes its toll of him, and all he is.

A community also influences public education by the way its members rate the community's schools. The drop in public confidence in public education over the last several decades is well documented. In 1993, the National Opinion Research Center found that only 22 percent of Americans had confidence in public education institutions. The 1998

Phi Delta Kappa/Gallup Poll (Phi Delta Kappa International, 1999) suggests why this is so. "People assign low grades to the nation's schools. These are the ones they do not know, and the ones on which their information comes from the media." The same report makes a recommendation: "The demographic breakdowns for this poll make it clear that educators need to redouble their efforts to reach out to nonwhites by listening to them, addressing their problems, and providing opportunities for more involvement in school matters."

The results of the 2000 Phi Delta Kappa/Gallup Poll (Phi Delta Kappa International) of the public's attitudes toward public schools should be of interest to educators at all levels. The findings show a

> turning away from high-stakes testing; the leveling off and the downward trend in support for choice involving private or church-related schools; the fact that lack of financial support has jumped into first place as the biggest problem; the preference for balance in the curriculum over a focus on "the basics"; and the clear support for public schools that is evident throughout the poll.

The poll shows that

> Respondents continue to indicate a high level of satisfaction with the local schools. . . . Public satisfaction is also evident in the fact that 59 percent of Americans believe that reforming the existing system of public schools, rather than seeking an alternative system, is the best way to bring about school improvement. When given the specific choice, 75 percent would improve and strengthen existing public schools while just 22 percent would opt for vouchers, the alternative most frequently mentioned by public school critics.

The poll also asked where and by whom the public believes decisions regarding local schools should be made. The responses affirm the principle of local control.

The need for schools to work with the whole community, not just the families of school children, is the topic of an increasing number of reports. *Learning Together: The Developing Field of School Community Initiatives* (Melaville, 1998) summarizes the reasoning:

> Schools have a first-order responsibility for ensuring young people's academic success, but that doesn't diminish the responsibility of the rest

of the community to help create the conditions in which young people can succeed more broadly not only in school, but also in their careers, in their civic responsibilities and eventually as parents. School-community initiatives provide a valuable setting in which to connect both school and community resources. The diversity of these initiatives is daunting.

The *National Standards for Parent/Family Involvement Programs* (National PTA, 1998) lists "Collaborating with the Community" as one of the six standards (the first five are described in chapter 4) and specifies quality indicators of successful programs.

Standard VI. Collaborating with the Community

Community resources are used to strengthen schools, families, and student learning. As part of the larger community, schools and other programs fulfill important community goals. In like fashion, communities offer a wide array of resources valuable to schools and the families they serve. The best partnerships are mutually beneficial and structured to connect individuals, not just institutions or groups. This connection enables the power of community partnerships to be unleashed.

Quality Indicators. Effective programs:

- Distribute information regarding cultural, recreational, academic, health, social, and other resources that serve families within the community.
- Develop partnerships with local business and service groups to advance student learning and assist schools and families.
- Encourage employers to adopt policies and practices that promote and support adult participation in children's education.
- Foster student participation in community service.
- Involve community members in school volunteer programs.
- Disseminate information to the school community, including those without school-age children, regarding school programs and performance.
- Collaborate with community agencies to provide family support services and adult learning opportunities, enabling families to participate more fully in activities that support education.

• Inform staff members of the resources available in the community and strategies for utilizing those resources.

PUTTING FAMILY, SCHOOL, AND COMMUNITY PARTNERSHIPS ON TODAY'S REFORM AGENDA

Davies (2002), the founder of the Institute for Responsive Education, took a look at today's school-reform efforts. He expected to find substantial action toward involving families and communities in schools in the last five years. He found the "surge of interest in acceptance of the ideas of parent involvement and partnership gratifying," but that "practices in most schools have hardly caught up with the flourishing rhetoric." He offers a prescription for action for educators, parent leaders, and policymakers at all levels who are ready to build the partnerships they are talking about. However, he adds two cautions, one for educators and one for partnership advocates:

> A caution for educators: if partnership programs are to be worth the effort, time, and money that they require, they must be able to demonstrate in tangible ways how they contribute to increasing the social and academic development of children in school. This means that programs must be (1) carefully designed, with the participation of all those affected by them; (2) based whenever possible on research evidence; (3) faithfully executed; (4) objectively evaluated; and (5) sustained over time.
>
> A caution for partnership advocates: partnerships with families and communities are not the whole answer to school reform that is geared toward equity. They are not a substitute for well-trained, well-paid, and effective teachers and administrators; good books and materials; diverse instructional strategies; commitment to high standards of academic content; good, varied tools for assessing student achievement; ample time for student learning; and safe, orderly, and well-managed schools. Partnership is not the whole answer, but it is one important strategy for school reform.

Davies' prescription for action consists of seven recommendations:

Teachers and principals. Teachers and principals make or break any effort to form partnerships among families, schools, and communities. However, plans for partnerships are often developed with little or no teacher input, and principals are often directed by the central office to just do it themselves. Top-down management dooms the partnership effort from the start.

Democratic principles. Successful partnerships require attention to the essential elements of the democratic process, including recognizing different interests and respecting all participants regardless of color, religion, or educational status. Various methods of conflict resolution—mediation, negotiation, and compromise— are also necessary aspects of the democratic process. Along with partnerships comes power sharing. Realistic and workable ways must be found to involve parents and other community representatives in planning, establishing policy, and making decisions regarding educational issues.

Reaching out to where the parents are. Schools that are friendly and welcoming have an easier time creating good, workable partnership programs. However, making schools attractive and friendly is not enough if educational equity and high standards are the goals. Schools must reach out to those who are thought of as hard to reach. A variety of approaches are necessary and often include recruiting and training parents and other community residents to visit homes to offer information about the schools, academic standards, and how families can support children's learning at home; reaching out by teachers, principals, and parent coordinators to family members in community settings rather than waiting for them to come to the school; and offering services to meet family needs through the school working with health and social service agencies and then communicating with families about education matters.

Grassroots activism. A revival of parent activism is a key element in rebuilding support for public schools and persuading more schools and districts to make the necessary changes so that all of their students can achieve higher academic standards.

Both choice and voice. Parent choice is a legitimate and important part of the process of empowering parents and improving schools, as is giving parents an effective voice in decision making in schools. As many reasonable opportunities as possible for choice should be developed, but only within the public school framework, such as magnet and alternative public schools, schools-within-schools, cross-district transfers, and early access to post-secondary education. For parent choice to be genuinely empowering, special steps must be taken to inform families about what they need to know in order to make informed choices.

Increased family responsibility. With parent power comes increased parent responsibility. In order to close the huge gaps between white and minority children and between the middle class and those with lower social status, it is important to spread the responsibility between the home and the community as well as to the school. However, assigning more responsibility to low-income and minority families must be backed up with major efforts to help these families fulfill their responsibility of rearing and educating their children.

Linking school reform and community development. Public schools are seldom able to be much better than their neighborhoods and surrounding communities. Neighborhoods and communities are seldom able to stay healthy and attractive without good schools. Linking schools and community development is important because achieving educational equity requires progress in the areas of access to affordable housing, good health care, jobs, transportation, safe streets, and reduction of alcohol and drug abuse.

Davies adds that his recommendations are really a plea for changing the culture of schools so that partnership is a way of life that offers benefits to all who are engaged and becomes a tradition rather than a funded project.

WORKING WITH THE COMMUNITY

As Epstein (2001) points out, students are central to successful partnerships. Successful partnerships recognize the shared responsibilities of home, school, and community for children's learning and development. "In partnership, educators, [students], families and community members work together to share information, guide students, solve problems, and celebrate successes."

Today's school–community partnerships differ from those of the past in that they reflect a deeper awareness of the devastating effects of noneducational barriers to learning, such as poverty, poor health, or an unstable home life. Collaborative efforts with businesses, universities, medical and social service agencies, foundations, and community-based religious and civic organizations are based on the recognition that there is not a single solution to school improvement. The challenge in developing partnerships and collaborative efforts is ensuring that all parties are working together to set and reinforce consistent messages and standards for all children.

The Education Policy Studies Laboratory at Arizona State University invited a group of distinguished education scholars to review the research on a series of education reform topics, including efforts to better link public schools with their communities. Their findings are presented in the publication, *School Reform Proposals: The Research Evidence* (Molnar, 2002). The reviewers found that the challenge in linking schools and communities is "to devise the right mixture of services and programs in organizational situations that are highly idiosyncratic." The recommendations included:

- Educational leaders and policymakers should be encouraged to reconceptualize the public school as a vital economic resource that must be nurtured.
- Schools and other social organizations wishing to provide school-linked services should carefully consider the scope, funding needs, organizational and professional complexities, and types of services to be offered. While perhaps not as compelling or intellectually stimulating, incremental types of school-linked services should be pursued if providers are dedicated to institutionalizing the project.
- Funding for new community improvement projects should be kept consistent and stable. The bigger and more complex the project, the greater the need for adequate funding.

Working with the community is a two-way process. Diverse stakeholders in public education—students, teachers, school administrators, parents, business people, community groups and organizations, and members of the community—must be involved as participants, not merely as audiences, in discussions and actions on behalf of school improvement, increased student achievement, and strengthened families.

Over the past several decades, grassroots community involvement programs have moved from relative obscurity into the limelight of educational, health, and human service policy and practice. Key policymakers and many educational organizations now argue that these kinds of grass-roots connections are critical to school reform and, ultimately, to improved school outcomes.

In 1994, the U.S. Department of Education (*Strong Families, Strong Schools: Building Community Partnerships for Learning*) established the Partnership for Family Involvement in Education (PFIE). PFIE was intended as a way to build lasting alliances among businesses, community and religious organizations, families, and schools in the common cause of improving schools and promoting student achievement. The department's role in the partnership is to provide a network of support for those companies and organizations that are working to make education a community affair. The partnership (Partnership for Family Involvement in Education, 1999) is designed to facilitate partners' networking in order to pool resources and ideas, share best practices, and be recognized for these efforts. It keeps partners informed of current educational issues and trends and provides resources and publications to make programs more effective.

Responding to controversy surrounding public schools' ability to engage in successful partnerships and collaborative initiatives, the Harvard Family Research Project (1995) conducted a series of studies centered on three questions:

1. What kinds of programs are schools starting in order to work with parents of children from birth to age six to promote child development?
2. What can pioneering programs teach about the challenges of developing and implementing these programs in conjunction with public schools?
3. Can schools link and work with other community services in order to develop more comprehensive services to strengthen and support families?

The resulting publication, *Raising Our Future: Families, Schools, and Communities Joining Together,* is a national resource guide for school-based programs designed to serve the families of young children. It profiles an array of service arrangements under school sponsorship and provides detailed information on such operational features as service, curriculum, staffing, and funding. The guide is intended to provide examples and increase understanding of the key ingredients in building schools' capacity to sponsor family support programs.

Three national groups—the National Committee for Citizens in Education, the Academy for Educational Development, and the Center for Law and Education—with support from the Lilly Endowment, Inc., took the lead in another research project into grassroots programs involving schools, families, and communities working together to help children succeed in school and have a brighter future. The project, Supporting Our Kids (Bamber, Berla, and Henderson, 1996), had two charges: (1) to define a set of simple concepts to stretch people's thinking about how families could be involved in the whole range of public education, prekindergarten through high school; and (2) to produce a set of tools that local communities could use to get started. The project defined "student achievement" more broadly than good grades and high test scores; it included the qualities students needed to become healthy, happy, well informed, hard-working citizens. It examined programs that extended partnerships across all grades and viewed the raising of children as a job shared by the entire community. *Learning from Others: Good Programs and Successful Campaigns* (Bamber et al.) profiles some seventy projects and describes how they focused on helping children learn and grow.

In March 1999, the Annenberg Institute for School Reform released *Reasons for Hope, Voices for Change* based on an eighteen-month effort to identify, map, and describe a variety of options for public engagement in public education projects across the United States. It summarizes the work of hundreds of schools and communities and offers a look at how local civic, business, and school initiatives are developing the skills necessary to involve communities in educational improvement.

THE ROLE OF SCHOOL PRINCIPALS

Working with the community is like any other process—someone must begin it. School leadership is often in the best position to begin the collaborative process. Timpane (as cited in Decker and Boo, 2000) points out, "No one else can speak with as much legitimacy and effect in every community in the land. Few others can, frankly, stand the heat; attitudes and behaviors of long standing will not change overnight; a new sense of trust and common purpose will not bloom immediately."

According to Blank and Kershaw (1999), each school and community must develop, test, and refine strategies for gathering perceptions and collaborating on results while maintaining a school environment that is supportive of learning. They must learn to communicate effectively, promote supportive relationships, develop shared expectations, involve others productively, and support teaching and learning. These collaborative endeavors must prize diversity and inclusiveness and develop numerous connections and a range of opportunities to address the needs of the hard-to-reach, the disadvantaged, and single working parents, as well as those parents who are typically active supporters. Blank and Kershaw emphasize that it takes strong building-level leadership to initiate partnership activities, maintain control, and sustain momentum.

A principal's willingness and ability to engage in collaboration are essential to the success of the initiative. Historically, collaborative skills have not ranked high on the list of leadership abilities needed to be an effective principal, and few principals or other school personnel receive training in working with parents and families or the community at large.

Giles (1998) sees the successful principal of the future as an educational entrepreneur. Being an entrepreneur involves creating an environment in which teachers, families, and others involved in a partnership feel safe enough to take risks, and even fail, in an effort to create positive change. This entrepreneurial principal must be willing to share the responsibilities of leadership, but must, at the same time, be able to work effectively in two very different cultures: the hierarchy of the broader educational bureaucracy of which the school is a part, and the evolving collaborative structure of the school. As an educational entrepreneur, the principal needs to know not only how to negotiate the bureaucracy to attract and keep resources but also how to prevent institutional regulation from interfering with the process of establishing and maintaining community partnerships.

Recognizing the ever-expanding responsibilities of school principals, the National Association of Elementary School Principals (NAESP) (2001) released a publication that details the individual responsibilities of principals in today's educational environment. *Leading Learning Communities: Standards for What Principals Should Know and Be Able to Do* is a comprehensive guide for elementary and middle-level principals for crafting their responsibilities in key instructional areas, including setting school goals and standards, improving student performance, providing meaningful professional development for faculty and staff, effectively using data and testing tools, and engaging the local community.

The guide encourages principals to actively engage the community in creating shared responsibility for student and school success and in building greater ownership for the work of the school. The community engagement section of the guide states (NAESP, 2001):

> Principals must be willing to tell the bad news along with the good. . . . A principal committed to public engagement understands that the community needs avenues to learn about and reflect on academic standards, the school's goals, how the school is using its resources and what the data shows about the school's progress. Although true public engagement in schools is powerful, it is time-consuming and complicated. It requires ongoing collaboration and communication. When done well, though, all members of the community share the responsibility and authority for creating a successful school.

The section also points out that teachers are important to a school's engagement effort because "as the most visible and often most respected people in education, teachers frequently have a role in communicating with the public and key community stakeholders."

COLLABORATIVE LEADERSHIP

Leading a collaborative in which no one has control over all of the people and organizations involved is different from leading in a traditional organizational setting. Participants in a national dialogue on leadership for collaboration (Institute for Educational Leadership, 1993) identified the following qualities and skills of collaborative leaders:

Listening and communicating. Collaborative leaders consciously reach out to talk with and learn from the consumers of their services and the frontline workers who deliver those services. They value and nurture dialogue with leaders in order to gain a greater understanding of needs, concerns, and possibilities and to build bridges within and across organizations and sectors in the community.

Building visions. Collaborative leaders have skills to develop visions—clear pictures of how people, organizations, and communities must come together to build a better future for children and families. They work to communicate that vision throughout their communities, adapting the vision to achieve an ever-increasing commitment to making it a reality.

Risk taking. Collaborative leaders do more than take risks themselves. They create a climate in which other people are willing to take risks, knowing that mistakes are to be viewed as learning experiences and will not lead to punitive action.

Respect for diversity. Collaborative leaders convey not only tolerance, but also acceptance, inclusion, and celebration. They strive to strengthen communications among different people and groups, and bring people who reflect the diversity of their communities to collaborative dialogue.

Knowledge and skills in group process. Collaboration involves numerous meetings at which people must sort through problems, seek alternative solutions, and make decisions. Collaborative leaders have the group-process skills needed to run effective meetings. They ensure the active involvement of all participants, giving them a sense of ownership in the process and obtaining their commitment to follow through on the group's decisions.

Conflict management. Rather than overlooking tough issues about which conflict might arise, collaborative leaders have the skills to manage conflict. They recognize that by working through conflicts, groups strengthen their capacity to solve complex problems.

Decisiveness. Collaborative leaders are able to move groups toward decisions in ways that maintain both individual identity and group cohesion.

Consensus building. Collaborative leaders use the group's vision to drive toward consensus on real changes that push people and agencies beyond traditional boundaries.

Motivation/passion. Collaborative leaders motivate others by communicating the group's vision and constantly nurturing other leaders and the many people with whom they work. Their passion provides fuel for others and helps groups overcome obstacles to positive outcomes.

Empowering. Collaborative leaders give the work of the collaborative to the partners who are at the table. They recognize that nurturing leadership in others is as essential to the prudent exercise of leadership as is leading itself.

Reflection. Collaborative groups can be described as learning communities in which people challenge old ideas and assumptions and learn new ways of acting. Collaborative leaders facilitate the group's reflection so that learning can be captured and new behaviors internalized.

Flexibility. Collaborative processes do not follow a linear path. Collaborative leaders must remain flexible, adapting yesterday's ideas and today's plan to tomorrow's realities.

Knowledgeable about other systems. To make interagency collaboration work, leaders should have knowledge of systems other than their own. This knowledge enables them to ask better questions, moving people to think beyond the established framework of their agencies.

While it is true that the principal is usually the first-line gatekeeper—the individual who will determine whether a school reaches out to involve families and the community in the education of children—it is also true that staff administrators, supervisors, teachers, and support personnel are important in creating a welcoming environment and successful outreach. A team approach is necessary in developing meaningful educational partnerships that support academic achievement.

Katzenbach and Smith (1993) recommend six rules for effective team leadership that are applicable to the emerging roles of both principals and teachers as they work with families and other community members, agencies, and organizations:

1. Keep the purpose, goals, and approach relevant and meaningful. All teams must shape their own common purpose, performance goals, and approach.
2. Build commitment and confidence, keeping in mind that there is an important difference between individual accountability and mutual accountability. Both are needed if any group is to become a real team.
3. Strengthen the mix and level of skills. The most flexible and top performing teams consist of people with all the technical, functional,

problem-solving, decision-making, interpersonal, and teamwork skills the team needs to perform. Team leaders should encourage people to take the risks needed for growth and development.

4. Manage relationships with outsiders, removing obstacles as necessary. Team leaders are expected by people both outside and inside the team to manage much of the team's contacts and relationships with the larger organization.

5. Create opportunities for others. The leader's challenge is to provide performance opportunities for the team overall and for individuals on it.

6. Do real work. Everyone on the team, including the leader, should do real work in roughly equivalent amounts.

ESTABLISHING COLLABORATIVE RELATIONSHIPS

Withrow (1999) describes what the American public expects its schools to do today and in the future:

> What we expect of our schools is cumulative. Schools are still expected to produce ethical, moral, civilized people who can help us sustain our democracy. They are expected to prepare a new wave of immigrants for life in America. And as demands increase, expectations grow, and life accelerates, our schools are expected to produce people who can effectively lead us into a global knowledge/information age. . . . Transformation expected of us is not new. It is simply one of the great benefits and ongoing challenges of living in a free and dynamic society—a society we can only keep that way through sound education.

Given such lofty goals, it is not surprising that many observers believe that establishing collaborative initiatives is the only way schools can fulfill public expectations. As Giles (1998) says:

> The mixed results of the plethora of reform initiatives over the past several years suggest . . . that collaborative initiatives . . . which mobilize local community resources and institutions, engage parents and educators in a process of critical reflection about their schools, and use power effectively, offer the best possibility for addressing the very serious problems faced by schools and communities today.

Parson (1999), observing that "schools have talked about becoming more collaborative for more than a decade," suggests a set of components on which to base a collaborative relationship:

- Credibility: The initiators must have a high level of credibility.
- Shared concerns: Concerns that are shared are the force that brings people together.
- Trust building: Before any collaborative actions can be taken, partners must begin the process of building mutual trust.
- Resources: To be successful, every collaborative effort must have resources committed to its program of work.
- Shared decision making: Decision making must be done openly with the participation of all partners.
- Consensus process: Consensus must be arrived at to obtain the support of all partners.
- Realistic early goals: The early goals should be obtainable in a fairly short period of time in order to build momentum.
- Evaluation: A commitment must be made to evaluate the results of the collaborative effort.
- Celebration: Every success should be celebrated.
- Moving to a higher level: As success is achieved in the initial stages, subsequent goals should be set at higher, more challenging levels.

Parson adds two provisions that should be acknowledged and accepted by those establishing the collaborative: First, there should be a provision for bailout. Any individual or group should be able to exit gracefully if the proposed collaboration does not fit its situation or circumstances. Second, there also should be a provision for being prepared to fold the tent. If the reasons for forming a specific collaborative disappear, there may be a need to move on to other concerns, perhaps with other partners.

Mattessich and Monsey (1993) review the research on a variety of successful collaboratives and identified factors that increase the chances for success. They group those factors into six general categories:

Environment. If a history of collaboration or cooperation exists in the community, potential partners are more likely to have an understanding of the required roles and expectations and trust the process. The collaborative group (and, by implication, the agencies in the group) is perceived as a leader—at least in relation to the goals and activities it intends to accomplish. Political leaders, opinion makers, persons who control resources, and the general public support (or at least do not oppose) the missions of the collaborative group.

Membership characteristics. Members of the collaborative group share understanding and respect for each other and their respective organizations: how they operate, their cultural norms and values, limitations, and expectations. The collaborative group includes representatives from each segment of the community that will be affected by its activities. Members see collaboration as in their own self-interest, and collaborating partners believe the benefits of collaboration will offset costs, such as loss of autonomy and turf. Collaborating partners are able to compromise, recognizing that the many decisions within a collaborative effort cannot possibly fit the preferences of every member perfectly.

Process/structure. Members of the collaborative group feel ownership of the way the group works and the results or product of its work. Every level (upper management, middle management, operation) within each organization in the collaborative group participates in decision making. The collaborative group remains open to varied ways of organizing itself and accomplishing its work. Collaborating partners clearly understand their roles, rights, and responsibilities and how to carry out those responsibilities. The collaborative group has the ability to sustain itself in the midst of major changes, even if it needs to change major goals or members in order to deal with changing conditions.

Communication. Collaborative members interact often, update one another, discuss issues openly, convey all necessary information to one another and to people outside the group. Partners establish formal and informal communication links. Channels of communication exist on paper so that the flow of information occurs. In addition, members establish personal connections, producing a better, more informed, and more cohesive group working on a common project.

Purpose. The goals and objectives of a collaborative group are concrete and clear to all partners and can be realistically attained. Collaborating partners have the same vision, with clearly agreed-upon mission, objectives, and strategies. The shared vision may exist at the outset of collaboration, or the partners may develop a vision as they work together. There is a unique purpose so that the mission and goals or approach of the collaborative group differ, at least in part, from the mission and goals or approach of the member organizations.

Resources. The collaborative group has an adequate, consistent financial base to support its operations. The individual who convenes the collaborative group has excellent organizational and interpersonal skills and carries out the role with fairness. Because of these characteristics (and others), the convener is granted respect and legitimacy by the collaborative partners.

More recently, the National Assembly of Health and Human Service Organizations (2001) undertook a literature review project funded by the Charles Stewart Mott Foundation to identify the most promising practices in school community collaborations. Although the project focused primarily on the literature related to after-school program collaboration, the findings apply to the collaborative relationship in general. The resulting publication, *After School Collaboration: When It Works, Why It Works: A Literature Review* outlines the ten elements of successful school–community collaboration that were mentioned the most by the writers of the articles that were reviewed:

1. Collaborative vision should be a routine way of approaching all of the decision making related to the school–community collaboration. No member of the collaboration should be a tenant in the other's location—the emphasis should be on partners, not tenants. Turf issues should not be allowed.
2. There should be a structure ensuring clear communication between school–community collaboration members. Resentment or differing views should not be allowed to fester without an opportunity to voice them, nor should misinformation be allowed.
3. Key stakeholders should be involved in the school–community collaboration from the beginning—never feeling that the collaborative

group will not care or reach out to them. These should include youth, members of diverse community groups, parents, and others who may be involved in the collaboration's programs.

4. School–community collaboration needs to take into account the specialties of the members, including differing perceptions of children's learning and development. There should be a mix of instructional and community activity—a mix of play, service, and learning. There should be strong links between school programs and community programs.

5. All members of the school–community collaboration should have clear roles and responsibilities. A clear planning structure should be developed.

6. School–community collaboration should be focused on clear goals with a method of measuring success. There should be a clear consensus among members of what needs to be achieved.

7. All members of the school–community collaboration should have a sense of how much time and effort it takes to accomplish the goals and should take into account the responsibilities that the members have outside of the collaboration.

8. Funding should be ensured by developing relationships between the school–community collaboration members and funding sources (government, foundation, corporate, and others). Costs, financial responsibilities, and budgeting within the collaborative should be well documented.

9. School–community collaboration participants should work to remain energized and focused. Mentoring, training, staff development, and other efforts should be used to ensure focus and avoid burnout or loss of interest.

10. School–community collaboration should be responsive and active in the neighborhood and the political process.

The National Association of Partners in Education (NAPE, 2001) has established a process to help schools develop partnerships with the community. NAPE suggests that it is important to think about all the steps at the outset and refer to them repeatedly during development and implementation, and points out that, depending on the situation, some steps may be more important than others.

- Awareness: Informing key populations that a partnership is being considered as a means of improving the school by relating to the community.
- Needs assessment: Gathering and interpreting information in order to formulate the goals and objectives of the partnership.
- Potential resources: Identifying people, materials, equipment, and funding available within a school, school district, business, agency, and community to help meet identified needs.
- Goals and objectives: Determining a broad-based statement of purpose for the partnership and statements of intended outcomes that are measurable, are specific, and determine the focus of the evaluation.
- Program design: Selecting specific strategies for achieving the partnership's goals and objectives.
- Management: Defining the partnership's administrative structure and the rules and regulations under which it will function.
- Recruitment: Engaging people, organizations, and resources in the partnership and responding to needs identified by the school and the community.
- Assignment: Matching people with the jobs that need to be done and allocating financial resources and materials to identified needs.
- Orientation: Preparing people for involvement by ensuring that they understand the roles, rules, policies, and procedures.
- Training: Preparing individuals or groups to perform specific tasks in predetermined situations.
- Retention: Making the necessary efforts to keep individuals involved and maintain a strong, effective partnership.
- Evaluation: Monitoring and data collection, interpretation, and analysis for the purposes of decision making and program improvement.

BARRIERS TO COLLABORATION

A major obstacle to collaboration is that agencies may have different definitions of the same issue. This obstacle is expressed in the actual collaborative process, in the mindsets of people engaged in the collaborative effort, in the ways in which resources are allocated, and in the policies that govern the delivery of services.

Determining the methods of communication and problem solving used to establish goals and objectives, agreeing on roles, making decisions, and resolving conflicts are common process-oriented barriers. These barriers relate to the formulation of a broad and practical vision, including overcoming power and control issues; lack of trust; defeatism/skepticism; an "it's-not-my-job" attitude; ignorance of how others work; danger of setting lowest-common-denominator goals; and differing philosophies. Barriers caused by the individual members of the collaborative may include the difficulty of ensuring a full buy-in by staff and overcoming resistance to change.

Barriers related to resources can take several forms. There may be insufficient funds to provide the necessary services, erosion of trust among potential collaborators who increasingly must compete for scarce resources, and conflict over who pays for what. Lack of time to engage in collaborative activities is also a resource-related barrier. Resource issues are intimately related to process issues, since the dictates of self-preservation make it difficult to share scarce resources.

Policy can also be a barrier to collaboration. The federal, state, and local rules, regulations, policies, guidelines, and definitions each agency brings to the table affect the ease or difficulty with which partners can work together. Included in this category are semantic differences (using similar words with different meanings or terms with unclear meanings) and differences in state and federal statutory requirements (eligibility and reporting regulations, separate funding streams, confidentiality rules, and other policies that interfere with joint efforts).

THE PARTNERSHIP CONTINUUM

In education, "partnership" encompasses three levels of working relationships that can be viewed as a continuum. *Cooperation* is at one end, implying a simple working together toward a common end. *Coordination* occupies the middle range, implying sharing resources and the joint planning, development, and implementation of programs. *Collaboration* is at the other end, implying a higher degree of sharing and a more intensive, concerted partnership, including joint allocation of resources and joint monitoring and evaluation.

Using this continuum in the context of service delivery, Melaville and Blank (1991) explain:

A collaborative strategy is called for in localities where the need and intent is to change fundamentally the way services are designed and delivered throughout the system. In those communities not yet ready for collaborative partnerships, cooperative initiatives to coordinate existing services offer a reasonable starting point for change. Ultimately, however, these efforts must become increasingly collaborative if they hope to achieve the goal of comprehensive service delivery.

There is no single model for an educational partnership. The extent of cooperation or collaboration depends on each partner's willingness to share resources—human, physical, and financial. Table 5.1 illustrates what a continuum of school–community partnerships (Decker and Associates, 1994) might include.

The type of involvement and partnership will vary from school to school depending on local needs and circumstances. The goal is to build shared ownership for education and the well-being of children. Table 5.2 outlines a partnership continuum of activities and responsibilities representing progressively greater levels of collaboration, shared responsibility, and participation in decision making (Saskatchewan Education, 1999).

Table 5.1.   The Partnership Continuum

One-on-One (Sponsor → Beneficiary)	Cooperative Agreements (Sponsor ↔ Beneficiary)	Comprehensive Collaboratives (Sponsors ↔ Beneficiaries)
• Tutoring • Mentoring • Field trips • Guest speakers • Summer jobs • Paid work-study • Scholarships • Incentives and recognition awards • Demonstrations • Use of business facilities • Loaned executives • Volunteer services • Mini-grants for teachers • Teaching assistance • Donations of equipment/ supplies • Public relations	• Needs assessment • Planning • Research and development • Training in new technology • Teacher/administrator professional development • Advocacy policy, laws • School-based health clinics • Magnet schools • Funds to support innovation • Advice on restructuring schools • Focused programs such as dropout or teen pregnancy prevention	• Needs assessment • Broad-based multi-agency planning • Research and development • Long-term institutional commitment • Commonly defined vision • Goals/objectives by consensus • Shared authority/ decision making • New roles/relationships • Advocacy policy/laws • Integration of multiple cross-institutional programs • Comprehensive services focused on whole child • Full-service school

Table 5.2. Continuum of Parent and Community Involvement Partnerships

Meeting Basic Needs	Developing Openness and Two-Way Communication	Supporting Learning in Home and the Community	Participating in Voluntary and Advisory Roles	Building Collaboration and Partnerships	Participating in Governance
Activity and Program Examples	Activity and Program Examples	Activity and Program Examples	Activity and Program Examples	Activity and Program Examples	Activity and Program Examples

At home . . .
• safe, caring home environment
• adequate food, clothing
 	
In school/ community . . .
• nutrition programs
• clothing exchanges
• "safe rooms"
• parenting education
• community kitchens
• home-school liaison
	At home . . .
	• advise teacher of student's likes and dislikes, change to routine, etc.
	• discuss concerns and successes with teacher
	• review information sent home from school
	• attend meetings and school events
	
	In school/ community . . .
	• welcoming school environment
	• parent, student, teacher conferences
	• school newsletters
		At home . . .
		• being interested in and encouraging children's learning
		• creating a place to study/work
		• reading to children
		• making learning part of everyday life
		
		In community . . .
		• mentoring
		• creating safe, stable communities
		
		In school . . .
		• family literacy programs
		• assignments to encourage family involvement
			• attending/assisting with school events
			• fund raising
			• volunteering
			• room for volunteers/ parents
			• guest speakers
			• tutoring students
			• newsletter coordination
			• leading clubs
			• parent centers
			• providing advice on school issues/ programs
			• advising on school policy issues such as code of conduct, discipline, curriculum, program adaptation, schedules, etc.
				• financial and "in kind" contributions
				• business partnerships and sponsorships
				• integrated services
				• community development
				• youth community service/work
				• in-school day care
				• early intervention
				• preschool
				• shared facilities
				• adopt-a-school
				• community service work
					• planning, problem solving
					• making decisions about
					  – budget
					  – program adaptations
					  – priorities
					  – criteria for staff and/or staffing
					• training in leadership and decision-making skills
					• program assessment
					• shared management of project, program, or school
					• partnerships with organizations, agencies, and governments

(continued)

Structure
- self-help groups
- school–community liaison program
- school-level organizations—parent council, school council, home–school association
- community association

- home visits
- surveys of parent opinion
- message board of school events and activities
- newspaper columns
- learning contracts among parents, teachers, and students
- summer/holiday learning projects

Structure
- school–community liaison program
- school-level organizations—parent council, school council, home–school association
- community association
- district boards/committees

Structure
- school–community liaison program
- school-level organizations—parent council, school council, home–school association
- community association
- district boards/committees

Structure
- volunteer programs
- school–community liaison program
- school-level organizations—parent council, school council, home–school association
- community association
- district boards/

Structure
- advisory committees
- interagency committees
- school-level organizations—parent council, school council, home–school association
- community association
- district boards/

Structure
- school councils, parent advisory council
- school–community council
- district boards/committees
- comanagement board
- associate schools
- district board of education

TYPES OF EDUCATIONAL PARTNERSHIPS

In an examination of school–community initiatives, Melaville (1998) found that most initiatives were built around one or more of the following goals:

- Improved educational quality and academic outcomes for youth.
- More efficient and effective health and social service delivery for children and families.
- Increased recognition of the developmental needs of young people and the importance of building on their strengths.
- Expanded efforts to strengthen the human, social, and economic foundations of neighborhoods and communities.

Melaville noted: "Growing appreciation of the need to blend purposes and strategies around a central vision and mission is . . . likely to make collaboration easier among multiple reform initiatives in the community." Some of those reform initiatives are described below.

Volunteer Programs

Volunteer programs are the oldest and best-known home, school, and community initiatives. They take advantage of the American tradition of volunteering that remains strong today. The Network for Good (2002) reports that 109 million American adults (56 percent) volunteer annually and 59 percent of teenagers volunteer an average of 3.5 hours each week.

School volunteer programs involve recruiting and training individuals to work in support of schools and education. Typically, school volunteers fall into one of four categories: *One-time volunteers* have limited time, usually part or all of one school day. They may volunteer to help with field trips, assist with a special event, share a special skill or expertise on a particular topic, or participate in a career education day. *Off-campus volunteers* can work only from home or another non-school site. They may have small children, or they may be older or handicapped. These individuals often help develop educational materials or do clerical work, such as typing or checking papers; provide a meeting place and leadership for off-campus youth clubs, such as Scouts and Brownies; or provide a service such as child care or transportation to allow others to visit a teacher or work at school. They may help with telephone campaigns or other publicity needs or make telephone contacts to request community agencies' and groups' assistance in a special project. *Short-term volunteers* may offer mini-courses or short-term enrichment programs, help with building improvements, assist with assemblies and plays, or provide some other in-school service on a short-term project. *Extended volunteers* can work several hours a week over a semester or a year as a tutor or mentor, serve as a classroom or library aide, supervise lunchroom/playground activities, provide classroom or office clerical services, help with a particular subject, such as art or music, or assist in coordinating the volunteer program itself.

Traditionally, parents—primarily mothers—have been the main source of school volunteers. However, as family demographics and work schedules have changed, so have the sources of volunteers and the character of volunteer programs. Schools have had to reach beyond families to the community and the student body to recruit volunteer assistance. Senior citizens have become a welcome pool of assistance in all kinds of volunteer activities, as well, especially tutoring, mentoring, and acting as foster grandparents. Students themselves also have been effective as tutors and mentors for their peers.

Inger (1992) reminds educators not to overlook minority populations, even though they may be more difficult to reach. Specifically, he suggests that schools "tap into an important and underutilized source of strength—the Hispanic extended family. Aunts, uncles, grandparents, cousins, godparents, and even friends all play a role in reinforcing family values and rearing children." This is a resource that schools can and should draw on.

Developing a volunteer program is often a school's first step in building partnerships to meet educational needs. Obviously, the commitment of teachers and administrators to using volunteers, knowledge of the role of volunteers, and attitudes and skills in using volunteers are basic to a volunteer program's success.

Careful, thorough planning and organization are needed in recruiting volunteers and in assigning tasks. Stehle (1993) emphasizes advance planning in order to avoid several common recruitment mistakes. Time should be taken to do a careful needs assessment so that recruiting efforts are targeted to needed job skills. A scattershot approach probably will not attract the specific kinds of volunteers and skills required. Also, time must be taken to interview prospective volunteers to make sure that the school has *meaningful* assignments that will take full advantage of their skills and interests. Issues of school safety and security clearances must also be considered.

The issue of retaining volunteers also requires some time and attention. Decker and Associates (1994) offer the following advice for retaining volunteer support:

- Nurture the volunteers' feeling of belonging to the educational team. With a sense of pride and ownership, they can become tremendous boosters of public education.
- Monitor the volunteer/teacher placements. Be sensitive to problems and encourage flexibility when change is indicated.
- Provide ongoing in-service training when appropriate.
- Train teachers to work with volunteers. Many problems can be avoided if volunteers and teachers have mutual expectations.
- Provide feedback about volunteers' performance and suggestions for teaching, discipline, or human relations techniques.
- Hold informal and formal recognition activities throughout the year.
- Use suggestions from evaluations when possible.

After-School Programs

After-school programs are increasing rapidly, with strong support from the federal government and state and local policymakers. A recent survey by the National Association of Elementary School Principals (NAESP) (*After-School Programs*, 2001) shows that in an era in which schools are asked to do more for children, both academically and socially, public schools are stepping in as providers of after-school programming. "Two-thirds (67 percent) of elementary school principals said that their schools now offer optional programs for children after regular schools hours. Another 15 percent of the principals say they are considering offering an after-school program in the future."

NAESP (*After-School Programs*, 2001) survey findings of principals whose schools had after-school programs include:

- Six in ten (59 percent) principals report that their programs began within the past five years and three in ten (29 percent) said their programs are less than three years old.
- Nearly all (95 percent) after-school programs are located on-site at the schools. Of schools identified as having programs, 27 percent also have before-school programs.
- Principals believe their extended-day programs are well worth the effort. Nine in ten (91 percent) rate their programs as successful and identify improving student academics (34 percent) and providing a safe place for students (26 percent) as their programs' biggest achievements.
- Almost all (96 percent) of the principals said their programs offer students help with their homework. Two-thirds (67 percent) say students' after-school learning activities are linked to their regular classroom learning. Most say they provide literacy and reading (69 percent) and math enrichment (85 percent), science (69 percent), the arts (63 percent), and computers and technology instruction (62 percent).
- After-school programs offer more than academics. More than three-fourths (78 percent) of the principals say their programs offer recreation and sports activities, and many offer opportunities to develop social skills such as leadership (50 percent) and conflict resolution (49 percent).

According to NAESP, the rationale for establishing after-school programs is threefold (NAESP, 2001):

- Attendance in after-school programs can provide youth with supervision during a time when many might be exposed to or engage in antisocial or destructive behaviors.
- After-school programs can provide enriching experiences that broaden children's perspective and improve their socialization.
- After-school programs can help improve the academic achievement of students who are not accomplishing as much as they need to during regular school hours.

The Children's Aid Society (2002) examined research evidence to determine whether after-school programs did in fact accomplish the goals implied in the threefold rationale for establishing them. Its *Fact Sheet on After-School Programs* shows:

- After-school programs help reduce youth crime and provide a safe environment. About 40 percent of young people's waking hours are discretionary time that is not committed to other activities such as school, homework, meals, chores, or working for pay. Experts estimate that at least 5 million latchkey children come home to empty houses. Violent juvenile crime triples during the hours from 3 P.M. to 8 P.M., and it is during these same hours that children face the most serious danger of becoming victims of crime. Recent studies confirm the relationship between availability of after-school programs and reduced juvenile crime.
- Children, participating in high-quality, constructive after-school programs demonstrate higher school attendance, higher language redesignation rates, and improved performance on standardized tests. In addition, economically disadvantaged children who participate from 20 to 35 hours per week in constructive learning activities during their free time get better grades in school than their peers who do not participate.
- In addition to improved academic achievement, children who participate in high-quality after-school programs experience additional benefits, including better work habits, emotional adjustment, and peer relations; improved social skills; and increased ability to maintain self-control, avoid conflict, and make constructive choices for their personal behavior.
- Teenagers, as well as younger children, benefit from participation in high-quality after-school programs.

Fashola (1999) acknowledges that research on after-school programs is at a rudimentary stage, but points out that a number of promising models exist. The amount and type of school–community collaboration in after-school programs is affected by the design and staffing of the program and whether the program operates in the same building as the school-day program or in another location. Among programs intended to increase academic achievement, those that provide greater structure, a stronger link to the school-day curriculum, well-qualified and well-trained staff, and opportunities for one-to-one tutoring seem particularly promising. Programs of all types, whether academic, recreational, or cultural in focus, appear to benefit from consistent structure, active community involvement, extensive training for staff and volunteers, and responsiveness to participants' needs and interests.

While the value of after-school programs is generally accepted, there is concern that after-school programs are not equitably distributed among the students. Low-income youth are much less likely than their more affluent peers to have access to them. The Children's Aid Society (2002) reports:

> According to the National Education Longitudinal Study, sponsored by the U.S. Department of Education, 40 percent of low-income eighth graders—compared with only 17 percent of high-income respondents—do not participate in any organized after-school activities. The likely explanation for this difference is access, not interest, since virtually every survey of American youth suggests that they want to participate in well designed, organized after-school programs.

The Children's Aid Society also reports that expanding after-school programs is widely supported. "Ninety-four percent of voters say that there should be some type of organized activity or place for children and teens to go after school every day, and 75 percent of voters (near a 10 percent increase since 2000) believe that federal or state tax dollars should be used to expand daily after-school programs and to make them accessible to all children."

The NAESP (2001) survey shows that even with widespread public support and their demonstrated success, after-school programs face challenges. Principals identify funding (56 percent) and staffing (49 percent) as the most troubling issues and the ones most likely to stand in the way of expanding their programs.

Advisory Committees and Task Forces

Advisory committees and task forces are commonly used to involve the community in educational planning and decision making. A task force is usually an ad hoc group formed to focus on a specific issue or assignment. An advisory committee is typically a continuing body that focuses on broad aspects of a school program. Although some advisory groups are elected, membership is usually developed through appointment and volunteering. An advisory group may report to the superintendent, the school board, the principal, or the community.

Establishing effective advisory committees and task forces requires a strong commitment and a great deal of work. However, there are a number of good—even self-interested—reasons for undertaking the serious work involved in developing and nurturing effective advisory groups. First, and most obviously, community members who become significantly involved with schools develop an understanding of competing interests, are more willing to accept compromise, and tend to support decisions that are made after broad-based consultation. There are some other advantages. Special interests tend to balance out. Policy decisions are more likely to be based on complete and accurate information about the community. In addition, a sense of community cohesion usually develops.

The impact and credibility of an advisory group depends less on the way members are selected than on the degree to which the membership accurately reflects the total community in ethnicity, socioeconomic level, and gender. The group's impact and credibility also depend on the support it gets from school staff, the substance of its assignment, and clarity of the task to everyone involved.

Decker and Decker (1991) offer the following guidelines for advisory groups:

- State the goals clearly and precisely.
- Involve a representative cross section of the community and the school, but keep the group size manageable.
- Decide on a leadership structure and chain of command.
- Establish a time schedule with specific intermediary goals and keep the group on course.
- Determine if and—precisely—how the group will work with or respond to the news media.
- Staff the advisory group properly in terms of administrative and other support personnel.
- Maintain a clear understanding of what will happen to the group's report.

- Discharge and thank the committee in a meaningful and appropriate manner.

The source of the following *Fable about Practically Nothing* is unknown, but it serves to illustrate how the best-intentioned advisory group can go wrong.

Once upon a time, there was an advisory council that had only four members. It was an organization not unlike our civic clubs, service clubs, church councils, even our professional and technical societies. The four members were named *Somebody, Everybody, Anybody*, and *Nobody*. All four declared that they supported the aims and objectives of the advisory council. But *Everybody* was either a golfer, bowler, gardener, or fisherman and used her spare time and talents in that way, or stayed at home with friends. *Anybody* wanted to go to meetings of the council, but didn't because he was afraid that *Somebody* might give him a job to do, and he just wanted to belong, not work. *Nobody* went to the meeting of the advisory council.

Of the four, *Nobody* was the best. For instance, when the advisory council needed a chair for an important committee, *Everybody* thought that *Anybody* should be willing to take on an important job like that, and *Somebody* observed that *Everybody* ought to. Guess who finally jot the job? That's right—*Nobody*. And when the four learned that there was a new resident in the community who was eligible for membership on the advisory council, *Everybody* thought that *Somebody* ought to invite her to join. *Anybody* could have extended the invitation, but did not. And can you guess who finally did get around to asking her? That's right—*Nobody* took the job.

And do you know what finally happened to that advisory council? With *Nobody* doing the jobs that had to be done, the advisory council amounted to Practically Nothing, which is the real name of a great many councils, despite their fancy assumed names and high ideals. Now the moral of this story is this: When you join an advisory council, you must be willing to work at accomplishing its aims and objectives, for if you do not, others will call you *Nobody*, regardless of your real name, and your advisory council will become Practically Nothing.

School–Business Partnerships

The most publicized school–community partnerships have been those between schools and businesses. Businesses have offered student internships, job counseling, and job-site visits. They have participated in career fairs, assisted administrators in solving management problems, donated money and equipment, funded newsletters and voice-mail systems, served on task forces of various types, provided experts to speak in classrooms and at assemblies, and even used their influence to affect political and financial issues of concern to schools.

Involving the business community in helping prepare students for the workplace is not a new idea. Vocational students have benefited from participation in cooperative vocation education programs for decades. What is new is the way in which traditional efforts are expanding to reach students from elementary school to college, and the positive way people in the business world are responding to this initiative.

For more than twenty-five years, the mission of Communities in Schools (2002) has been to connect community resources with schools in order to help young people learn, stay in school, and prepare for life. CIS brings resources into the schools from community agencies and businesses that have agreed to collaborate. Historically, businesses have been the backbone of this endeavor.

The U.S. School-to-Work Opportunities Act of 1994 sunset in October 2001 (National School-to-Work Learning Center, n.d.). It provided seed money to schools to create partnerships with businesses that seek to make education relevant by allowing students to explore different careers and see what skills are required in a working environment and to obtain skills from structured training and work-based learning experiences, including the necessary skills of a particular career as demonstrated in a working environment. School-to-Work programs also provided students with valued credentials by establishing industry-standard benchmarks and developing education and training standards that ensure appropriate education for each career.

New Jersey was one of eight states to receive initial funding from the 1994 act. Reporting on New Jersey's School-to-Work initiatives (now called School-to-Careers initiatives), Timberman (1999) describes a guide that promotes the advantages of such collaborative relationships to potential partnership employers. The guide lists these benefits: an expanded pool of qualified workers; a reduction in turnover; a voice in curriculum development to meet industry needs; a reduction in training costs; and an ability to improve the quality of life and work skills in the community. She also reported on studies of school-to-work in Philadelphia and Boston, indicating that "students who worked had higher attendance rates, lower dropout rates, lower suspension rates, higher graduation rates, and higher promotion rates than students who did not work."

Under the provisions of the School-to-Work Opportunities Act, there was no single school-to-work model, but each local initiative had to contain three core elements (School-to-Work, 1999):

1. School-based classroom instruction based on high academics and business-defined occupational skill standards.
2. Work-based career exploration, work experience, structured training, and mentoring at job sites.
3. Connecting courses integrating classroom and on-the-job instruction; matching students with participating employers; mentor training; and building additional bridges between school and work.

Although the School-to-Work Opportunities Act is no longer in effect, the National School-to-Work Learning Center (n.d.) reports that relevant content from its website will be integrated into the websites maintained by the U.S. Department of Labor's Employment and Training Administration and the U.S. Department of Education's Office of Vocational and Adult Education. One of the three key areas of the Office of Vocational and Adult Education's (n.d.) new initiative, Preparing America's Future, is "preparing every American youth to complete high school and be well prepared for postsecondary education and employment." It is expected that other school-to-work initiatives will be developed under the Bush Administration.

Workplace schools are still a relatively rare form of public–private partnership, but they are growing in number. Companies such as Honeywell, IDS Financial Services, Target, Mall of America, First Bank, American Bankers Insurance Group, and Hewlett-Packard have set up schools for their employees' children. Workplace schools, sometimes called "satellite schools," are hybrids: a business provides a classroom building and maintains it while the public school district provides teachers, books, and lessons.

Broder (1999) reports on the Baldrige in Education initiative, a project of the National Alliance for Business (NAB) that has the backing of major business organizations, the National Education Association, and many state officials. The late Malcolm Baldrige, Secretary of Commerce in the Reagan Administration, recognized that American companies had to restructure themselves to compete effectively worldwide, so he started a competition for companies that involve management and workers in a drive for quality and customer satisfaction. The Baldrige in Education initiative applies the Baldrige process to public education. Broder explains that the project focuses on long-term results because, quoting the NAB project director, while "random acts of improvement can boost school performance, it is only when those changes are properly aligned in a strategic plan that major, long-term results emerge."

In addition to direct involvement with schools and school programs, the private sector can encourage and support family involvement in education. The U.S. Department of Education (1994) suggests some ways:

> Although a number of businesses have been investing in overall school reform, many are now realizing the importance of increasing family involvement. "Family-friendly" businesses have at least one of the following policies: allowing time for employees to get involved with schools; initiating, implementing, and funding specific programs that promote family involvement in education; and providing resources to employees on how to become more involved in their own children's education.

Employers can also encourage and recognize employees who volunteer in schools. They can give employees release time or provide flexible scheduling, or can give tangible rewards for volunteering. They can also encourage all employees to continue their education, especially those who do not have high school diplomas. Many employers have discovered the benefits of adjusting work schedules or providing scholarship assistance for employees who wish to upgrade their skills or retrain in a new area.

Although businesses can significantly contribute to the learning experiences of students, educators must honestly weigh both the advantages and the disadvantages that may be derived from a specific school–business partnership. An ERIC Clearinghouse on Educational Management *Policy Report* (2001) examined several facets of school–business partnerships, including corporate sponsorships, school-to-career activities, commercialism on the Internet, and student privacy and other legal and ethical issues. The report points out, "When there is not a clear and direct educational benefit to students, the arrangement is not a genuine educational partnership."

Eight principles for corporate involvement have been adopted by the National Association of State Boards of Education, National Parent-Teachers Association, American Association of School Administrators, National Council of Social Studies, and National Education Association (ERIC, 2001). The principles are intended to ensure that educational values are not distorted or diluted within the context of a school–business partnership. Adhering to them will help educators protect the welfare of students and the integrity of the learning environment.

1. Corporate involvement shall not require students to observe, listen to, or read commercial advertising.
2. Selling or providing access to a captive audience in the classroom for commercial purposes is exploitation and a violation of the public trust.
3. Since school property and time are publicly funded, selling or providing free access to advertising on school property outside the classroom involves ethical and legal issues that must be addressed.
4. Corporate involvement must support the goals and objectives of the schools. Curriculum and instruction are within the purview of educators.
5. Programs of corporate involvement must be structured to meet an identified educational need, not a commercial motive, and must be evaluated for educational effectiveness by the school or district on an ongoing basis.
6. Schools and educators should hold sponsored and donated materials to the same standards used for the selection and purchase of curriculum materials.
7. Corporate involvement programs should not limit the discretion of schools and teachers in the use of sponsored materials.

8. Sponsor recognition and corporate logos should be for identification rather than commercial purposes.

Service Learning

Service learning is a growing type of collaboration between schools and community agencies. Summarizing the language of the National and Community Service Act of 1990, the National Youth Leadership Council (1990) defines it as follows:

> Service learning is student learning and development through active participation in thoughtfully organized service experiences that meet real community needs and that are coordinated in collaboration with the school and community. The service learning is integrated into the students' academic curriculum and includes structured time to talk, write, and think about what they did and saw during the actual service activity.

This type of collaboration views young people as resources rather than as problems and uses the community as a laboratory for youth development. Service opportunities emphasize accomplishing tasks to meet human and community needs and using the service experience to accomplish intentional learning goals. Students have opportunities to use newly acquired skills and knowledge in real-life situations in their own communities. The service opportunities enhance what is taught in school by extending student learning beyond the classroom and into the community and help foster the development of civic responsibility and a sense of caring for others.

The development of service learning programs received increased impetus from the 1997 Presidents' Summit for America's Future. Summit participants identified "opportunities for service" as the fifth developmental resource need for all youth. Benson and Walker (1998) summarized the important benefits to be gained by adding service learning to a school's educational curriculum.

- Service answers the need of all young people, rich and poor, for practical experience and an understanding of democratic values in action and the need to learn how to work with people of different backgrounds and experiences. Working together in common, sustained service is one way to close the racial and ethnic gaps that divide America.

- Service is a vital way to learn citizenship, responsibility, and discipline, build skills, enhance self-esteem, develop problem-solving abilities, introduce new career options, and prepare young people for future work.
- Service can improve academic motivation, school attendance, and school performance and can establish a pattern of future service that will continue through a lifetime of active citizenship.

Service learning can be an important vehicle for bridging the gap that often exists between students and schools, schools and communities, and students and communities. Besides the academic, social, personal, and career benefits to students, service learning activities benefit the school, the community, and the service learning partners. Table 5.3 (Lyday, Winecoff, and Hiott, 1998) summarizes these benefits.

Service learning activities can be designed for students of all ages, kindergarten through adults. There are three basic types of activities: direct service, indirect service, and advocacy. The three types are distinguished by the purpose of the service activity, who is served, and how the service is delivered. Lyday et al. explains:

- *Direct service* activities require the student to come into direct, personal contact with the recipients of the service. This type of service is often the most rewarding to students, since they are directly involved with the recipient and receive immediate feedback. Direct service also requires the strongest partnerships and greatest amount of planning and preparation, since students must have the knowledge, skills, and attitudes needed to make the experience beneficial for everyone involved. Examples include working with senior citizens, reading to or tutoring another person, and serving meals to the homeless.
- *Indirect service* activities are easier to manage because students work behind the scenes and much of the work can be done at school. This type of service might include collecting toys at holiday time, landscaping the schoolyard, cleaning up a vacant lot, or gathering needed items for a homeless family. The required

Table 5.3.   Benefits of Service Learning

Benefits to School	Benefits to Community	Benefits to Partners
• Makes curriculum relevant • Develops student's responsibility for their own learning • Links school to community in positive ways • Develops problem-solving, teaming, higher-order thinking, time management, and other vital workplace skills • Expands learning environment beyond the classroom • Motivates reluctant learners • Promotes problem-solving and conflict management skills • Helps reduce school problems: behavior, attendance, tardiness	• Mobilizes youth as a resource instead of a community problem • Addresses real community needs • Builds good, productive citizens • Promotes a "sense of community" for many students who do not have stability in their lives • Develops next-generation leaders • Develops an ethic of service and commitment to the community • Provides shared responsibility for student learning • Helps nurture and train the future workforce • Makes good economic sense • Helps build healthy communities	• Provides much-needed resources • Helps achieve partner goals • Introduces next-generation leaders to the partners' important work • Bonds agencies with schools and helps build new partnerships • Provides opportunities to enhance public image • Introduces students to career options in the partner's areas of service • Gives the partnership a different lens through which to view and assess its work • Challenges some ingrained ways of doing business • Infuses youthful vitality

partnerships are more loosely structured than those required for direct service and do not require the same rigor of scheduling, co-ordination, training, and supervision.

• *Advocacy* requires that students lend their voices and use their talents to eliminate the causes of a specific problem. Students work to make the community aware of a problem and attempt to get the community involved in seeking a solution. This type of service might include research on a community problem; the development of brochures and pamphlets related to the problem; a series of presentations to other students or community members; and a concerted effort to influence political, personal, or community decision making. The partnerships can range from loose coordination with a single agency to a complex array of relationships with multiple community groups.

The service learning project model also affects the nature of the partnership between the school and the agency or organization. In a one-shot model, teachers and students link one service project to their classroom studies, requiring coordination with one agency, one time, on a given date. In an ongoing project, teachers and students link service to their classroom studies on a regular basis throughout the semester or the school year.

Ongoing, direct service projects require continuing communication, interaction, and planning with the agencies and clients involved. In the student placement model, students—individually or in teams—complete internships of a set number of hours in agencies and organizations over the course of the semester or school year, and the agency becomes the students' classroom. The school–agency partnership is more involved, requiring contact, contracts, and written agreements between the school and partnering agencies to ensure meaningful experiences for both the students and the agencies in which they serve.

Many types of service-learning opportunities are possible, but successful programs appear to have common characteristics (National Youth Leadership Council, 1989). They are an integral part of the educational program—not an add-on. Contact between schools and community agencies is structured to ensure that mutual goals are met. They have practices in place that give students feedback from faculty and community sponsors and include a planned method for examining service experiences in relation to gains or changes in skills, knowledge, and attitudes. They give students genuine responsibility because consequences depend on their performance. They involve systematic monitoring of student and client activities so that service experiences will be seen as important.

In 2000, the W. K. Kellogg Foundation, a longtime supporter of service learning, appointed the National Commission on Service-Learning (2002) to study the current state of service learning in U.S. schools. Researchers spent a year reviewing research data, visiting schools, and questioning students, teachers, and other advocates in order to determine the prevalence and practice of service learning. The results of this comprehensive study were summarized in the report *Learning in Deed: The Power of Service-Learning for American Schools.*

The report noted that, according to the National Center for Education Statistics, by 1999 nearly one-third of all public schools—and nearly half of all high schools—were organizing service learning as part of their curriculum. However, researchers found that despite rapid growth, "the number of schools offering service learning is still limited, and in many of these, only a few teachers participate." They pointed out that "the overwhelming majority of American primary and secondary school students still lack the opportunity to participate in this demonstrably effective means of promoting scholarly achievement, and overcoming academic and civic disengagement."

The National Commission on Service-Learning found the documentation from the year of research and discussion so convincing that service learning was a low-cost, high-impact way of addressing the problems of academic and civic disengagement that it recommends: "Every child in American primary and secondary school should participate in quality service-learning every year as an integral and essential part of his or her education experience."

Other School–Community Partnerships

Other kinds of partnerships with agencies and organizations are responding to the recognized need for more school-readiness programs, before-school and after-school enrichment and recreation programs, child care, and the cooperative delivery of health and human services. The federal initiative, 21st Century Community Learning Centers Program, and a new national association, America's Promise—The Alliance for Youth, are urging public, private, and nonprofit organizations to focus their combined talents and resources on improving the lives of the nation's youth. These two initiatives are among an increasing number that are promoting the concept of school–community partnerships that turn public schools into full-service community centers open all day, all week, year-round, with on-site health and dental clinics, mental health counseling, child care, extended-day programs, tutoring, adult education, parent workshops, cultural programs, and summer camp. The daytime academic curriculum is integrated fully with the before-school, after-school, and evening programs, and the schools are open to everyone in the community—children, siblings, teens, parents, and other adults (Parson, 1999).

Full-service schools are based on the premise that no single agency or organization can substantially improve the lives of children and families, especially at-risk children and families. Table 5.4 (Dryfoos, 1994) suggests some of the components that together make up a full-service school.

Table 5.4.   Full–Service Schools

Full Service Schools		
Provided by School	Provided by Schools or Community Agencies	Support Services Provided by Community Agencies
• Effective basic skills • Individualized instruction • Team teaching • Cooperative learning • School-based management • Healthy school climate • Alternatives to tracking • Parent involvement • Effective discipline	• Child care • Extended day programs • Comprehensive health education • Health promotion • Preparation for the world of work (life planning) • Adult education	• Health/dental screening and services • Individual counseling • Substance abuse treatment • Mental health services • Nutrition/weight management • Referral with follow-up • Basic services: housing, food, clothing • Recreation, sports, culture • Mentoring • Family welfare service • Parent education, literacy • Child care • Employment training/jobs • Case management

A REALISTIC LOOK AT COLLABORATION

School alone cannot address the increasingly complex and diverse needs of families and communities that affect both the educational climate and the educational resources available to carry out the school's mission of successfully educating all students. The need for collaboration is obvious. Developing collaborative relations should be an important part of a school's comprehensive home, school, and community partnership plan.

Bruner (1991) recommends keeping seven key points in mind while developing collaborative relationships:

1. Collaboration is not a quick fix.
2. Collaboration is a means to an end, not an end in itself.
3. Developing interagency collaboration is extremely time-consuming and process-intensive.
4. Interagency collaboration does not guarantee the development of a client-centered service system nor the establishment of a trusting relationship between an at-risk child or family and a helping adult.

5. Creative problem-solving skills must be developed and nurtured in those expected to collaborate.
6. Among these skills are the ability to deal with the ambiguity and stress that increased discretion brings.
7. Collaboration is too important to be trivialized.

Obviously, comprehensive school–community collaboration takes time to develop because it is built on the success of other attempts to use community partnerships to meet educational goals. Parson suggests that as collaborative efforts are begun and increase in complexity, several common elements must be incorporated into the design:

- Collaborating agencies and organizations must work as equal partners, sharing all aspects of their joint efforts.
- Services must focus on families in order to have an effect on children and their ability to benefit from educational programs and be able to respond to the diversity in children and families.
- Educational, social, and community services must be integrated into a seamless experience for children and their families.
- The issue of *school-based* as opposed to *school-linked* services is not as important as the question of how each individual community can make the best use of its resources to improve the quality of education and life.
- Collaborative partnerships are based on trust and understanding, which must be developed over time.

A REMINDER

Good planning and organization are essential to success in all types of partnerships and collaborative initiatives. It is crucial to not lose sight of the fact that collaboration takes place among people, not institutions. People must be the focus of every collaborative effort.

A national survey by the League of Women Voters (Duskin, 1999) found that "contrary to conventional wisdom, Americans are engaged in civil society. They just aren't participating in traditional civic institutions. Instead, citizens are actively engaged in their communities and are interested in becoming more involved." The survey found that 56 percent of Americans are somewhat involved in community activities and issues, and 46 percent would like to be more involved. According to the survey:

A new form of involvement is emerging as America heads into a new century—a trend that reflects the growing pressures that people experience juggling the multiple tasks and responsibilities of daily life. Today, community engagement is localized and personalized, and it tends to be channeled through individual and group-based activities rather than through established organizations. Above all, people want to spend their volunteer time accomplishing real change. One of the key factors in whether people are going to get involved nowadays is whether they feel they are going to be able to make a difference. . . . By and large, Americans believe they can be most effective in small groups working on specific issues. Accordingly, people are spending more time solving neighborhood problems than trying to influence politicians. . . . There is a growing tendency to want to connect personal responsibility and individual freedom. They [the participants in the study] see the community as the place to do this.

A more recent survey by the Public Education Network and *Education Week* (2001), examined registered voters' level and areas of concern for public education, individuals' views of their civic responsibility for public education, actions they are willing to take to improve education, the kinds of information they want about education, the sources they trust to give that information, and key barriers that inhibit Americans from taking greater civic responsibility for quality schools. The report, *Action for All: The Public's Responsibility for Public Education*, (Public Education Network, 2001) "gives new insight on how to transform our shared concerns into quality schools, creating a road map for purposeful action and strategies for reconnecting schools to an untapped resource, the community." The Executive Summary presents the conclusion from the survey data: the best way to involve the most members of a community is to have them become educated voters and "education voters." It points out:

The bad news is that Americans say they have only three hours or fewer available to them each week to do anything to improve public schools. The good news is that the public actions required to ensure that schools are improving are not that difficult, expensive, or time consuming.

What Americans say they can and should do is to better perform their traditional civic duties—becoming better informed about education, increasing the pressure on elected officials to do whatever it takes to get better results for a broader range of students, and exercising the responsibility to vote as knowledgeable education consumers.

In fact, if Americans were to do one thing that could make schools better it would simply be to become "education voters," who know the issues, know the candidates' positions, and use the power of the voting booth to improve schools.

REFERENCES

Annenberg Institute for School Reform. (1999). *Reasons for hope, voices for change.* Brown University, Providence, R.I. Retrieved September 7, 2002, from www.annenberginstitute.org/publications/publications/reports.

Bamber, C., Berla, N., and Henderson, A. T. (1996). *Learning from others: Good programs and successful campaigns.* Washington, D.C.: Center for Law and Education.

Benson, P. L., and Walker, G. (1998). *Why the five fundamental resources matter: A reassessment of the evidence.* America's Promise. Retrieved March 4, 2002, from www.americaspromise.org/fivepromises/whymatter.cfm.

Blank, M. A., and Kershaw, C. (1999). Designing collaborative partnerships. *NASSP Practitioner,* 25, 4.

Broder, D. S. (1999). Business has a vital role in education. (Charleston, S.C.) *Post and Courier.* July 15.

Bruner, C. (1991). *Thinking collaboratively: Ten questions and answers to help policy makers improve children's services.* Washington, D.C.: Education and Human Services Consortium.

Children's Aid Society. (2002). *Fact sheet on after-school programs.* Retrieved February 7, 2002, from communityschools.org/afterschoolfactsheet .html.

Communities in Schools. (2001). *About communities in schools.* (1999). Retrieved September 7, 2002, from www.cisnet.org/about.

Davies, D. (2002). The 10th school revisited: Are school/family/community partnerships on the reform agenda now? *Phi Delta Kappan,* 83, 5.

Decker, L. E., and Associates. (1994). *Home-school-community relations: Trainers manual and study guide.* Charlottesville, Va.: Mid-Atlantic Center for Community Education.

Decker, L. E., and Boo, M. R. (2001). *Community schools: Serving children, families and communities*. Fairfax, Va.: National Community Education Association.

Decker, L. E., and Decker, V. A. (1991). *Home-school-community involvement*. Arlington, Va.: American Association of School Administrators.

Dryfoos, J. (1994). *Full-service schools*. San Francisco: Jossey-Bass.

Duskin, M. S. (1999). Community activism: An untapped reservoir. *The National Voter,* 49, 1.

Epstein, J. L. (2001). *School, family, and community partnerships: Preparing educators and improving schools*. Boulder, Colo.: Westview Press.

ERIC Clearinghouse on Educational Management. (2001). Can schools befriend businesses without compromising their mission? *ERIC information: Policy report.* Eugene: University of Oregon.

Fashola, O. S. (1999). Implementing effective after-school programs. *Here's how,* 17, 3. National Association of Elementary School Principals.

Giles, H. C. (1998). Parent engagement as a school reform strategy. *ERIC Digest.* Retrieved September 7, 2002, from eric-web.tc.columbia.edu/digests/dig135.html.

Hart, J. K. (1913). *Educational resources of villages and rural communities*. New York: Macmillian.

Harvard Family Research Project. (1995). *Raising our future: Families, schools, and communities joining together*. Cambridge, Mass.: Harvard Family Research Project.

Inger, M. (1992). Increasing the school involvement of Hispanic parents. *Clearinghouse on Urban Education Digest,* 80. Retrieved April 3, 2002, from eric-web.tc.columbia.edu.

Institute for Educational Leadership. (1993). *Leadership for collaboration: A national dialogue*. Washington, D.C.: Institute for Educational Leadership.

Katzenbach, J. R., and Smith, D. K. (1993). *The wisdom of teams*. New York: Harper-Collins.

Lyday, W. J., Winecoff, H. L., and Hiott, B. C. (1998). *Connecting communities through service learning*. Columbia: South Carolina Department of Education.

Mattessich, P. W., and Monsey, B. R. (1993). *Collaboration: What makes it work*. St. Paul, Minn.: Amherst H. Wilder Foundation.

Melaville, A. (1998). *Learning together: The developing field of school community initiatives*. Flint, Mich.: Charles Stewart Mott Foundation.

Melaville, A., and Blank, M. (1991). *What it takes: Structuring interagency partnerships to connect children and families with comprehensive services*. Washington, D.C.: Education and Human Services Consortium.

Molnar, A. (Ed.). (2002). *School reform proposals: The research evidence.* Retrieved September 7, 2002, from www.asu.edueduc/epsl/news.htm.

National Assembly of Health and Human Service Organizations. (2001). *After school collaboration: When it works, why it works: A literature review.* Washington, D.C.: National Assembly of Health and Human Service Organizations.

National Association of Elementary School Principals. (2001). *After-school programs.* Retrieved September 9, 2002, from www.naesp.org/afterschool/aspnews.

National Association of Elementary School Principals. (2001). *Leading learning communities: Standards for what principals should know and be able to do.* Retrieved February 20, 2002, from www.naesp.org/nprc.

National Association of Elementary Schools Principals. (2001). *NAESP redefines role of school principal.* Retrieved September 9, 2002, from www.naesp.org/comm/prss10-29-01.

National Association of Partners in Education. (2001). *Seven stage partnership process: Creating and managing highly collaborative development of community–school partnerships.* Alexandria, Va.: National Association of Partners in Education.

National Commission on Service-Learning. (2002). *Learning in deed: The power of service-learning for American schools.* Columbus: Ohio State University.

National Opinion Research Center. (1993). Public opinion and demographic report: Confidence in institutions, *American Enterprise, 4.*

National PTA. (1998). *National standards for parent/family involvement programs.* Chicago: National PTA.

National School-to-Work Learning Center. (n.d.). Announcement of sunset of the School-to-Work Opportunities Act of 1994. Retrieved September 9, 2002, from www.stw.ed.gov. [new websites are www.doleta.gov or www.ed.gov/offices/OVAE]

National Youth Leadership Council. (1989). *Growing hope: A sourcebook on integrating youth service into the school curriculum.* St Paul, Minn.: University of Minnesota, Center for Youth Development and Research.

National Youth Leadership Council. (1990). *National service learning initiative.* St Paul: Minn.: University of Minnesota, Center for Youth Development and Research.

Network for Good. (2002). *Volunteering tradition.* Retrieved September 8, 2002, from www.networkforgood.org/volunteer/volunteertradition.html.

Office of Vocational and Adult Education, U.S. Department of Education. (n.d.). *Preparing America's future.* Retrieved September 9, 2002, from www.ed.gov/offices/OVAE/paf.html

Parson, S. R. (1999). *Transforming schools into community learning centers.* Larchmont, N.Y.: Eye on Education.

Partnership for Family Involvement in Education. (1999). *Partners for learning: Preparing teachers to involve families.* Retrieved March 4, 2002, from pfie.ed.gov.

Phi Delta Kappa International. (1999). *Fast facts PDK/Gallup poll: Local schools supported, but more outreach needed.* Retrieved March 5, 2002, from www.pdkintl.org/whatis/ff4poll.

Phi Delta Kappa International. (2000). *32nd annual Phi Delta Kappa/Gallup poll.* Retrieved January 29, 2002, from www.pdkintl.org/kappan/kpol0009.

Public Education Network. (2001). *PEN releases "action for all."* Retrieved September 9, 2002, from www.publiceducation.org/news/041601.htm.

Saskatchewan Education. (1999). *Parent and community partnerships in education: Policy framework.* Regina: Saskatchewan Education.

School-to-Work Opportunities Act of 1994. (1999.) Retrieved February 3, 2001, from www.stw.ed.gov/general/whatis.

Stehle, V. (1993). Finding new ways to recruit and keep today's volunteers. *Chronicle of Philanthropy,* June 29.

Timberman, L. (1999). Foster a relationship between the business community and schools. *Journal of Educational Relations,* 20, 2.

U.S. Department of Education. (1994). *Strong families, strong schools: Building community partnerships for learning.* Washington, D.C.: U.S. Government Printing Office.

Withrow, F. (with Long, H., and Marx, G). (1999). *Preparing schools and school systems for the 21st century.* Arlington, Va.: American Association of School Administrators.

WEBSITES FOR MORE INFORMATION AND LINKS TO OTHER RELEVANT SITES

America's Promise, www.americaspromise.org
Association for Volunteer Administration, www.avaintl.org
Charles Stewart Mott Foundation, www.mott.org
Children's Aid Society, communityschools.org
Corporation for National Service, www.learnandserve.org
Energize Especially for Leaders of Volunteers, energizeinc.com
National Association of Elementary School Principals, www.naesp.org
National Association of Partners in Education, www.napehq.org
National Dropout Prevention Center, www.dropoutprevention.org
National Network for Collaboration, crs.uvm.edu/nnco
National Network of Partnership Schools, scov.csos.jhu.edu/p2000
National PTA, www.pta.org

National Service Learning Clearinghouse, www.servicelearning.org

National Youth Leadership Council, www.nylc.org

Partnership for Family Involvement in Education, pfie.ed.gov

Youth Serve America, www.servenet.org

U.S. Department of Education, www.ed.gov

Office of Vocational and Adult Education, www.ed.gov/offices/OVAE

U.S. Department of Labor, Employment and Training Administration, www.doleta.gov

CHAPTER 6

School Public Relations: Bridging the Gap

Voter support for public education has declined dramatically since the 1960s. Taxpayers have become increasingly reluctant to invest in something they perceive to be declining in quality, and many do not believe that they benefit directly from public education.

A comprehensive public relations program directed at the general public should try to build an understanding that everyone in the community benefits when schools are able to carry out their mission of academic success for all children. In *How Our Investment in Education Pays Off*, The American Association of School Administrators (AASA) (1993) addressed the question: Why support public schools?

> Everyone in society reaps the benefits of education. Whether or not we have children in school, each of us will one day depend on an educated workforce to sustain a viable and healthy economy. If we hope to maintain or improve the quality of life in our communities, attract new industries, and continue to prosper as a nation, then top-notch schools are essential.

The AASA publication lists seven ways in which investing in education pays off for society:

1. Provides greater earning power: Education increases the likelihood of getting higher-paying and professional jobs. It leads to greater employability and prepares students for the jobs of the future.
2. Enriches the quality of life in our communities: Education increases a community's standard of living. It creates and nurtures

cultural experiences and opportunities. It reduces crime by providing skills, direction, and hope.

3. Promotes equal opportunity: Public schools educate all children.
Schools help all children achieve. Education promotes an understanding of others.

4. Maintains our free-market economy: Education ensures that children will be well prepared for the challenges of the workforce.
Schools give future workers the skills they need to compete. Education preserves the middle class, preventing a two-tiered society of
haves and have-nots. Schools promote the understanding and use of
technology.

5. Enhances our personal fulfillment: Education encourages students to strive for excellence. In addition to academic skills, education gives students life skills: students learn self-discipline, pa-
tience, responsibility, and sharing. It gives students the
opportunity to explore interests and develop talents.

6. Ensures our world leadership status: Education helps our students
compete in the global economy. Other nations are investing in education, so maintaining our international competitiveness and our
standard of living depends on an educated workforce. Guarantee-
ing our national security also rests ultimately on education.

7. Preserves our democracy: Education creates a common vision of
democracy that cannot thrive in an uneducated population or in a
society in which only an elite few are educated. Schools empower
students to become active, concerned citizens.

THE HEART OF THE PROBLEM

The 1998 Phi Delta Kappa/Gallup Poll (Phi Delta Kappa International,
1999) points to a central problem in school public relations: The schools
to which people assign low grades do not exist. Respondents assign low
grades to schools generally or to schools in communities in which they
do not live—not to the schools they know. The schools that rate low are
perceived to exist on the basis of information received from the media.
This conclusion may comfort educators in terms of their own schools,
but the pollsters warn: "Educators should . . . not ignore people's per-

ceptions that public schools in other communities are bad."

The emphasis here should not be on the erroneous conclusions based on media impressions and misinformation, but on the lack of adequate, high-quality information issued by school leaders. A study of school districts in four Midwestern states (Kowalski and Wiedmer, 1995) confirmed the findings of several earlier studies showing that public relations were a low priority for schools and "most superintendents appeared to be PR passive." In the targeted districts—which included districts that were small city/town, rural, suburban, and urban, and ranged in size from less than 1,500 students to more than 7,000 students—researchers found:

- About 42 percent of the districts did not have a plan or policy directing public relations activities.
- More than one out of three districts (35 percent) did not have a plan or policy for communicating with the media in the event of an emergency or crisis.
- Approximately one out of five districts had no one—not even the superintendent—designated as responsible for public relations.
- Approximately 15 percent of the districts never published a newsletter, and another 38 percent did so only once or twice a year.
- Nearly three out of four districts (74 percent) did not have regularly scheduled radio or television programs.
- Only 28 percent of the districts reported extensive efforts to prepare printed promotional materials (pamphlets, brochures), and only 8 percent reported extensive efforts to prepare visual promotional materials.
- The most widely used public relations technique was the issuance of news releases. Slightly more than half of the superintendents indicated that this was done frequently in their districts, although two superintendents said they never issued news releases.

DEFINING SCHOOL PUBLIC RELATIONS

Public relations is not publicity, nor a communications function designed to tell "good" news or cover up "bad" news. Public relations is a school's management function basic to its successful operation. The National School Public Relations Association (NSPRA) (2002) explains:

> Today's educational public relations program is a planned and systematic management function designed to help improve the programs and services of an educational organization. It relies on a comprehensive, two-way communication process involving both internal and external publics with a goal of stimulating a better understanding of the role, objectives, accomplishments, and needs of the organization. Educational public relations programs assist in interpreting public attitudes, identify and help shape policies and procedures in the public interest and carry on involvement and information activities which earn public understanding and support.

Public relations is not based on image building or communications designed only for purposes of advocacy or persuasion. Public relations is a continuous effort to understand the concerns of relevant populations (students, families, staff, taxpayers, and the like) and respond to those concerns. The key concepts are *understanding*—or, more precisely, mutual public understanding—and *responding*. An educational administrator's role is facilitation of a process that is more dialogue than monologue. Martinson (1995) adds, "If persuasion occurs, the public should be just as likely to persuade the organization's management to change attitudes or behavior as the organization is likely to change the public's attitudes or behavior."

WHY SCHOOL PUBLIC RELATIONS?

The National School Public Relations Association (2002) emphasizes the *public* in school public relations.

> Public relations needs to be in the public's interest. It needs to be grounded in solid two-way communication techniques and used as a vehicle to build trust, confidence and support for doing the best for all children in our schools. NSPRA firmly believes that school systems and schools have a public responsibility to tell parents and taxpayers how the schools are

spending their money, and to seek their insights on helping the school district deliver a high quality, efficient educational program. The public has a right to know and be engaged in their schools. And they need someone in the schools trained in communication so they can get clear answers and guidance on how to work with their schools.

In the following passage, NSPRA contends that excellent public relations is needed by schools now more than ever.

- This is the media age. Schools' communication needs have increased dramatically and become more complex. Schools have to be able to communicate through both print and electronic media and in face-to-face communication, as well as handle relations with the multitude of media.
- Public education is under attack from taxpayers, business groups, and others. Schools need to publicize positive news about student and staff achievements and programs and to develop a coordinated, proactive approach that anticipates problems before they develop. If there is no positive communication from the school or school district, critics' voices are the only ones that will be heard.
- The scope of successful school public relations has expanded from the mostly written communication of the past to a greatly increased need for face-to-face communication with a variety of publics. Community relations programming, realtor orientations, breakfasts with chamber of commerce members and clergy, and American Education Week open houses are becoming common ways to build informed support and solid community relationships.

If educators are to respond to the public's increasing demand for information and accountability, they need to understand (1) the difference between publicity and genuine public relations, (2) the difference between a publicity campaign of pure advocacy and a public relations programdesigned to facilitate mutual understanding, and (3) the power of public relations to serve as a two-way link between an organization and its publics in order to build understanding and resolve conflicts (Martinson, 1995).

COMMUNICATION

The process of communicating with others is not as simple as some people believe. As the playwright George Bernard Shaw observed, "The greatest problem of communication is in the illusion that it has been accomplished."

All types of communication, oral and written, have five basic components (Decker and Associates, 1994):

- Source—the person with an idea to communicate.
- Message (structure and content)—what the person wants to communicate, expressed in words, gestures, and symbols.
- Channel—how the idea is expressed: sight, sound, touch, smell, taste, or a combination; selecting the right channel is important if the idea is to reach the intended receiver.
- Receiver—the person(s) to whom the message is directed. Considering the receiver's characteristics is crucial as the source develops the idea into a message and chooses a channel to express it.
- Effect—an indication of whether or not the receiver understood the message.

Oral communication is also affected by nonverbal behaviors (Clark, 2000). Eye contact helps regulate the flow of communication; it signals interest in others and increases the speaker's credibility. Facial expressions convey emotions. Smiling is a cue that transmits happiness, friendliness, warmth, and liking, and it often makes people more comfortable and more willing to listen. Gestures capture the listener's attention, making the conversation more interesting and facilitating understanding. Posture and body orientation affect how the audience interprets a message. A speaker who stands erect and leans slightly forward communicates that he or she is approachable, receptive, and friendly, whereas speaking with back turned or looking at the floor or ceiling conveys discomfort or lack of interest. Cultural norms dictate a comfortable distance for interacting with others. Variations in tone, pitch, rhythm, timbre, loudness, and inflection help keep listeners' attention.

Successful oral communication involves the listener as well as the speaker. Listening is not the same as hearing. Hearing is involuntary and refers simply to the reception of aural stimuli. Listening is a selective activity that involves both reception and interpretation of aural stimuli; it involves decoding sound into meaning. Listening may be passive or active. Passive listening is little more than hearing Active listening involves listening with a purpose; it requires that the listener attend to the words and feelings of the sender for optimal understanding.

It has been suggested that an active listener listens first to what someone is *saying*, then tries to listen to what a person is *not saying* and to what a person *wants to say but doesn't know how*. What the listener perceives as said is as important as what is actually said. The listener's perceptions can affect the meaning assigned to the words and the meaning of the complete message.

Effective communication occurs only when the receiver understands the exact information or idea that the sender intends to transmit. Several kinds of barriers can keep the message from being understood in the way the sender intends it. These barriers may be internal or external (Decker and Associates, 1994):

- Filters—senders and receivers may have different opinions, concerns, or value systems.
- Jargon—specialized terms, acronyms, or unfamiliar expressions.
- Semantics—words that mean or imply different things to different people.
- Information overload—too much information and/or not enough time to comprehend it.
- Nonverbal behavior—body language, facial expressions, gestures, proximity, vocal elements.
- Emotional climate—fear, anger, hostility, or distrust.

The most effective channel for communication is oral and face-to-face, especially one-on-one. The more people involved, the greater the chance the message will not be received or will be misunderstood. Written communication, however carefully thought out and precisely worded, is more likely to encounter barriers—filters, semantics, and information overload. Thus, when the intent of the communication is to advocate or persuade, person-to-person exchanges such as telephone calls, dialogues, or workshops are preferable. When the intent is to inform, mass media sources—media memos, newsletters, brochures, news releases, radio and television spots, videotapes—may be viable options. Designing an effective school public relations program involves analyzing the needs and problems in communicating with two primary groups: the internal and the external publics of the school.

The Internal Public

Most experts in school public relations agree that a solid internal communications program is essential. Bagin (2001), past president of the National School Public Relations Association and consultant on school public relations, emphasizes that, before anything can be done externally, people who work in the school need to be informed and knowledgeable about the school and its educational mission and policies, and realize their role in public relations.

The school's internal public is defined as all those directly connected to and affected by the school and its operation: the professional and support staff, students, and families. These are also the people who affect the internal climate of a school. Their importance to a school's public relations cannot be overstated because the internal climate of a school affects student achievement, staff morale, and the type and level of community support a school enjoys. Norton (1998) emphasizes:

> Schools are people; the interpersonal relationships within the system are of paramount importance for bringing about a climate that serves to support and enhance the performance of all people in a school. . . . Effective communication necessitates a climate of trust, mutual respect, and clarity of function. Thus, a healthy school climate enhances the chances that communication within the system will be *heard and internalized.*

The 1988 Phi Delta Kappa Commission on Developing Public Confidence in Schools found that the employees of a school rank first as the general public's information sources, and their impressions are the most powerful determinants of a school's image (Woodland, 2001). To many people, the staff is the school. As Yantis (1995) points out: "There is a close relationship between the internal social, psychological, and emotional environment of a school and the type of external relations a school has with its community. Low staff morale and poor personal relationships within the school quite often carry over to unsuccessful school–community relations." Bagin, Gallagher, and Kindred (1994) issue the same warning: "School and community relations are the result of a constant flow of images from the school and its employees, and negative comments or actions project a negative image."

Yantis emphasizes the administrator's role in developing a staff-based approach to community relations:

> Excellent school and community relations is a well-planned and continuous endeavor. School administrators cannot routinely manage the schools and assume that a reactive approach to the community will suffice. They must also recognize that the administration by itself cannot foster and maintain the level of community relationship that is necessary today. Effective administrators must undertake a proactive role in developing a total staff approach to community relations. In fact, when planning the community relations program, a wise administrator will quite likely consider the staff first, knowing that a knowledgeable staff with a positive attitude can go a long way toward building a positive and realistic public image of the schools.

All staff communicate with each other and the public about the school, and are viewed by the community as primary sources of information about the school and it's programs. Every staff member—from administrator and teacher to nurse, custodian, bus driver, and contract worker—needs to know his or her importance as a member of the public relations team and believe that responsibility for creating good public relations is within their job description. A school's public relations plan needs to contain provisions for (1) orientation of staff to their respective roles in public relations, (2) ongoing staff development on how to enhance public confidence in schools, and (3) ongoing information-sharing about program changes, new directions, and so on to keep all staff up to date and informed.

Obviously, the public relations plan should also provide for keeping students and families informed. They, too, have a vested interest in high-quality public relations because of the importance of good school–community relations in carrying out the mission of the school: the academic success of all children.

The External Public

To say that everyone who is not part of a school's internal public is part of its external public sounds simplistic, but it is true. Some people—alumni, grandparents, volunteers, and others who have some kind of a collaborative relationship with the school—may perceive themselves as having an indirect or secondary connection to a school. Others may think that they have little or no connection to public schools and, therefore, have no reason to support them.

A comprehensive public relations program must include strategies directed at all segments of the external public to build and maintain the understanding that everyone in the community benefits from the academic success of children. Whether or not community members believe that a school is able to carry out its mission of educating all children—or at least making good progress toward carrying out that goal—depends on how well the school's public relations program has informed its external public, appropriately involved them, sought their opinions or invited them to participate in decision making, and provided them with opportunities to be of service to the school.

WHY IMAGE MATTERS

Marketing consultants often advise clients that image is more important than reality because image—the sum of perceptions, attitudes, beliefs, ideas, and feelings about something—makes people act in certain ways and shapes attitudes toward a product, service, or organization. Carroll and Carroll (1994) emphasize that this advice applies to schools and school systems as much as it does to the private sector. "Whether perceptions or beliefs about a school system are deserved or undeserved, positive or negative, they account for much of what happens inside the voter booth when budgets or referenda are on the ballot."

A public school's image depends on how the school *appears* to the public. A person's impression of a school is based partly on observed *objective* characteristics and partly on *subjective* experiences and reactions. Carroll and Carroll (1994) advise paying attention to things that can improve or degrade a school's image, including:

- Newspaper articles
- Publications distributed from the school
- Radio and television reports
- Condition of physical plant, grounds, offices, classrooms, bulletin boards, cafeteria
- Curriculum design
- Standardized test scores, especially SAT
- Colleges where the school's seniors are accepted
- Dropout and teen pregnancy rates
- Student and staff drug and alcohol use
- Athletic programs
- Special facilities and equipment (swimming pool, computer hardware and software)
- School–business partnerships
- Student and staff volunteerism in the community
- Teacher and administrative staff outreach and service to community

Because image does matter, one of the first steps in developing a school's public relations program is finding out what the community's image of the public school actually is. Assessing a school's image benefits the staff in several ways (Carroll and Carroll, 1994): First, it requires that a school look at its internal and external publics and systematically identify community perceptions so that planning can be based on fact, not speculation. Second, it helps to build better public relations by letting community members know that their opinions are important. Third, it provides school staff with baseline data to measure long-term increases in support, monitor changes in image over time, and keep in touch with the opinions of key community groups.

The techniques for assessing a school's image are much the same as those used for conducting a needs assessment. The objectives should be clearly defined, written, and formally agreed upon. The research design should be realistic and achievable, involving decisions on whether data will be collected only from targeted groups or from a sampling of the entire community. The design should ensure that the desired information is gathered in the most judicious, expedient, cost-effective, and reliable manner possible. This may involve a blending of qualitative and quantitative research methods.

Carroll and Carroll (2001) stress that public schools need to practice *outside-inside* marketing so that resulting strategies and actions are based on information and data coming from the community to the school, not on decisions "often made in isolation. . . . [D]ecision making [should not be] an insular process, occasionally interrupted by poorly attended public hearings." Educators need to assess systematically the needs, wants, perceptions, preferences, and satisfaction of the total community using techniques such as surveys, focus groups, and in-depth interviews. They point out that "using such strategies builds long-lasting, meaningful relationships with the community and fosters a loyalty to the public school. Relationship building is the key to getting and keeping community support and to do this, public schools must start 'outside' with their communities."

Assessing a school's image takes resources and time, but schools that assess and monitor their images—and, as a result, work to improve them—have several advantages over those that do not (Carroll and Carroll, 1994):

- They are likely to be more effective in securing community support for school projects and changes.
- "Them versus us" attitudes are minimized.
- Family support and involvement increases.
- Morale improves, since the staff feels part of a winning team.

Based on data from image assessment, a school can develop a plan to enhance positive factors and decrease the impact of negative ones. The planned actions and supporting data must be communicated to targeted groups.

MARKETING COMMUNICATIONS

A school's public relations strategies should include marketing communications—that is, communications directed at persuading the external public of the value of supporting public education in general and a specific school in particular. Marketing communications are tools used to persuade; their major purpose is to provide information to, and develop a relationship with, community groups.

There are three basic types of marketing communications: advertising, publicity, and personal contact. Advertising includes traditional methods—purchased time or space and outreach materials, such as fact sheets, brochures, newsletters, and videotapes. Publicity includes newspaper and magazine articles, press releases, radio and television coverage, discussion panels, guest appearances, and other special efforts. Personal contact involves public speaking, special events, and tables or booths at community gatherings.

Carroll and Carroll (1994) suggest using a combination of advertising, publicity, and personal contact to get a school's message out to the community. They recommend eight strategies.

Strategy 1: Seize all opportunities that communicate quality to the community. Quality is not a homogeneous concept; it may mean academics, job placement rate, literacy rate, before- and after-school programs, community service learning opportunities, and so on. A public school needs to find out how quality is measured or judged by key community groups.

Strategy 2: Identify all community groups that should hear good news about the school. Identify key community groups and use marketing communications tools targeted at those groups to share good news and highlight quality.

Strategy 3: Use repetition to make the message memorable. Delivering a message once is not enough.

Strategy 4: Name a public relations coordinator. Although marketing is part of the whole staff's job, the public relations coordinator has the major responsibility of overseeing a school's public relations plan. This individual is usually the one who works with the media and coordinates communications efforts. For large schools, the marketing coordinator's position may be full-time; for smaller schools, the coordinator may work part-time, or the assigned tasks may be the responsibility of a designated member of the school staff; for the smallest schools, the coordinator may be the principal or the superintendent.

Strategy 5: Develop a solid relationship with the media. Work diligently to be accessible to the media and give them clear, consistent, and accurate information.

Strategy 6: Issue Press Releases and Public Service Announcements (PSAs). A press release is a concise, factual, non-promotional document that includes all the facts (who, what, where, why, when, and how) about an event, program, or happening that a publication or broadcast station needs to cover a story. PSAs are newsprint or broadcast announcements that are printed or aired free for nonprofit organizations. Radio PSAs are usually short, written announcements read on the air by station personnel without sound effects or music.

Strategy 7: Build a collection of useful communication items, both in writing and in pictures. The collection may consist of examples of good written communications such as those written by the coordinator or other school personnel on specific programs and activities or on public education in general. The collection may include letters to the editor, editorial columns, articles, op-ed pieces, newsletters, pictures with headlines that tell a story, and the like.

Strategy 8: Develop your marketing communications with senior citizens in mind. The support of senior citizens requires special cultivation in most communities because this growing group is often on a fixed income and may have the perception that public education is of no personal benefit to them.

SOCIAL MARKETING

According to Weinreich (1995), social marketing began as a discipline in the 1970s when Kotler and Zaltman realized that the same marketing principles that were being used to sell products to consumers could be used to *sell* ideas, attitudes, and behaviors. Social marketing employs general marketing strategies to deal with social issues and affect behavioral change. It differs "from other areas of marketing only with respect to the objectives of the marketer and his or her organization. Social marketing seeks to influence social behaviors not to benefit the marketer, but to benefit the target audience and the general society."

Weinreich explains that like commercial marketing, the primary focus in social marketing is on the consumer—learning what people want and need—and the marketing message talks to the consumer, not about the product. The planning process takes this consumer focus into account by addressing the elements of the *marketing mix*. "This refers to decisions about the concept of a *product, price,* distribution (*place*), and *promotion* . . . often called the Four P's of marketing." Social marketing also adds a few more P's: *partnership, policy, and politics.*

At a meeting convened by the Harvard Family Research Project, social marketing was presented as a strategy to generate family–school partnerships (Sensiper, 2002). Sensiper (2002) and Weinreich (1995) explain the marketing mix in the context of generating family, school, and community partnerships.

> *Product.* A continuum of products exists, ranging from tangible, physical products to services, practices, and more intangible ideas. The product or program must be one that has recognizable benefits for those participating. In order to have a viable product, people must first perceive that they have a genuine problem or need, and that the product offering is a good solution. It takes research to discover the consumers' perception of the problem or need and the product, and determine how important people feel it is to take action toward achieving a solution.
>
> *Price.* There is always a *cost* involved in efforts to increase participation in involvement programs. This cost may be monetary or it may require the consumer to give something intangible, such as time or effort, or risk disapproval. If the costs outweigh the benefits for an individual, it is unlikely the product will be adopted. Determining the cost-benefit ratio may not be a clear-cut process. If the product is priced too low or free of charge, it may be viewed as low in quality. If the price is too high, some people may not be able to afford it. Remember also that language may be a cost on the part of the marketer and the consumer when it is a barrier to communication.
>
> *Place.* Place describes the way the product reaches the consumer. For a tangible product, it is the distribution system. For an intangible product, place refers to decisions about the channels through which consumers are reached. An element of place is determining how to ensure accessibility. Planning meetings at convenient times in comfortable locations and creating a friendly, positive atmosphere promotes open communication and meaningful sharing.

Promotion. Promotion is only one element, but because of its visibility, promotion sometimes mistakenly is perceived as comprising the whole of social marketing. The focus is on creating and sustaining a demand for the product. Research is needed to determine the most effective and efficient methods to reach the target audience and increase demand. Promotion may be through one-on-one contact, advertising, public relations, promotional samples, media advocacy, public service announcements, or any other *selling* vehicle.

Partnership. Education, social, and health issues are so complex that no one agency alone can offer a viable solution. Team work in the form of agency cooperation and collaboration is needed to be effective. Research is needed to determine which agencies and organizations have similar goals and to identify ways in which they can work together in partnership toward the solution of a problem or the fulfillment of a need.

Policy. Social marketing programs can motivate individuals, but they are difficult to sustain unless the environment in which the product is offered is supportive. Often a policy change, is needed. Media advocacy programs can be an effective complement to a social marketing program.

Politics. The issues addressed by social marketing programs are often complex and frequently controversial. Some political diplomacy may be needed to gain community support, get access to a target audience, or deal with potential adversaries.

In addition, Weinreich (1995) offers ten tips to help build social marketing into an overall home, school, and community partnership program:

1. *Talk to consumers.* Social marketing is a consumer-driven process and all aspects of a program must be developed with the wants and needs of the target audience as the central focus.
2. *Segment the audience.* There is no such thing as selling to the general public. To be most effective, target audiences need to be segmented into groups that are as similar as possible and messages need to be created for each segment. Segmentation may

be by sex, age, geographical location, race/ethnicity, and behavior. Remember that some target audiences may be reached more successfully when the message comes through a secondary group.

3. *Position the product.* To counteract the factors or costs working against the adoption of a product, it is often necessary to acknowledge potential problems and address them before they start. Positioning the product determines what people in the target audience think about your product as compared to the status quo or the competition. Product positioning is usually based on either the benefits of the product or the removal of barriers to selling that product.

4. *Know the competition.* Social marketers need to be aware of any competing messages directed at the target audience. Environmental factors may affect people's reaction, political changes may require a new approach, news events may change the context in which people hear the message, and efforts of other agencies or organizations may affect how the message is portrayed.

5. *Go to where the target audience is.* People usually will not go out of their way to find a product's message. Messages need to be in places where the target audience will encounter them. Research into audience demographics of local media outlets and creativity may be needed to match a target group's characteristics with the most effective media.

6. *Utilize a variety of approaches.* The most effective social marketing programs use a combination of mass media, community, small groups, and individual activities. When a simple, clear message is repeated in many places and formats throughout the community, it is more likely to be seen and remembered.

7. *Use models that work.* A model used frequently is one that incorporates elements of well-established behavior theories that portray people moving through several steps in a continuum before adopting a new behavior. This model provides a useful framework for segmenting the target audience. A program can be designed to address people in each stage over a period of time or address those at a particular stage in the process.

8. *Test market.* All products, promotional materials, and services should be tested with a target audience to gauge their effectiveness. Using a focus group is one of the methods most associated with social marketing. Surveys are a more generalizable method to research people's knowledge, attitudes, and behaviors related to a particular topic.

9. *Build partnerships with key allies.* By pooling resources with other agencies and organizations working toward a goal, a social marketing program can have a greater impact and gain access to new audiences or better access to a target audience.

10. *Evaluate.* Evaluation occurs throughout the social marketing process. As a program is developed, messages and products need to be tested with members of the target audience and refined. When the program is implemented, activities need to be monitored and assessed to determine if they are occurring as planned. Periodically, the program needs to be evaluated to see if it is having its desired effect. The actual impact of a social marketing program may be difficult to assess accurately, especially in the short run. However, at whatever level the evaluation is performed, the information gained should be used to improve the program in the future.

WORKING WITH THE NEWS MEDIA

Schools deal with two things very dear to most people: their children and their tax dollars. People want to know how well schools are teaching students, and they want to know how their tax dollars are spent. In many communities, fewer than 25 percent of the households have children in school. The other 75 percent probably heavily rely on the news media for information about schools. The 1998 PDK/Gallup Poll's (Phi Delta Kappa International, 1999) identification of the media's negative impact on public confidence in public education underscores the importance of working with the media to ensure that attitudes toward schools are not based on misinformation or misunderstanding.

Working with the news media is only one part of a school's overall public relations plan, but it is such an important part that expending time and effort to do it well can pay big dividends. Doing it poorly can have disastrous effects. Public confidence takes a long time to build, but only a short time to destroy.

One of the facts that school leaders—both new and experienced—know is that, like it or not, they will have contact with the news media on a fairly regular basis. Still, as Mullen (1999) points out, many seem to have an inherent fear of the media, even though they know that working effectively with the media can make their jobs easier by accurately informing community members about what is going on at the school.

Working with the media involves a variety of encounters, from a full-scale news conference to a brief telephone call. The contact may be initiated by either educators or reporters. Taking time to get acquainted, especially with the reporters who cover education, is important. Whether the contact centers on a crisis situation or on a routine story, it is always easier to work with someone you know and trust.

In an orientation guide for new school spokespersons, Mullen (1999) recommends that, in addition to taking time to know media personnel, the new spokesperson defines three positive points—facts, issues, or messages—he or she wants everyone to know about the school. First, if unsure of which messages to promote, the spokesperson should think of how the various issues of the day affect community members, identify school strengths and vulnerabilities, brainstorm with others, and keep asking *why, so what*, and *prove it* until three solid points are defined. Second, the spokesperson should anticipate a reporter's questions by making a list of questions that have been asked in the past or could be asked, including questions the person never wants to get. Then he or she should practice answering them, making sure to find a way back to the three positive points. Third, the spokesperson should personalize responses as much as possible, using *we* and *you,* and keeping in mind the 10 C's of a good source: be concise, candid, conversational, clear, correct, calm, compassionate, compelling, complete, and credible.

In an American Association of School Administrators publication, *Working with the News Media*, Ordovensky and Marx (1993) stress that each school and school system should identify one person who will be the media liaison with full responsibility for media relations. The media relations director for a school system should work directly with the superintendent, hold a position in the school system's cabinet, and be involved in and informed about the details of all programs and important decisions. The designated person should have the authority to speak for the school system on any issue that might arise, and to call on others for their knowledge and expertise in addressing various topics. The media relations director should not be chastised for reporting facts—some organizations are prone to shoot messengers rather than solve problems.

Ordovensky and Marx give practical tips for working with print or broadcast media:

- Rule number one for all occasions: Whatever you say, be sure it's true. Do not even think about obscuring the facts or saying things that are untrue.
- Know your audience and address it. Just as you would organize your presentation a bit differently for a PTA meeting, a chamber of commerce luncheon, or a school assembly, consider a reporter's audience when responding to a reporter's questions.
- Remember that brevity is a virtue. Since reporters are generally limited either by time or space, compose your comments in easy-to-understand, colorful segments. Beware of the temptation to make the same point repeatedly.
- Avoid education jargon. Jargon exists in every field. It is a kind of shorthand that people use to communicate within a profession or line of work. If your audience is not likely to understand a term, either do not use it or offer a brief, uncomplicated explanation.
- Stick to the story. If a reporter is visiting with you about a bond issue, site-based management, or test scores in math, for example, avoid drifting into other subjects.
- Do not blame reporters for things they cannot control. A reporter generally has little or no control over whether the story will actually be used; how the story is positioned and presented in relation to other stories; the length of a story, either in print space or air time; what is cut from the story to make it fit the required time and space; or the headline.
- Know what is public information. Reports and surveys financed by public dollars are public documents. A reporter can legitimately

ask to see any such reports, and schools are required to provide them. Anything said at a public meeting, by any participant, can be publicly reported.

- Remember, humans err. Educators occasionally make mistakes. So do reporters. If an error appears in a story, resist the temptation to explode. The reporter simply may have misunderstood something you said. Keep in mind that good reporters base their livelihoods on their credibility. If they lose it, they are out of business.

- Return calls promptly. When reporters call, chances are they are working on a story for the next newspaper or newscast. Often, they must complete their stories within one or two days. Move a reporter's message to the top of your stack.

- Know what "off-the-record" means. Always assume that any conversation with a reporter is on-the-record and might be published. Reporters work on that assumption. So should you. On occasion, if you have a working relationship with a reporter and want to share unquotable information or background, you can ask to go off-the-record for a minute. If the reporter agrees—and in most case he or she will—you can speak without fear of being quoted.

- Think before you speak. Try to select those words that will most precisely convey your ideas. If necessary, pause for a few seconds to form your answer. Always speak to those who may not have enough information to understand you, and do so in clear, plain language.

- Remember that "I don't know" is not a guilty plea. If you do not know the answer to a question, do not try to make up something that could be inaccurate.

- Remember that "no comment" is a comment. In reality, these two words imply that the speaker has something to hide or is being condescending. Most reporters will assume both are true. Simply say you cannot answer the question and why (something like, "That's a personnel issue involving a school employee, and I don't think a public statement would be appropriate").

- Be fair to all media. You can go a long way toward building and maintaining credibility by adopting a policy of scrupulous fairness. Distribute even the most routine news releases at the same time to all media outlets. Do not deliberately, even inadvertently, time your news releases to give one news organization an advantage. If you invite one news organization to cover an event, invite them all. If you expect both broadcast and print coverage at an event or news conference, allow adequate time.

- Look for news pegs. Know what aspect of a potential story will grab the reader's attention. Generally, some aspect of every story makes it topical or ties it to a community or worldwide concern. Schools are in an excellent position to work with various reporters on many beats. The entertainment reporter (school musical, dances, student art shows), business reporter (economics class), environmental reporter (science projects), and others might find special interest in various school activities. However, if a specific person has been assigned to cover education, make this reporter your first contact.
- Be sensitive to deadlines. Reporters are busiest each day during the two hours immediately preceding their deadlines. That is generally not a good time to call and chat unless you have information they need to complete a story.
- Set up a good internal reporting system. Many school systems distribute reporting forms to staff inviting them to submit possible story ideas. It is also a good idea to appoint a person in each school building to spot potential news stories. Every school district will benefit from efforts to help staff develop a nose for news.
- Never ask a reporter to show you a story before it is published. The news media are free and independent, and a request to review a story before publication would probably be seen as an attempt to censor or change it.

Ordovensky and Marx conclude with a valuable reminder:

> Any organization that expects fair, balanced, accurate, interesting coverage by the media must be fair, balanced, accurate, and interesting with the media. . . . Both schools and the news media need to understand that occasional conflict is a fact of life. Mutually productive relationships should be sound enough to weather the storms of controversy.

KEY COMMUNICATORS

Many schools' public relations plans include a strategy for using another group of people besides news media personnel to bridge the gap between the school and the community. Often called "key communicators," they are supportive people—internal and external—who are kept well informed about the school. Their job is twofold: (1) to spread accurate and supportive information quickly to other members of the community, and (2) to be listening posts in the school and community, alerting school administration to rumors and concerns.

The people selected as key communicators are individuals who can be counted on to be supportive of the school and its successful operation, especially during times of stress. They should represent a cross section of the community. A key communicator can be almost anyone who is respected and listened to in his or her circle of contacts, regardless of the size of the circle. They might be business people, loyal volunteers, bus drivers, crossing guards, substitutes, parents of students and former students, former students themselves, or interested senior citizens.

To establish and maintain good communications with key communicators, school public relations personnel should:

- Identify people who share opinions with others about the school.
- Personally call each individual and invite him or her to become a key communicator. Invite all to come to one meeting, stressing that there will not be additional meetings. Briefly explain the concept of the program. Assure them that you are aware of their interest in the school and that you would like them to be a key communicator to receive and share information—to be two-way communicators.
- Send interested individuals envelopes containing such items as school newsletters, a sample staff bulletin, a school calendar, and the like.
- Ask these people to call you. Explain your need to know if something is occurring that affects the students or the school. Ask them to let you know if they hear something that sounds like a rumor. Promise that you, in turn, will keep them informed.
- Set up a way to contact your key communicators quickly and efficiently—a telephone chain, fax, or e-mail relay for quick response if the need arises, or pre-addressed envelopes for more detailed or less urgent communication. If an incident occurs at school, contacting these people with an explanation before the story reaches

the newspapers or is exaggerated by the rumor mill will pay great
dividends in credibility.

• Remember to say thank you, both individually and to the group. At
the end of the year, invite the key communicators to school. Thank
them for their interest and support. Perhaps give them a certificate,
a small gift, or admission tickets to a school event.

TAKING ADVANTAGE OF TECHNOLOGY

While technology cannot replace face-to-face communication, word
processing, e-mail, voice mail, faxing, videoconferencing, paging,
chatting, surfing the Web, and CD-ROMs have become common tools
for communicating ideas and accessing information. Bryan (1998)
points out that educational technology is pervasive in the administrative and instructional aspects of schools and encompasses both
instructional design and delivery techniques.

Electronic communication provides twenty-four-hour public access to
school information and allows the school to communicate the same message in different languages. Homework hot lines and e-mail to and from
teachers also make possible a kind of two-way communication not con-
strained by geography, time, or language barriers.

Machine translation is a technology that automatically translates text
from one language to another. For example, an English-to-German
machine translation system translates English (the source language) to
German (the target language). An IBM report (2002) on emerging
technologies underscores the fact that machine translation is undergo-
ing continuous refinement. Currently nine language pairs are supported: English to/from French, English to/from Italian, English
to/from German, English to/from Spanish, English to/from simplified
Chinese, English to/from traditional Chinese, English to/from Japan-
ese, English to Korean, and English to Brazilian Portuguese. The report
emphasizes that

The source and/or the target language medium might be text or speech,
but most [machine translation] systems work with text. If speech source
or speech target is of interest, then speech recognition or speech synthesis modules could convert speech to or from text, and the machine trans-

lation could work with the text form. . . . Machine translation is particularly useful for translating Web pages, email, and chat. It not only translates the text, but it also carefully preserves links and pictures and renders fonts nicely in the target text.

Today's audio technology makes it possible to break the language barrier between a speaker and an audience of diverse languages. This emerging technology is helping in solving communications problems resulting from an ever-increasing diversity of students in the public school system. As an article in *EDCAL* (TALK systems, 1999), the official newspaper of the Association of California School Administrators, points out:

These problems are exacerbated when the student's parents speak little or no English. Adding to the dilemma is the fact that for students to do well, parental involvement is a must. What is a school administrator to do when faced with a parent group meeting in which attendees may speak two or more different languages?

The Parent Institute (1999) reports that schools in about twenty-five states are now using TALK Systems to solve the growing problem of getting and keeping non-English-speaking parents involved in their children's education. A lightweight, portable, and wireless transmitting and receiving system allows voice interpretation in up to ten languages to be transmitted to an unlimited number of listeners equipped with earphones. Thus, regardless of the primary speaker's language, interpreters may simultaneously transmit in different languages to different people in the same room. Two-way communication is possible because anyone in the audience can use an open microphone to ask questions, and the interpreter can translate the questions for all to hear. One benefit is that "the equipment has helped integrate parents of different cultures into a greater parent community . . . because TALK Systems allow the listener to sit anywhere in a room, parents need no longer be segregated into language groups. By being together and listening to each other's questions, they discover they all have similar concerns about their kids."

The TALK System is relatively inexpensive. The Parent Institute reports that, although the systems have been mainly used in "parent-teacher and parent education meetings, and with bilingual advisory committees, . . . [it is] also being used in parent-teacher conferences, school board meetings, field trips and in classrooms as an alternative to bilingual education." Teacher aides, volunteers, parents, and students typically serve as interpreters, as well. Being an interpreter has the benefit of showing students the value of being bilingual and the potential for using bilingualism in future careers.

A study for the Institute for Public Relations (Pavlik, 1996) points out some of the uses of technology in the field of public relations.

> Properly used, the Web represents the ultimate communication tool for building relationships between an organization and its publics, both internal and external. The Web can deliver messages incorporating all modalities of human communication, whether text, audio, graphics, still pictures, animation or full-motion video. It can even deliver immersive virtual reality environments where organizations can demonstrate products or services, tours of offices and other facilities, or educational environments. More importantly, the Web offers interactivity and customization of information never before available to a large-scale audience or public.

The growth of local cable television has given rise to the production of a variety of local, community-produced programs and provides yet another means of communicating with local audiences. Urging superintendents to be "electronic superintendents," Donlevy, Hilliard, and Donley (1996) point out that local cable television can allow "an 'electronic superintendent' to reach community members in their homes at least as a supplement to standard communication channels such as newsletters and meetings, but possibly as a means to attract new attention and dialogue about school issues." They emphasize that not only can such a show enable the superintendent to communicate regularly with the various district audiences on items of concern to all stakeholders, but to do so at small cost to the district.

Technology is also being used in much broader ways to create "virtual schools." In one project, part of a National Science Foundation initiative, the college of human relations and education and the computer science department at Virginia Tech University in Blacksburg, Virginia, are working with county schools to develop a network-based virtual school (Parson, 1999). They are developing "an unbounded educational environment with no walls, no halls, no bells, where virtual collaborative classrooms encompass the entire community and exploit connections among diverse educational resources: schools, libraries, homes, businesses, government, local and global networks, and individuals."

Blacksburg residents are also linking themselves to an "electronic village" through technology. The idea is to link community members to each other, to information sources, and to worldwide networks. The Blacksburg Electronic Village (www.bev.net) is an example of a collaborative venture involving the town government, Virginia Tech University, and the regional telephone company.

GETTING A PUBLIC RELATIONS PROGRAM UNDERWAY

The process of developing a comprehensive school public relations program is similar to the process used in the development of any strategic plan. It should:

- Be strategic in that it contributes to the school's and school district's mission and overall objectives.
- Market the school and the district and their educational values, as well as the programs, facilities, and services.
- Focus on both internal and external publics, especially targeting those stakeholders with whom public relations need to be improved.
- Be part of a schoolwide and a districtwide effort that supports and is supported by other organizational functions (such as operation, programming, and home, school, and community outreach efforts).
- Recognize that the success of public relations and ultimately the entire home, school, and community partnership initiative depends on the quality and strength of the relationship with all the community's educational stakeholders, with an emphasis on long-term satisfaction.
- Be viewed, budgeted, and evaluated as an investment, not as an expense.

A detailed public relations plan should have eight integrated components: the organization's mission, goals, and objectives; a needs/situation assessment; public relations objectives; internal and external populations segmentation, targeting, and positioning; the mix of strategies; a budget; implementation plan; and evaluation. The National School Public Relations Association and the National School Boards Association supply reference materials and written examples. Most larger school systems are willing to share their plans and offer assistance to smaller districts. The school or school district may also want to use an advisory committee representing educators, students, families, businesses, and community members in all of their diversity.

Staffing the Program

School public relations personnel perform several functions (National School Public Relations Association, 2002):

- Communication with internal and external publics: Handle all aspects of the school's or the district's publications, such as its external newspaper and internal newsletter.
- Media relations: Serve as media liaison. Write news releases for local newspapers, television, and radio; work to get media coverage of education news.
- Budget/bond issue campaigns: Stay closely informed about the entire budget-making process and promote community input. Develop budget/bond issue campaigns and publications.
- Communications planning/crisis communications planning: Develop a communications plan, detailing how to reach internal and external publics; develop a communication plan for reaching publics, gathering facts and dealing with media in the event of a crisis.
- Public relations research, surveys, polls, informal research: Conduct formal and informal research to determine public opinion and attitudes as a basis for planning and action.
- School/district imaging and marketing: Promote the school's/district's strengths, achievements, and solutions to problems.
- Student/staff recognition: Vigorously publicize student and staff achievement. Develop staff and retirement recognition programs.
- Information station: Answer public and new resident requests for information, maintain extensive background files, and keep historical and budget records. Plan for school/district anniversary celebrations.

- Public relations training: Provide public relations training to staff and other school-related groups (such as the school advisory council, and the PTA) in areas such as talking to the media, communicating in a crisis, and recognizing nonteaching staff as part of the school public relations team.
- Community relations liaison: Serve as liaison with community groups such as civic associations and service clubs. Help plan/publicize school's/district's parent, senior citizen, and community service programs. Develop ways to bring the community into the school.
- The I's: Help keep both I's of the school/district open by working to keep the public *informed* and *involved* in the schools.
- Public relations counsel: Provide public relations counsel, taking a proactive stance. Anticipate problems and provide solutions.

Public relations personnel need a number of operational capabilities ("Training Educational Communication-School PR Specialists," 1997) to be effective:

- Thorough understanding of educational services, objectives, processes, and potentials.
- Ability to identify relationships between education and other human needs and wants.
- Comprehension of social conditions and trends.
- Familiarity with political structures and decision-making processes.
- Comprehension of ethical public relations operations.
- Understanding of how people respond to communication messages.
- Knowledge of how people change their opinions and attitudes.
- Awareness of how perception affects acceptance or rejection of new facts and ideas.
- Comprehension of the function of reward and threat in a message's content.
- Awareness of the nature of rumor.
- Ability to work cooperatively with teachers, education leaders, community leaders, media personnel, and other influential members of the community.
- Knowledge of how leadership can be developed in others.

- Comprehension of how civic and advisory groups can be used effectively.
- Understanding of how the media functions.
- Ability to compose messages to attract attention, arouse interest, and evoke action.

In spite of compelling evidence of the importance of public relations, Kowalski and Wiedmer (1995) found that probably no more than 20 percent of school boards have adopted a public relations policy and employed a full- or part-time public relations person. Budget constraints may be cited as a reason for not having a public relations program and a person designated to carry it out, but the real reason is more likely that, despite the evidence, public relations is not viewed as a priority.

When public relations is a priority, creative resource allocation and staffing can usually be formulated. In larger districts, it is not difficult to justify hiring at least a part-time public relations coordinator with an adequate operations budget. In smaller districts or at the local school level, the superintendent or principal will have to personally perform many of the public relations' tasks, especially those needed on a regular basis. However, even in these cases, it is usually possible for the superintendent or principal to designate several people—from staff or the community—to be responsible for certain aspects of the plan. For example, the various tasks of a comprehensive public relations plan could be divided so that a staff member is given time to write a newsletter and news releases. Trained volunteers could be used to conduct surveys and publicize student and staff achievements. Students can be trained to research community opinions and attitudes. As Litrenta (1999) points out, students gain valuable experiences in data collection and analysis and are an efficient, timesaving, and cost-effective way for a public relations coordinator to acquire valid data.

STEPPING FORWARD

Houston and Bryant (1997) note that school public relations are improving. Schools are becoming "aware of the mixed message they often send to the public. We welcome them into the school on one hand and wave them away with the other. We say we want them involved in their schools, and we create all these mechanisms that hold them at arm's length." More school officials are now attempting to reach across the gulf that separates schools from the public they serve. Chase, president of the National Education Association (1996), quotes a bumper sticker that says, "Change is good. You go first." Noting our natural human ambivalence about change, he observes that some schools and school districts are daring to go first with new ideas and initiatives to revitalize public schools. Many of these schools are reaching out to families, social service agencies, businesses, and the public in general to build broad support for learning. Central to their public relations efforts is the concept of keeping the "public" in public education and involving the community in raising the child. A variety of public relations efforts are starting to bridge the gap that separates schools from communities.

One technique—initiating conversations with the public—is gaining popularity. Schools are using town meetings and community forums as a means of taking the public's pulse on education issues. Some are patterning local forums on forums sponsored by Phi Delta Kappa in cooperation with the Center for Education Policy and the National PTA. These forums are structured around three fundamental questions: (1) What are the purposes of the public schools? (2) How effective are the public schools in achieving those purposes? and (3) What changes are necessary to make the public schools as effective as we want them to be? (Rose and Rapp, 1997)

Education leaders—school boards, superintendents, and principals—should raise these questions in their communities at every opportunity. How they analyze and deal with the answers they receive will determine, collectively across America, if the gap between those who operate public schools and their publics will be bridged.

REFERENCES

American Association of School Administrators. (1993). *How our investment in education pays off.* Arlington, Va.: American Association of School Administrators.

Bagin, D. (2001). Perspectives on school public relations: Challenges yet to be met. *School Public Relations Journal, 22,* 4.

Bagin, D., Gallagher, D., and Kindred, I. (1994). *The school and community relations.* Boston: Allyn and Bacon.

Bryan, V. C. (1998). Technology and education: Leadership issues. In A. C. Jurenas (Ed.), *School administration: Knowledge, constructions and theory.* Dubuque, Iowa: Kendall/Hunt.

Carroll, S. R., and Carroll, D. (1994). *How smart schools get and keep community support.* Bloomington, Ind.: National Educational Service.

Carroll, S. R., and Carroll, D. (2001). Outside-inside marketing. *School administrator web edition.* Retrieved September 9, 2002, from www.aasa.org/publications/sa/2001_08/carroll.htm.

Clark, D. (2000). *Big dog's leadership page: communication.* Retrieved September 9, 2002, from www.nwlink.com/~donclark/leader/

Decker, L. E., and Associates. (1994). *Home-school-community relations: Trainers manual and study guide.* Charlottesville, Va.: Mid-Atlantic Center for Community Education.

Donlevy, J. G., Hilliard, A., and Donley, T. R. (1996). The electronic superintendent. *Journal of Educational Public Relations,* 17, 1.

Houston, P., and Bryant, A. (1997). The role of superintendents and school boards in engaging the public with the public school, *Phi Delta Kappan,* 78, 10.

IBM. (2002). *alphaWorks emerging technologies: Machine translation.* Retrieved March 8, 2002, from www.alphaworks.ibm.com/tech/mt.

Institute for Public Relations. (1996). *A report on the issues facing communications professionals, executive summary.* Retrieved February 3, 2001, from www.instituteforpr.com/projects2.

Kowalski, T. J., and Wiedmer, T. (1995). Most superintendents appear to be PR passive. *Journal of Educational Public Relations,* 16, 1.

Litrenta, L. E. (1999). PR directors can benefit from student researchers. *Journal of Educational Relations,* 20, 2.

Martinson, D. (1995). School public relations: Do it right or don't do it at all. *Journal of Educational Relations,* 16, 3.

Mullen, M. (1999). How to work with media reporters. *Journal of Educational Relations,* 20, 3.

National Education Association. (1996). *Stepping forward.* Retrieved March 5, 2002, from www.nea.org/newunion/stepfwd/.

National School Public Relations Association. (2002). *Getting a public relations program started.* Retrieved September 9, 2002, from www.nspra.org/main_schoolpr.

Norton, M. S. (1998). School climate has a major impact on school improvement. *Journal of Educational Public Relations,* 19, 4.

Ordovensky, P., and Marx, G. (1993). *Working with the news media.* Arlington, Va.: American Association of School Administrators.

Parson, S. R. (1999). *Transforming schools into community learning centers.* Larchmont, N.Y.: Eye on Education, Inc.

Pavlik, J. V. (1996). *Managing the information superhighway: A report on issues facing communication professionals.* Retrieved September 9, 2002, from www.instituteforpr.com. [link Internet and New Technology].

Phi Delta Kappa International. (1999). *Fast facts PDK/Gallup poll: Local schools supported but more outreach needed.* Retrieved March 5, 2002, from www.pdkintl.org/whatis/ff4poll.htm.

Rose, L., and Rapp, D. (1997). The future of the public schools: A public discussion. *Phi Delta Kappan, 78,* 10.

Sensiper, S. (2002). *Generating family-school partnerships through social marketing.* Retrieved March 13, 2002, from www.gse.harvard.edu/%7Ehfrp/projects/fine/resources/research/sensiper.html.

TALK systems. (1999). *EDCAL, 28,* 31. Retrieved March 8, 2002, from www.talksystems.com/slide4_article_a.htm.

The Parent Institute. (1999). Break down the language barrier to parent involvement. *What's Working in Parent Involvement,* January.

Training educational communication-school PR specialists. (1997). *Journal of Educational Public Relations, 18,* 1.

Weinreich, N. K. (1995). *What is social marketing?* Retrieved September 9, 2002, from www.social-marketing.com/whatis.html.

Woodland, B. (2001). Beyond image: Learning-based communications. *School administrator web edition.* Retrieved September 9, 2002, from www.aasa.org/publications/sa/2001_08/woodland.htm.

Yantis, J. (1995). Community relations start with the internal school climate. *Journal of Educational Relations, 16,* 3.

WEBSITES FOR MORE INFORMATION AND LINKS TO OTHER RELEVANT SITES

Institute for Public Relations, www.instituteforpr.com
National School Public Relations Association, www.nspra.org
Public Relations Society of America, www.prsa.org

CHAPTER 7

Dealing with Political Realities

Educators have long been advised to stay out of politics. The advice is strongly rooted in the profession and continues to be espoused. For example, former President Clinton, in his 1997 State of the Union address, strongly admonished Congress and the American public that politics must stop at the schoolhouse door.

Acknowledging the widespread aversion among educators to engage in political activities in the achievement of educational goals, Berg and Hall (1999) stress:

> For those of us who work with present and future educational leaders, it is imperative that a more realistic stance be established. . . . In short [quoting Carter and Cunningham 1997], 'if the administrator does not become one of the political players, he or she will be dominated by others, powerless and at the mercy of the political system.'

Today, no one seriously disputes the proposition that politics plays a significant role in decisions about schools and educational practices. Schools and educators have been cast as saviors or scapegoats: they are expected to remediate society's social and economic ills, but if their attempted reforms fail to produce quick fixes, critics make scapegoats of their visible leadership. Murphy (as cited in Decker and Associates, 1994), dean of the Harvard Graduate School of Education, says the truth of this point is borne out by the fact that the average tenure of big-city school superintendents is less than three years. Keedy and Björk (2001) flatly state that "the superintendency, now more than ever, is a political position."

Many people in the community have a stake in education—even if they see it only as an expenditure of their tax dollars—so it is not surprising that they want a voice in the ongoing debate about schools. Even in communities that have a commitment to equal opportunity for all children, actuating that commitment almost inevitably involves money—public money—for such things as early childhood education, smaller classes, expanded technology, and more comprehensive social services. It is a reality that *any* decision about the expenditure of public money involves politics and the community power structure.

Educators need to understand political power—where it comes from and how it can be used to improve schools—but many educators continue to resist political engagement.

> Overtly political efforts to move an agenda forward, build coalitions of support and, when needed, force concessions which encourage broad-based community involvement are more and more the standard than the exception. Still, political engagement remains, in many administrators' thinking, an intrusion in the business of schooling. Much remains to be done to move these educational leaders away from thinking that the nobility of their mission guarantees public support. . . . Recognition that confidence in the schools comes as much from influential individual and political support as it does from student outcomes is a concept many educators only grudgingly accept, if at all. (Berg and Hall, 1999)

POLITICS

Education is political because school administrators have authority over the allocation of public resources and because the public expects schools to transmit values. Education is both the *object* of political activity by influences outside the school and the *subject* of political activity because its practitioners can shape policies and behaviors within the school system.

As Cortes (1993) explains, politics is about collective action initiated by people, "about relationships enabling people to disagree, argue, interrupt one another, clarify, confront, and negotiate, and through this process of debate and conversation to form a compromise and a consensus that enables them to act." This is the process that enables people to change the nature of schools—or any other institution—recreating and reorganizing the way in which people, networks, and institutions operate.

If the process of debate and conversation leads to consensus, people must be given the opportunity to develop practical wisdom and the kind of judgment that includes understanding and responsibility. Cortes argues, "In politics, it is not enough to be right, that is, it is not enough to have a position that is logically worked out; one also has to be reasonable, that is, one has to be willing to make concessions and exercise judgment in forging a deal." Understood in this sense, decisions made by voting are "not to discover what people want, but to ratify decisions and actions the political community has reached through argumentative deliberations."

In Keedy's and Björk's (2001) opinion, "The political process not only is an institutional centerpiece within a democratic society, it is essential to the viability of local schools." Educators, especially superintendents, encounter three types of politics. *Participatory politics* occurs when group membership is fluid, alliances are ad hoc, and it reflects complex and changing interactions among interest groups and individuals. *Partisan politics* encompasses circumstances in which distinct political groups or parties compete over educational issues. *Patronage politics* occurs in the context in which programs, jobs, or funds are allocated or withheld on the basis of personal affiliations.

Citizen Politics

Public Life Project (1992), sponsored by the Humphrey Institute of Public Affairs at the University of Minnesota, is based on the conviction that the politics of a serious democracy is the give-and-take, messy, everyday work of citizens themselves. Politics is the way citizens deal with public problems—the issues of their common existence—in many settings, not simply through government. It is the way people *become* citizens—accountable players and contributors.

This kind of citizen politics should play a role in each of the following traditional modes of political problem solving (Project Public Life, 1992):

Institutional politics. Examples are Congress, schools, and boards. The strength of institutional politics is that it has broad-scale effects, that mechanisms and processes are in place, and that there is accountability through voting. The barriers are that it lacks active citizen involvement, that experts own the knowledge, and that power is fragmented in a hierarchical system. *Using citizen politics* reclaims the public mission and organizes leadership that represents the hierarchy, working laterally as well as hierarchically.

Community politics. Examples are neighborhood crime watch and groups organized to rehabilitate local parks. The strength is that it draws on diversity to solve problems and demonstrates citizen leadership. The barriers are that it takes time and is limited in scale. *Using citizen politics* expands the role of neighbor to citizen and brings local lessons to larger audiences/arenas.

Helping politics. Examples are soup kitchens, Adopt-a-Grandparent, and Big Brother/Sister. The strength is that it connects individuals, educates participants, and provides immediate assistance. The barrier is that it risks becoming a professional service, cannot solve problems on a larger scale, and does not examine the policy behind the need. *Using citizen politics* explores self-interests and roles, and understands the nature of building diverse public relationships.

Protest politics. Examples are marches, demonstrations, boycotts. The strength is that it is a successful organizing tool, increases a feeling of community and shared concerns, and brings attention to an issue. The barrier is that it is a reaction that rarely sets an agenda, is difficult to sustain, and sets up enemies and innocents. *Using citizen politics* builds public mission, identifies diverse self-interests, understands power as relational, and creates public spaces for problem solving.

These modes of public problem-solving are not isolated from one another. Each is related to the other, either as a result of or response to inadequacies of any one political mode for solving large, complex problems. Project Public Life proponents contend that by making each type of politics more public—more open, diverse, participatory, democratic—the practice of public problem-solving is enhanced.

Community Politics

The Kettering Foundation (2000) explains another kind of politics—community politics. Community politics is based on the premise that changing political practices, particularly the way in which issues are framed, choices are made, and action is taken, will result in greater public engagement. The practice of deliberation is the cornerstone of community politics. It is the Kettering Foundation's contention that

> The promise of community politics is that communities can learn to work better, to increase the capacity of their citizens to join together to face common problems. . . . At the heart of community politics is an integrated set of ideas that, when put into practice, create opportunities for citizens to make choices and act on problems that affect their common well-being. . . . Ultimately, it is about developing ways to allow a deeper, deliberative form of public engagement to take root in the habits, traditions, and culture of their community on an *ongoing* basis.

There are five basic elements of community politics (Kettering 2000).

Element 1. Naming and framing issues for deliberation. The way a problem is named determines who will get involved and the response that may emerge. For a broad array of citizens to become engaged with an issue, it must be named in a way that connects with or reflects what is valuable to them. In order to make sound decisions regarding what should be done about a problem, people must consider a range of approaches to the problem. Most importantly, issues must be presented in a way that reveals the inevitable conflicts among and within each approach. Framing an issue in a way that reveals the conflicts among several approaches makes deliberation possible.

Element 2. Making choices through deliberation. Deliberation is a natural kind of taking and reasoning people use when a difficult

decision has to be made and involves weighing the costs and consequences of various approaches to a problem against what people
consider most valuable. The goal of deliberation is not a clear
agreement or a compromise, but rather a general sense of direction
and purpose bound by limits. Deliberation produces a reading on
how the public thinks about an issue, after people have had the
chance to engage each other. It creates a public knowledge about
whether there is a shared sense of direction or purpose even when
citizens cannot agree fully and are unwilling to compromise. Informed and shared public judgment is the foundation for wise
policymaking.

Element 3. Acting publicly. Deliberation can stimulate citizens and organizations to take action on particular issues by triggering a sense
of possibility. It contributes to public action, not by developing
consensus, but by discovering a sense of purpose or direction. Out
of this sense of direction, people—individually or together with
other citizens or organizations—can start acting in mutually reinforcing ways around an issue, though they may still disagree on
certain aspects of the problem.

Element 4. Connecting citizens and officeholders. Community politics arises out of a vision of politics in which the public takes on a
central role with greater control over, and greater responsibility
for, issues important to them. Its goal is to supplement and reinforce, not replace, the activity of officials. There are no prescribed
models or answers to demonstrate how citizens and officeholders
can interact most constructively. However, whatever the approach,
all are working to find innovative and workable ways for citizens
and officeholders to become partners—coproducers—of sound,
sustainable policy.

Element 5. Judging progress. Judging progress simply refers to the
process of taking stock—a form of evaluation in which people
involved in the common work of community politics ask themselves: "How are we doing?" The judging process is about creating opportunities for citizens themselves to come together to
assess the value of what they have done and what they have
learned from it. It is key to sustaining momentum for community
politics.

COMMUNITY ORGANIZING

In December 2000, the National Coalition for Parent Involvement in Education and the American Youth Policy Forum conducted the final forum in the *Urgent Message* series. The topic was the presentation of the results of a study on community organizing efforts taking place across the United States (National Coalition for Parent Involvement in Education, 2001) The study of community organizing groups working to improve public education in low-performing schools and districts is believed to be the first to document community organizing in education, and vastly expands the concept of family and community involvement. For the study, "organizing" was defined as: "A base that takes collective action and focuses on concrete change in policy and practice, democratic decision making, ongoing recruitment and leadership development, and a lasting organization dedicated to altering power relationships."

Study results showed that the number of organizing groups is growing—groups in which families and communities are breaking away from the terms of engagement defined by the school and are coming up with their own courses of action for building support for key interventions. The results reveal a wide gap between educator-led school reform organizations and community-led organizing groups.

> Issues central to the learning community of educators in school reform differ greatly from those central to the agendas of community organizing groups and their constituencies. For example, issues central to the learning community of educators include professional collaboration and the creation of learning communities. They are concerned with new teacher support, and the role of the district in reform. Whereas, the issues central to the agendas of community organizing groups are distribution of resources, superintendent selection, safety, high stakes testing, tracking, to name of few. . . . The study [also shows] that a combination of collaborative and confrontational tactics has helped to neutralize rigid representatives and decision-making structures inside schools.
>
> Most importantly, what has risen from the efforts of these concerned parents and community members is the creation of the political context to make change happen, wherein groups are establishing new, stronger accountability relationships between schools and parents, youth, and communities.

POWER

Understanding politics requires an understanding of power, because both power and politics are involved in the allocation of resources for the *public good*.

Two kinds of power—unilateral and relational—exist in communities (Cortes, 1993). Unilateral power treats the opposition as an object to be instructed and directed; it tends to be coercive and domineering. Relational power involves a personal relationship, subject to subject. This kind of power involves, not just the capacity to act, but the capacity to allow oneself to be acted upon. A kind of empathy permits a meaningful understanding of other people's subjects and allows them to understand one's own.

Understanding politics also requires an understanding of the relationship between leadership and power. The Center for Leadership Studies (1999) points out:

> Only an empowered leader can successfully direct followers. Power is the resource that enables a leader to influence followers. Given this integral relationship between leadership and power, leaders must not only assess their leadership behavior in order to understand how they actually influence other people; they also must examine their possession and use of power. . . . Inappropriate use of power, or inappropriate use of certain power bases will ultimately undermine a leader's credibility.

Hersey and Natemeyer (1979) identified seven bases of power:

1. *Legitimate power* is based on the position of the leader. The higher the position, the higher the legitimate power tends to be. A leader high in legitimate power influences others because they believe that he or she has the right, by virtue of position, to expect suggestions to be followed.
2. *Information power* is based on the leader's access to information that is perceived as valuable to others. This power base influences others because they need the information or want to be in on things.
3. *Expert power* is based on the leader's possession of expertise, skill, and knowledge that gains the respect of others. A leader high

in expert power is seen as possessing the expertise to facilitate the work of others, and respect for this expertise leads to compliance.

4. *Reward power* is based on the leader's ability to provide rewards for other people. They believe that their compliance will lead to gaining positive incentives, such as increased pay, promotion, or recognition.

5. *Referent power* is based on the leader's personal traits. A leader is generally liked and admired by others because of personality. A liking for, admiration of, and identification with the leader influences others.

6. *Connection power* is based on the leader's connections with influential or important persons inside or outside the organization. A leader high in connection power induces compliance from others because they aim at gaining the favor or avoiding the disfavor of the powerful connection.

7. *Coercive power* is based on fear. It induces compliance because failure to comply is seen as leading to punishment, such as undesirable assignments, reprimands, or even dismissal.

The power structure of a community refers to the formal and informal networks that make things happen. Power is structured differently in different communities, and power structures change over time. Relational power comes into play when two or more people, groups, organizations, or agencies come together, argue their concerns, develop a plan, and take some sort of action. In citizen politics, the challenge is for people to get enough power to do the things they think are important. Gaining enough power usually involves building coalitions with other people and learning the rules of politics and power. One lesson is clear: effective political leaders learn from, and are influenced by, a community of collaborators and supporters. Effective leadership is both informed and collegial, and power and politics are intertwined.

POLICYMAKING

In a generic sense, a policy is a broad guideline describing a course of action approved by a governing entity in a given situation. Policymaking is the process by which a course of action is determined, worded, executed, and interpreted. It functions as a sorting-out process for the aspirations, needs, and concerns of the individuals and groups involved. Policy is an outcome of this process.

Policymaking is a special type of decision making that takes place in a political context. The focus is on the policymakers and the processes they establish to control access to the development of policies. Education policymakers are influenced by the representational and distributive nature of educational policy and the ongoing nature of the decision-making process. The participants and their orientations are basic factors in the policymaking process. As interests and values change, policy priorities also change.

Policymaking serves both problem-solving and power-balancing goals (Pisapia, in press). In problem solving, policies are adopted to help the organization pursue its goals more efficiently through technical processes. The resulting policies describe the extent to which the governing body intends to solve the problem, how it intends to solve it, the activities required to solve it, and the resources to be allocated. In power balancing, policymakers engage in a set of interactions they hope will shape the authoritative allocation of values. The policies developed represent an equilibrium: the balance of power among the various governing bodies, individuals, and groups charged with governing education or with an interest in the decisions. In its power-balancing aspects, policymaking is a political process designed to allocate money, jobs, prestige or status, and primary responsibility.

Policies tend to follow from political interaction and a complex set of forces that, together, produce effects. To understand who or what makes policy, one must understand the characteristics of the participants, what roles they play, what authority they hold, and how they deal with and control each other. Lindblom (1993) makes an important distinction between policymaking and problem solving. Policies tend to follow from political interaction rather than from rational analysis, while conventionally conceived problem solving is an intellectual process.

In the United States, policies regarding the allocation and use of resources result primarily from political interaction that blends the values and definitions of the *public good* of three political subcultures.

These subcultures may exist side by side or even overlap; differences in their cultural values significantly affect local and state educational systems. These subcultures are (Thompson, 1976):

Individualistic. In this culture, government is viewed simply as a utilitarian institution created to handle those functions that cannot be managed by individuals. Government need not have any direct concern with the question of the *good society* or the *general welfare.* The democratic order is viewed as a marketplace. Emphasis is placed on private concerns, and high value is placed on limiting community intervention in private activities. Government exists only to *give the public what it wants,* and public officials are normally unwilling to initiate, on their own, new programs or open new areas of governmental activity.

Moralistic. This culture emphasizes that politics is part of the people's search for the good society, and that the good life can be achieved only through the good society. Individualism in this view is tempered by a general commitment to use communal power to intervene in public activities when it is necessary to do so for the public good. Participation in community affairs is a civic duty for every citizen, and public officials have a moral obligation to promote the general welfare, even at the expense of individual loyalties and political friendships.

Traditionalistic. This culture views the maintenance of the existing social order as the main role of government. It accepts government as a positive factor in the affairs of the community—but only to the extent that government maintains and encourages the traditional values and patterns of life. Social and family ties are paramount, and real political power is confined to a relatively small and self-perpetuating group drawn from an established elite of *good old families.*

In addition to its political subcultures, every community has interest groups. The most common political tactics of interest groups are public relations strategies trying to create a favorable climate, electioneering trying to elect individuals who are sympathetic, and lobbying trying to influence decisions.

Four kinds of interest groups account for most of the influence directed at state and local governments:

1. Economically motivated groups: Government policies will either cost or save members money. Business and labor are the most obvious examples.
2. Professionally motivated groups: Government policies may affect their members' professional activities. Medical and teacher associations are examples.
3. Public agency groups: These groups provide opportunities for public officials to exchange ideas, lobby collectively, and get up-to-date information on developments and concepts that affect their own agencies. Examples are the U.S. Conference of Mayors and the National Association of Counties.
4. Ideological groups: Most of these groups claim to represent a public interest. Many are not permanent but arise in response to a specific issue. Environmental and religious groups are examples.

There are other groups, often not readily identifiable, that affect the political interaction of a community. Some may not be well informed about what is happening in local schools, may not understand the theory and practices behind educational jargon, or may feel excluded from serious discussion about school matters. Individuals in these groups are often targeted by opponents of various school initiatives and may receive biased information in order to enlist their support in opposition.

FRAMEWORK OF A HOME, SCHOOL, AND COMMUNITY PARTNERSHIP POLICY

Decision making in the development of a home, school, and community partnership policy must be done within the political context of a community. The process of developing a comprehensive policy should include input from teachers, administrators, families, students, and key community-based businesses, organizations, and groups.

The National Coalition for Parent Involvement in Education (2001) advocates that state and district policies should recognize:

- The critical role of families in their children's academic achievement and social well-being.
- The responsibility of every school to create a welcoming environment, conducive to learning and supportive of comprehensive family involvement programs that have been developed jointly with families.
- The need to accommodate the diverse needs of families by developing, jointly with families, multiple, innovative, and flexible ways for families to be involved.
- The rights and responsibilities of parents and guardians, particularly their right to have access to the school, their children's records, and the children's classroom.
- The value of working with community agencies to provide service to children and families.
- The need for families to remain involved from preschool through high school.

The coalition emphasizes that school-level policies should also add:

- Outreach to ensure participation of all families, including those who might lack literacy skills or for whom English is not their primary language.
- Recognition of diverse family structures, circumstances, and responsibilities, including differences that might impede family participation. (Policies should include participation by all persons interested in a child's educational progress, not just the biological parents.)
- Opportunities for families to participate in the instructional process at school and at home.
- Opportunities for families to share in making decisions, about school policy and procedures and about how family involvement programs are to be designed, implemented, assessed, and strengthened.
- Professional development for all school staff to enhance their effectiveness with diverse families.
- Regular exchange of information with families about the standards their children are expected to meet at each grade level, the objectives of educational programs, the assessment procedures, and their children's participation and progress.

- Linkages with social service and health agencies, businesses, faith-based institutions, and community organizations and groups to support key family and community issues.

Inclusion of these considerations results in a policy that contains a broad guideline describing a course of action. How the course of action is determined, worded, approved, executed, and interpreted is the result of a sorting-out process of the diverse aspirations, needs, and concerns of individuals and groups in a particular community. The result of this process should be a policy uniquely tailored to that community.

Discovering the Community Power Structure

An important first step for anyone who wants to make changes in schools or educational programs is identifying the leaders in the community's power structure. It is only then that appropriate communication linkages can be built, involvement strategies designed, and alternative plans developed. There are four basic ways to identify the power actors in a community (Hiemstra, 1997):

1. Positional method: Identifying the individuals who occupy key authoritative positions, usually formal roles, in the community's major organizations, groups, and strata. An important basic assumption is that power and decision-making ability reside in those who hold important positions in a community's formal organizations.
2. Reputational method: Identifying knowledgeable citizens who can provide the names of top community actors according to their reputations for social power. The basic premise is that a reputation for having the potential to affect community decisions is an accurate index of influence, and that such reputations are slow to change.
3. Decision-making method: Tracing the history of decision-making in a particular issue area. Influential people are those who can be identified as the main participants in any such activity. A basic assumption is that the social power to influence decisions within a community can be measured by a person's actual participation in various problem-solving or decision-making activities.

4. Social participation method: Making lists of the formal leaders of a variety of voluntary associations. The assumption is that social participation, active membership, and holding a leadership role are important prerequisites to the accumulation and use of community influence.

Hiemstra explains why it may be necessary to use more than one method to arrive at an accurate picture of a community's leadership:

In reality, each method may identify different power actors and leaders within a community. At times, the overlap of individuals determined by the various methods will be fairly small. The positional method yields institutional leaders, office holders, and highly visible leaders; the reputational technique identifies reputed leaders, generalized leaders, and frequently, non-visible leaders; the decision-making method can delineate both generalized and specialized activists; and the social participation method often identifies primarily "doers," those in the public eye, and voluntary association leaders. Thus it may be necessary for the educational change agent to employ more than one technique to obtain a comprehensive understanding of the community's leadership. . . . [Moreover,] actors will change over time. Consequently, any one method may need to be repeated periodically so that such changes can be determined.

Needed Political Skills

Bolman and Deal (1991) propose conceptualizing school organizations through a political frame of reference—a setting in which different interest groups compete for power and scarce resources. In their view, schools are "alive and screaming political arenas that house a complex variety of individual and group interests." The potential for conflict is everywhere because of the differences in needs, perspectives, and lifestyles among the various individuals and groups. Bolman and Deal see bargaining, negotiation, coercion, and compromise as part of everyday organizational life. They suggest that the following political skills are essential for school leaders:

- Agenda setting: The ability to establish both a purpose for the organization and a coherent strategy for achieving that purpose.

- Networking and coalition building: The ability to build personal relationships with members of the school community who can help neutralize potential opposition to the agenda and become allies in striving to achieve it.
- Negotiating and bargaining: The ability to manage the constant clash of different interests in the organization.

However, these skills alone will not make a successful school politician, according to Bolman and Deal. Attitudes must change, and school leaders must

Understand that politics are not something external to the school organization, or an unpleasant peripheral duty. Rather, politics must be understood as part of the very life blood of the organization and political skills seen as the tools through which the administrator achieves his or her major goal, the education of children.

SOURCES OF CONFLICT

Keedy and Björk (2001) emphasize that although school administrators might view politics as an enduring conflictual characteristic of public schooling, conflict itself is not bad. "Politics is a process through which individuals and groups openly express needs and interests and reconcile differences." They point out that educators face conflicts "over values and interests, heightened levels of political activism within communities, changing power structures, and challenges to traditional purposes and goals of public education."

Ascher, Fruchter, and Berne (2002) outline some of the current sources of disaffection and conflict facing educators.

- Business has been worried about the United States' loss of international competitiveness since the early 1980s and has been putting pressure on public education to raise its standards.
- Liberals and families of color have become discouraged by the failure of public education to realize the promise of the Supreme Court's desegregation decision in *Brown v. Board of Education,* and there is growing anger among minority and lower socioeconomic

groups at the failure to improve opportunities and outcomes for their children.

- At the same time, the protracted efforts expended on behalf of equal educational opportunity, particularly student busing, have created a backlash among some white families.
- Another source of discontent are the persistent problems resulting from the United States' property-based method of school financing. Awareness of the growing gap between rich and poor families has exacerbated the disparity of resources available for public schools.
- In many major U.S. cities, tax revenues have stagnated in the 1990s at the same time as increasingly poor urban populations have generated greater pressure for public services. In education, the increased competition for tax dollars has resulted in larger class sizes, teacher salaries lagging behind other professions, and school facilities less equipped to prepare students for success in a high-tech society.
- Exacerbating the problems resulting from the competition for tax dollars is the fact that public schools, particularly in troubled cities, are asked to respond to an increasing range of student needs generated by worsening economic conditions.
- Public education is also bearing the brunt of an anti-union and anti-government sentiment that has mushroomed in the United States in the 1980s and 1990s.
- The growing attack on public education has also been attributed to a long-term decline in civic consciousness and public engagement, and an increasing privatization of all areas of life.
- The concerted efforts of conservative and religious groups has influenced all of these trends, particularly the growth of anti-union and anti-government sentiment. These groups have blamed public schools for the decline in Christian and other traditional values of the United States, and branded them as part of "big government" and crusaded to replace public education with free-market solutions.

Keedy and Björk point out that "these prior complexities mask an even harsher reality: the weakening of 'common ground' (i.e., shared values and beliefs that undergird responsibility and the meaning of

citizenship)." They reiterate that the positions of education professionals, especially administrators, are

> highly politicized when viewed within the context of competing forces
> as to how public education will be defined. . . . The very existence of
> community interest groups requires [educators] to mediate and negotiate
> among competing groups to gain a consensus about how public schools
> might serve their communities.

Finding Common Ground

Educators, faced with concerns, criticism, and challenges from their
communities, often respond with anger and defensiveness. Vondra
(1996) points out, "[I]n some cases the name calling and behaviors
have become strident enough to erode trust among people inside and
outside of education on various sides of the issues. When voices become hostile, the school atmosphere can feel more like a war than a discussion on how to ensure a good education for students." Reaching
consensus on how education can best serve students is not only necessary to resolve differences, but also is in the best interests of everyone
in the community.

The process of seeking common ground relies on many of the same
techniques used to build communities and allocate social capital. In this
case, a school's "social capital" is the attention and resources it gets
from responsible adults in the community. Cortes (1993) notes that
thinking about relationships as *capital* helps put decisions about the allocation of resources into a helpful perspective.

> To create capital, individuals must invest labor, energy, and effort in the
> here-and-now to create something for later use. . . . Investment requires
> the ability and the discipline to defer gratification, to invest energy not
> only in the needs or pleasures of the present, but also in the potential de-
> mands of the future. Capital also requires maintenance and renewal. . . .
> Knowledge and skills must be updated and refined. Similarly, the part-
> ners in a venture must renew the means of trusting one another.

Almost all educational advocates acknowledge the difficulty in finding common ground. Although most Americans want decisive action to

improve schools, they disagree about both the problems and the solutions. Public support is up for grabs, and advocates of none of the contending perspectives can confidently count the public on their side.

Strategies for Achieving Change

Achieving educational change in policies and practices almost certainly requires efforts by a variety of people, probably in more than one organization. For this reason, no single approach is likely to accomplish all the goals and objectives. Hiemstra (1997) describes four basic strategies for achieving change and notes that unless the desired change is simple—and already has wide acceptance—a combination of strategies will be needed.

Strategy 1. Learn who the primary community leaders are. Understand how they control or affect the decision-making process, and establish an acquaintanceship or friendship with them. Those who propose or plan change need to involve or consult such influential persons at various stages of the planning process. If such involvement is not facilitated, the planner risks program blockage or failure.

Strategy 2. Identify with and use existing groups and organizations that will support the desired change. This approach involves the coordination of two or more groups. A professional planner or other expert is frequently needed to promote this cooperation.

Strategy 3. Affiliate with an organization whose function can include directing or guiding the change. Because such organizations often act as a change-agent, their employees are knowledgeable about the means used to achieve various changes, and have skills in human relations, problem diagnosis, and the use of resources to achieve specific goals.

Strategy 4. Form committees or groups around particular content areas or particular needs. This involves getting agencies or organizations with certain physical and organizational resources to cooperate with groups that have special skills or access to particular clients. This strategy is especially useful in addressing unique minority-group needs.

Many schools and school systems already have in place one vehicle for facilitating change: the school/community advisory council. Over the years, these councils have often functioned as advisory bodies in the development of educational policy.

Communication Skills and Processes

Finding common ground depends on several factors, but effective communication skills and processes are key. Ledell (1995) explains that finding common ground begins when everyone who has concerns and ideas about education—superintendents, administrators, teachers, community members, students, civic and community leaders—understands and practices certain basic strategies. Communication skills and methods are implicit in each.

- Listen in a variety of ways and in many places to a wide cross section of people, including those who disagree.
- Anticipate issues and separate them from personalities.
- Set up formal processes to monitor, measure, and disseminate the results of decisions made by boards of education, school committees, community advocacy groups, and similar groups.
- Create relationships built on trust and confidence and on processes designed to achieve efficiency, openness, and accountability.
- Acknowledge and support the proposition that all decisions and actions must be able to withstand public scrutiny, discussion, and debate.

The importance of effective communication was also emphasized by the report of the Millennium Communications Group (1999), commissioned by the Rockefeller Foundation. The report was part of the foundation's effort to revitalize citizenship at the local level by bringing collaborative problem-solving and conflict-resolution techniques to diverse groups of community stakeholders. The report, "Communications as Engagement," states that "actors need messages that will allow them to speak most powerfully to the aspirations and commitment of those who are already engaged . . . to enlarge the pool of those who are engaged, and to build a sense of momentum and forward progress among the population as a whole." The report recommends that the messages incorporate several themes:

- Drawing people into a process of involvement, engagement, and learning.
- Communicating diversity as an advantage, not a threat.
- Expanding understanding of the complex and interrelated nature of the problems faced.
- Demonstrating that the proposed initiative is a quality-of-life movement for everyone, not just an add-on.
- Repositioning the word "public" as that which belongs to all of the people—to *us,* not to an agency or to *them.*
- Creating a sense of accomplishment, momentum, and "can do" from the success stories that already exist.
- Creating and projecting a sense of wholeness that incorporates diversity.

Dealing with Criticism

One of the political realities that educators must accept is that they will always have critics in all shapes and sizes, with a variety of attitudes and motives. There are hostile critics, uninformed critics, professional critics, enlightened critics, and pressure groups.

Marx (1993) suggests these basic steps in dealing with a critic:

- Listen closely to what the critic has to say. Your major goal should be *mutual understanding*, not necessarily converting the critic to your point of view.
- Ask questions. Try to gain insight into the motivation behind the criticism. Get to know your critic.
- Keep in mind that some people just feel a need to complain but don't want to discuss the issue in depth.
- Avoid defensiveness, which often implies some kind of guilt. Maintain the offensive without being offensive. Always be open and honest.
- Try to reach some form of understanding. It is not necessary to be passive. Explain the school's role. Indicate that you want to reach an

understanding and maintain contact. Invite the person back for a second visit if necessary and make arrangements for a follow-up call.

Marx emphasizes that critics should be dealt with individually, if possible, not at public meetings. The following techniques should be used in responding to criticism:

- Be aware of the cultural and intellectual background of your critic. Do not over- or underestimate his or her intellectual background.
- Evaluate the emotional climate. Some hostile critics want to release tension more than they want to obtain an answer.
- Find out something about the person's interests and needs. Relate your comments to ideas or organizations the person deals with or understands.
- Give simple answers to the questions posed. Avoid long answers that can both destroy interest and create more hostility. Do not dwell on the history or background of problems unless asked to do so. Avoid side issues and exceptions.
- Speak in concrete terms, not theoretically, and avoid professional jargon. Include illustrations and examples.

When Things Get out of Hand

Sometimes, no matter how hard school personnel try, an atmosphere of skepticism degenerates into alienation and organized opposition. If this happens, Ledell and Arnsparger (1993) recommend using the following guidelines to get through the crisis and back to the basic communication strategy:

- Make sure you are clear about the issues. Do not respond to rumor or personal opinion. Gather available facts and materials circulated by critics.
- Do not overreact. Take time to review the available information. You may find that you can end the controversy by having a conversation with the individuals involved.
- Select in advance those who will be the spokespersons if things get out of hand. These individuals should handle all inquiries from the

media, families, and others in the community. The school and district should respond with one voice.

- Brief the entire staff. No one who works in the school or district should have to guess at what is going on. Tell them what has occurred, what steps are being taken, who the spokespersons are, and how they can help. Ask them to refer inquiries about the situation to one of the designated spokespersons.
- Prepare a written statement that can be given to people who ask for the school's response. It should answer most people's immediate questions.
- Provide an open forum at which the issues can be discussed and all points of view expressed.
- Invite the media and others into the school. Provide written information and a road map so they know what they are seeing.
- Do not be defensive. Respond freely and offer information to those requesting it. Be honest.
- Do not stonewall. Speak positively and enthusiastically about what the school and district are doing.
- Do not allow yourself to be insulted. You do not have a responsibility to respond to outrageous accusations or personal insults. When someone is in an irrational, aggressive frame of mind, keep your emotions under control. Do not accuse the critic of being irrational or out of control; tactfully suggest scheduling another time to talk.
- If personal safety becomes an issue, call the police immediately. Do not attempt to handle potential violence on your own.

POLITICS AND ACADEMIC SUCCESS

Politics are a fact of life in public schools because many people in the community have a stake in public education. Educators must understand and use politics and the community power structure to help them achieve their mission of academic success for all children. They must both master basic political skills and adopt an attitude that values politics as an honorable means of achieving educational goals. They have an obligation to engage and inform the public and protect schools from manipulation by special-interest groups who seek to misinform the public in order to advance their own agenda.

Educators must accept the fact that issues related to home, school, and community relations have entered into the arena of political policy and action. As a result, simplified answers are sometimes offered to complex questions of responsibility, choice, control, and blame. Even some of those who advocate sharing power with families and communities may, at times, be motivated by their own educational and social objectives (Beresford, 1992).

Whether overt opposition exists or not, educators must develop ways to communicate, through a democratic process, with a wide variety of people in the community. Without public understanding, support, and participation, initiatives to achieve the academic success of all children will be difficult, if not impossible, to sustain. The reality is that the greatest benefit of the process may be that members of the community will learn to work together to improve learning for all children.

REFERENCES

Ascher, C., Fruchter, N., and Berne, R. (2002). *Hard lessons: Public schools and privatization.* New York: The Century Foundation. Retrieved September 9, 2002, from www.tcf.org/Publications/Education/Hard_Lessons/Chapter1. html.

Beresford, E. (1992). The politics of parental involvement. In G. Allen and I. Martin (Eds.), *Education and community: The politics of practice.* London: Cassell.

Berg, J. H., and Hall, G. E. (1999). The intersection of political leadership and educational excellence: A neglected leadership domain. *AASA Professor*, 22, 4.

Bolman, L. G., and Deal, T. E. (1991). *Reframing organizations: Artistry, choice and leadership.* San Francisco: Jossey-Bass.

Center for Leadership Studies. (1999). *Power perception profile.* Retrieved March 18, 2002, from www.situational.com/leadership/accessories.

Cortes, E., Jr. (1993). Reweaving the fabric: The iron rule and the IAF strategy for power and politics,. In H. G. Cisneros (Ed.), *Interwoven destinies: Cities and the nation.* New York: W. W. Norton and Company. Retrieved March 18, 2002, from www.cpn.org/sections/topics/community/index.

Decker, L. E., and Associates. (1994). *Home-school-community relations manual.* Charlottesville, Va.: Mid-Atlantic Center for Community Education.

Hiemstra. R. (1997). *The educative community: Linking the community, education, and family.* Baldwin, N.Y.: HiTree Press. Retrieved March 5, 2002, from www-distance.syr.edu.

Hersey, P., and Natemeyer, W. E. (1979). *Power perception profile.* Escondido, Calif.: Center for Leadership Studies.

Keedy, J. L., and Björk, L. G. (2001). The superintendent, local boards, and the political arena. *The AASA Professor,* 24, 4.

Kettering Foundation. (2000). *The basics of community politics.* Dayton, Ohio: Kettering Foundation.

Ledell, M. (1995). *How to avoid crossfire and seek common ground.* Arlington, Va.: American Association of School Administrators.

Ledell, M., and Arnsparger, A. (1993). *How to deal with community criticism of school change.* Alexandria, Va.: Association for Supervision and Curriculum Development and Denver, Colo.: Education Commission of the States.

Lindblom, C. D. (1993). *The policy-making process.* Englewood Cliffs, N.J.: Prentice-Hall.

Marx, G., 1993. Lecture and handout, Falls Church, Va. (July).

Millennium Communications Group. (1999). Communications as engagement. Report to the Rockefeller Foundation. Retrieved February 3, 2001, from //cdinet.com/Millennium.

Murphy, J. (1994). Cited in Community power structure and political realities. In L. E. Decker, and Associates, *Home-school-community relations: Trainers manual and study guide.* Charlottesville, Va.: Mid-Atlantic Center for Community Education.

National Coalition for Parent Involvement in Education. (n.d.). *Developing family and school partnerships: Guidelines for schools and school districts.* Fairfax, Va.: National Coalition for Parent Involvement in Education.

National Coalition for Parent Involvement in Education. (2001). A report from the urgent message series: Study results from school reform organizing. *NCPIE Update* (December).

Pisapia, J. (In press). The governance system: The transformation of authority into educational policy. In *Public School Administration: Foundations and Futures.* Columbus, Ohio: Prentice-Hall.

Project Public Life. (1992). *The book: the political educator's guide to citizen politics.* Minneapolis, Minn.: University of Minnesota.

Report from the urgent message series: Study results from the field of school reform organizing. (2001) *NCPIE Update* (December).

Thompson, J. T. (1976). *Policymaking in American public education.* Englewood Cliffs, N.J.: Prentice Hall.

Vondra, J. (1996). Resolving conflicts over values. *Educational Leadership,* 53, 7.

CHAPTER 8

School Safety and Crisis Management

Schools function in a complicated, interconnected world. Events on school campuses in 1998 and 1999—urban and rural, demographically and geographically diverse—turned a spotlight on safety and security issues in our schools. They dramatically informed the nation that guns are brought to school, and some students will use them to kill. One after the other, school communities from Oregon to Virginia, Arkansas to Pennsylvania, and Mississippi to Kentucky were forced to face the fact that violence can happen to them. Repercussions of the shootings at Columbine High School in Littleton, Colorado, continue and are reflected in school shootings that have occurred around the country since then.

The definitions of "school violence" range from limited—for example, related to guns in school—to very broad, including all youthful misconduct. In a report, *In the Spotlight: School Safety*, the National Criminal Justice Reference Service (2002) uses the definition from the Center for the Prevention of School Violence: "Any behavior that violates a school's educational mission or climate of respect or jeopardizes the intent of the school to be free of aggression against persons or property, drugs, weapons, disruptions, and disorder."

Most schools are safe. However, the complacency once based on that fact is gone. Awareness that every school has the potential for violence has made educators aware of the need to be proactive in prevention and creative in developing strategies for responding to trouble.

ISSUES MANAGEMENT

The term "issues management" is misleading. The issue may be a trend or a condition, either in the school or in the broader society, that does, will, or may affect the school's mission of educating all children. What the educator hopes to manage is not the issue itself—which may well be beyond any individual's ability to control—but the school's response to it. One of the keys to success is preparedness: knowing which issues are already out there, which are lurking around the next corner, and having a general plan for responding to them.

Issues may be categorized as critical, ongoing, or emerging. Critical issues command attention now. A school crisis falls into this category if it requires an immediate response to prevent harm, to ward off additional damage, or to provide emotional support. Ongoing issues are those that have to be dealt with regularly. Emerging issues are just beginning to appear and may not even be recognized as issues because they are in an early stage.

Because more than a dozen deadly attacks by students with guns have occurred in public schools in the past several years, many people believe school safety is an ongoing issue that must be dealt with regularly. As Stephens (2001), executive director of the National School Safety Center, points out, "there are two types of school administrators: those who have faced a crisis and those who are about to." However, as the recent report, *Trends & Issues: School Safety* (Lumsden, 2002), reflects, "in reality . . . current data on youth crime and violence in this country provide reasons for both optimism and concern. . . . School safety must be approached from both an immediate and a long-term perspective and incorporate prevention as well as intervention strategies."

SCHOOL SAFETY

School safety is critically important to the total community. The public spotlight on school violence has moved the safety issue to crisis status in many communities. The U.S. Departments of Education and Justice (1998) attempted to present the first comprehensive picture of the nature and scope of crime and violence on school property nationwide in a joint report, *Annual Report on School Safety*. Summarizing the findings, former U.S. Secretary of Education Riley said, "This comprehensive report proves that the vast majority of America's schools are still among the safest places for young people to be." Specifically, the report found:

Schools are basically safe places. Forty-three percent of schools reported no incidents of crime; 90 percent reported no incidents of serious violent crime (defined as physical attack or fight with a weapon, rape, robbery, murder, or suicide); 47 percent reported at least one crime that was less serious or nonviolent; and 10 percent reported one or more incidents of serious violent crime.

Despite recent well-publicized occurrences, schools should not be singled out as especially dangerous places in a community. Most school crime is theft, not serious, violent crime. In 1996, theft accounted for 62 percent of all crime against students at school. About 26 of every 1,000 students aged 12 to 18 were victims of serious violent crimes away from school in 1996 in contrast to about 10 of every 1,000 students at school or going to and from school.

Teachers' concerns about their own safety are not without foundation. In the 1992–1993 school year, public and private school teachers reported, on average, about 30 violent crimes and 46 thefts for every 1,000 teachers.

Students in school today are not significantly more likely to be victimized than in previous years. The overall school crime rate declined between 1993 and 1996 from 164 to 128 school-related crimes for every 1,000 students. Crime victimization outside of school declined from about 140 to 117 crimes for every 1,000 students during the same time period.

Fewer students are bringing weapons to school, and there are consequences for those who do. Between 1993 and 1997, there was an overall decline from 12 percent to 9 percent among students in grades 9 through 12 who reported carrying a weapon to school in the previous month. In 1996 and 1997, states and territories expelled 6,093 students for bringing firearms to schools.

Some conditions, including the presence of gangs in schools, make students and teachers more vulnerable to school crime. Between 1989 and 1995, the percentage of students who reported the presence of street gangs in school increased from 15 percent to 28 percent, with increases reported in urban, suburban, and rural schools.

A majority of schools nationwide are implementing security measures on campuses. Measures range from zero tolerance policies for firearms, alcohol, and drugs, to controlled access to school buildings and grounds, to requiring visitors to sign in before entering school facilities. In the 1996–1997 school year, 96 percent of public schools reported having some type of security measure in place.

Despite the fact that most schools are safe, the issue of school safety must be taken seriously. "No school is immune," the report emphasizes (U.S. Departments of Education and Justice, 1999). "Creating a safe school requires having in place many preventive measures for children's mental and emotional problems as well as a comprehensive approach to early identification of all warning signs that might lead to violence toward self or others."

In its safe schools guide, the Center for Effective Collaboration and Practice (1998) presents convincing documentation that prevention and early intervention efforts can reduce violence and other troubling behaviors. "In fact, research suggests that some of the most promising prevention and intervention strategies involve the entire educational community—administrators, teachers, families, students, support staff, and community members—working together to form positive relationships with all children."

The guide outlines characteristics of school communities in which effective prevention, intervention, and response strategies operate best. These school communities

- Focus on academic achievement. They convey the attitude that all children can achieve academically and behave appropriately, while at the same time appreciating individual differences.
- Involve families in meaningful ways. They make parents feel welcome in school, address barriers to their participation, keep families positively engaged in their children's education, and support families in getting the help they need to address behaviors that cause concern.

- Develop links to the community. They develop and nurture close ties to families, support services, community police, faith-based communities, and the community at large, and benefit from the many resources these groups are willing to share.
- Emphasize positive relationships among students and staff. Research shows that a positive relationship with an adult who is available to provide support when it is needed is one of the most critical factors in preventing student violence. Effective schools make sure that opportunities exist for adults to spend high-quality, personal time with children. They also foster positive student interpersonal relationships, encouraging students to help each other and feel comfortable about getting help for each other when needed.
- Discuss safety issues openly. Children come to school with many different perceptions and misperceptions—about death, violence, and the use of weapons. Effective schools teach children appropriate strategies for dealing with their feelings and resolving conflicts, and teach them that the choices they make will have consequences for which they will be held accountable.
- Treat students with respect. A major source of conflict in many schools is the perceived or real problem of bias and unfair treatment by both staff and peers of students because of their ethnicity, gender, race, social class, religion, disability, nationality, sexual orientation, physical appearance, or some other factor. Effective schools communicate to students and the greater community that all children are valued and respected. There is a deliberate and systematic effort to establish a climate that demonstrates equal respect and a sense of community.
- Create ways for students to share their concerns. Peers are most likely to know about potential school violence in advance. Effective schools support and foster positive relationships between students and adults so students feel safe in reporting troubling behavior and potentially dangerous situations.
- Help children feel safe expressing their feelings. Effective schools create ways for students to feel safe when expressing their needs, fears, and anxieties to school staff.
- Have in place an appropriate system for referring children who are suspected of being abused or neglected. The system must

reflect federal and state guidelines. Offer extended-day programs for children. School-based before- and after-school programs that are well supervised and provide children a range of support services and activity options (counseling, mentoring, tutoring, community service, homework help) can be effective in reducing violence.

- Promote good citizenship and character. Effective schools reinforce such shared values as honesty, kindness, responsibility, and respect for others, while acknowledging that parents are the primary moral educators.
- Identify problems and assess progress toward solutions. Effective schools openly and objectively examine situations and circumstances that are potentially dangerous or intimidating for students and staff.
- Support students in making the transition from school to adult life and the workplace. Young people need assistance in planning for the future and in developing skills that will lead to success. In cooperative relationships with the community, effective schools provide students with community-service opportunities, work-study programs, and apprenticeships that help students connect with caring adults in the community.

Planning for Safety

The Center for the Prevention of School Violence (1999) emphasizes that school administrators must be acutely aware that the potential for violence exists *every day* and that awareness, grounded in information, is of the most value. The center recommends four things administrators can do to create information-based awareness:

1. Conduct site assessments. The physical environment should be reviewed annually, with daily attention, to determine if there are any areas in which the safety of students and staff might be in jeopardy. Law enforcement officials, particularly school resource officers, can help train school staff to identify potential trouble spots and develop strategies for reducing the likelihood of an incident.

2. Keep statistics and use them in decision making. Tracking disruptive and criminal incidents can help administrators make decisions about which prevention strategies and resources offer the most hope for solving particular problems.
3. Survey the entire school community. With information generated from surveys of students, staff, and families, administrators can pinpoint areas of concern and employ strategies to address them.
4. Know and involve students. Students must be involved in maintaining the safety and security of their own schools. They can be an invaluable resource. Staff needs to know students' typical patterns of behavior so that deviations can be recognized and addressed.

With the information generated in these four steps, administrators can develop safe-school plans that are directed at a school's specific needs. Strategies should address the "Three P's" the Center for the Prevention of School Violence identifies as being associated with the safety and security of schools. Riley (2000) explains the Three P's: place, people, and purpose. "Place" refers to the physical environment of the school. "People" refers to the relationships between and among people who are a part of the school community, including the potential for conflict. "Purpose" refers to a steady focus on the educational purpose of the school, so that the emphasis on safety and security does not have the effect of making a school take on the characteristics of a prison.

These Three P's relate to the conditions of being safe, orderly, and caring, as well as to the reason schools exist—education. The Center for the Prevention of School Violence (Riley, 2000) describes a "safe school" as "one whose physical features, layout, and policies and procedures are designed to minimize the impact of disruptions and intrusions that might prevent the school from fulfilling its educational mission." An "orderly school" is "one characterized by a climate of mutual respect and responsibility." A "caring school" is "one which is uniting and supportive of staff and students." Table 8.1 presents an analytical process to determine if a school is safe, orderly, and caring.

Table 8.1. How to Determine If Your School Is . . .

A Safe School	An Orderly School	A Caring School
A safe school is one whose physical features, layout, policies, and procedures are designed to minimize the impact of disruptions and intrusions that might prevent the school from fulfilling its educational mission. It is characterized by a climate that is free of fear. The perceptions, feelings, and behaviors of members of the school community reveal that the school is a place where people are able to go about their business without concern for their safety.	An orderly school is one characterized by a climate of mutual respect and responsibility. Students relate to each other and to teachers and school staff in acceptable ways. Expectations about what is acceptable behavior are clearly stated, and consequences for unacceptable behavior are known and applied when appropriate. Students and staff feel responsible for the successful operation of the school.	A caring school is one that is inviting and supportive of students and staff. Students and staff are provided with opportunities to relate to each other in appropriate ways. The perceptions, feelings, and behaviors of members of the school community reveal that the school is a place where people are comfortable, feel welcome, and are able to be successful.
Indicators of a Safe School: • The existence and implementation of a plan, policies, and procedures that address the safety of the school. • Measures: number of trespassers number of guns and other weapons number of break-ins incidents of vandalism rates of/reasons for absenteeism survey results school-specific indicators	Indicators of an Orderly School: • The existence and implementation of a plan, policies, and procedures that address the "orderliness" of the school. • Measures: referrals to the office reasons for referrals number of in-school suspensions number of out-of-school suspensions survey results school-specific indicators	Indicators of a Caring School: • The existence of a plan, policies and procedures that enable the school to provide a "caring" environment. • Measures: rates of/reasons for absenteeism number of/reasons for transfers staff turnover levels of involvement/participation survey results school-specific indicators

(continued)

Evaluating a School's Safety:
To evaluate the safety of a school, assessments of the safety concerns of members of the school community through surveys, for example, need to occur. Information from surveys and other safety measures needs to be used in the creation of the safe-school plan to address safety concerns. Continuous measurement of safety concerns needs to take place so that actions can be adjusted to address concerns.

Evaluating a School's Orderliness:
To evaluate the orderliness of a school, assessments of the reasons for disorder need to occur. From these assessments, a code of conduct reflecting behavioral expectations can be established as part of the safe-school plan. Review of the reasons for disorder should help establish the code of conduct. Adjustments to the code should be made based on continuous review of the school's orderliness.

Evaluating a School's Caring:
To evaluate how caring a school is, assessments of the perceptions, feelings, and behaviors of members of the school community need to occur. Such assessments will reveal how much these members feel cared for and will provide direction to school efforts intended to create a caring environment.

DISCIPLINE

In its guide to safe schools, the Center for Effective Collaboration and Practice (1998) points out that "a growing number of schools are discovering that the most effective way to reduce suspensions, expulsions, office referrals, and other similar actions . . . is to emphasize a proactive approach to discipline." Effective schools implement schoolwide campaigns that establish high expectations and provide support for socially appropriate behavior. They develop and consistently enforce schoolwide rules that are clear, broad-based, and fair. Rules and disciplinary procedures are developed collaboratively by representatives of the total educational community, are communicated clearly to all parties, and, as the center emphasizes, are followed consistently by everyone. Schools that are most effective:

- Develop a schoolwide disciplinary policy that includes a code of conduct with specific rules and consequences (including anti-harassment and anti-violence policies and due process rights) that can accommodate student differences on a case-by-case basis as necessary.
- Ensure that the cultural values and educational goals of the community are reflected in the rules, which should include a statement expressing the values that underlie the schoolwide disciplinary policy.
- Include school staff, students, and families in the development, discussion, and implementation of the rules, which should be perceived as fair.
- Make sure that consequences are commensurate with offenses and that rules are written and applied in a nondiscriminatory manner, accommodating cultural diversity.
- Make sure that negative consequences (such as the withdrawal of privileges) are combined with positive strategies that teach socially appropriate behavior and address external factors that might have caused the behavior.
- Include a statement of zero tolerance for possession of weapons, alcohol, or drugs. Provide services and support for students who have been suspended or expelled.

PROMOTION OF TOLERANCE

After the events of September 11, 2002, the National School Public Relations Association (2002) distributed a packet of articles directed at helping educators promote tolerance in schools. The overall message was that, in the aftermath of this national tragedy, it is important that educators all watch for any signs of racial tensions emerging among students, staff, and community.

An unfortunate consequent of international terrorism is the potential for some to look for scapegoats to unleash anger and frustration. Some students may target others from particular races, nationalities and religious groups for aggression. All students and staff need to be reminded that aggression toward these individuals cannot be tolerated. Administrators and teachers need to be particularly sensitive to student aggressive behaviors such as racial slurs, put-downs, threatening notes, defacement of property, and taunting. Let's not have minor infractions escalate into more serious incidents. So the time to address these infractions is now.

NSPRA (2002) makes a number of suggestions to help maintain a safe and respectful environment:

- Be vigilant for any signs of inappropriate behavior and reprisals against any students based on their faith or country of origin, for example, verbal or physical harassment such as insults, name calling, celebratory behavior, intimidation, and hate-based graffiti.
- Give students clear messages that all of them are expected to be respectful in all ways about the incidents.
- Remind students and staff to report any incidents to the principal immediately.
- Encourage students to talk to a teacher or administrator if they have concerns about the behavior of a fellow student or if they know of a student who is being harassed or intimidated. Explain that their cooperation is important for everybody's safety and that the best way they can help a fellow student who is having difficulty is by involving a staff member.

- Encourage students and staff to refrain from comments that undermine a positive and respectful environment or that may be hurtful to others.
- Try not to focus on who is *bad* and who is *good*, but rather on how hate and dissension can be debilitating. Emphasize how tragic it is that hate exists and the negative impact hate-based activities can have on all of us.
- Use this tragedy as a teachable moment to focus on the lesson that hate, distrust, and lack of tolerance is damaging at any level.

NSPRA emphasizes that in the multicultural environments of most of today's schools, educators need to pay attention to warning signs that tension is building. They should look for any self-segregation such as ethnic groups intentionally segregating themselves during lunch, breaks, recess, or after-school events. Any contention over group or team assignments should be carefully examined to determine the cause. Incidences of intolerance or insensitivity on or near the time of ethnic and cultural days of celebration should be noted. Graffiti and incidents of vandalism targeted at students or staff may signal that trouble is brewing.

A PLANNED RESPONSE TO CRISIS

There is no way to guarantee that a crisis will not happen at any given school. Schools and school systems need trained crisis-response teams and comprehensive crisis-response plans. Paine and Sprague (2000) point out that "developing comprehensive school safety plans has become an essential part of school-improvement planning. School leaders must make crisis response an ongoing, integral part of school-improvement planning." The authors suggest that preparation for a possible crisis should be a four step process.

Step 1. Form a crisis-response team within the school. A group of individuals should be identified who can serve as members of a team whose primary goal is assisting a school in responding to a crisis. A team approach is suggested because it can help reduce the fear and anxiety that accompanies a crisis, educate students and staff in the dynamics of grief and prepare them for what they might experience, and give members of the school community an opportunity to express their feelings in an accepting environment.

Step 2. Develop a written crisis- or emergency-response plan. A written crisis-response plan should be developed that describes intervention procedures and the responsibilities of the team members. The plan should address topics such as duties of specific crisis members, phone-tree directions, activities to help students deal with loss, media guidelines, communications guidelines, tips for handling special situations, grief and loss reactions in children and adults, and long-term follow-up.

Step 3. Coordinate the plan with community emergency personnel. When a draft of the plan is developed, the police, fire, hospital, and mental health services personnel in the community should be asked to review the plan. Strategies should be developed to coordinate the efforts of these agencies in case of a large-scale crisis. Maps of school buildings should be provided to law enforcement, fire department, and emergency personnel, including the location of important switches and valves. Mock emergency drills should be conducted to test the plan, including lockdown and evacuation procedures.

Step 4. Conduct training for staff, including information on the elements of the plan. This training is the only way to ensure rapid and sensitive response during an actual crisis.

Opalewski and Robertson (1998) state that although most school systems have basic crisis plans, many lack detailed plans that specify the who, what, where, when, and how of crisis response. Underscoring the need for comprehensiveness, Opalewski and Robertson ask if the plan covers:

- Catastrophic death, such as those resulting from a school bus accident
- An HIV-positive student who announces his or her status
- A memorial service held on school grounds
- Separate policies and procedures for accidental versus suicidal death

- Letters to parents and remembrance activities after a student's death
- Dealing with the media
- Returning personal property of deceased students or staff
- Death occurring on school grounds while school is in session
- Attempted suicide on school grounds and a plan for the individual's return to school
- Lesson plans for grieving students
- Policies for replacing a teacher who dies
- A catalog of community resources that can help in a crisis
- Establishing and staffing a crisis room
- Counseling procedures for the crisis room
- Debriefing personnel after a crisis
- Counseling and other follow-up activities after a crisis

CONFLICT RESOLUTION EDUCATION AND SCHOOL-BASED PEER MEDIATION

Safe and orderly environments in schools are essential to promoting high standards for learning and ensuring that all children have the opportunity to develop to their fullest potential. However, too often, youths face conflicts before, during, and after school. Many of these conflicts either begin at school or they are brought into school from the home or community. The Center for the Prevention of School Violence (*Stats 2000*, n.d.) cited the following statistics related to school violence selected from a number of recent reports and studies:

- Thirty-six percent of students reported seeing hate-related graffiti at school (*2000 Annual Report on School Safety*, U.S. Departments of Education and Justice, 2000).
- Students were two times more likely to be victims of serious violent crime away from school as at school (*Indicators of School Crime and Safety 2000*, U.S. Department of Education and Justice, 2000). Twelve percent of today's teens say that the behavior of students in their school was a positive influence, while 40 percent say it interferes with their performance (*State of Our Nation's Youth*, the Horatio Alger Association of Distinguished Americans, 2000).

- Nearly 5 percent of students ages twelve through eighteen reported that they had been bullied at school in the last six months. . . . [F]emales were as likely as males to report being bullied (*Indicators of School Crime and Safety 2000,* U.S. Department of Education and Justice, 2000).
- Fifteen percent of students in grades nine through twelve reported being in a physical fight on school property in the past twelve months (*Indicators of School Crime and Safety 2000,* U.S. Department of Education and Justice, 2000).
- Almost one in five students reported being threatened with a beating. . . . [T]his was a more common experience for middle school students (22 percent) than for high school students (16 percent) (*A National Study of School Environment and Problem Behavior: The National Study of Delinquency Prevention in Schools,* Gottfredson Associates, Inc., 2000).
- Forty-eight percent of students who belong to groups reported being subjected to hazing activities (*Initiation Rites in American High Schools,* Alfred University, 2000).

Many conflicts in schools arise out of differences. Cultural conflicts are based on differences in national origin or ethnicity, and social conflicts on differences in gender, sexual orientation, class, and physical and mental abilities. As the *Conflict Resolution Education Guide* (Crawford and Bodine, n.d.) points out, personal and institutional reactions to differences often take the form of prejudice, discrimination, harassment, and even hate crimes. These conflicts are complex because "they are rooted not only in prejudice and discrimination related to cultural and social differences but also in the resulting structures and relationships in inequality and privilege."

Former Attorney General Reno (n.d.) emphasizes that

A growing body of evidence suggests that we are not powerless to prevent these destructive behaviors. We can intervene successfully to prevent conflicts from escalating into violent acts by providing young people with the knowledge and skills needed to settle disputes peacefully. Conflict resolution education can help bring about significant reductions in suspensions, disciplinary referrals, academic disruptions, playground fights, and family and sibling disputes. It is important to understand that conflict resolution education is a critical component of comprehensive, community-based efforts to prevent violence and reduce crime. . . . As adults, we cannot solve young people's problems for them. We can, however, provide them with the knowledge, skills, and encouragement to resolve conflicts in a nonviolent manner, using words instead of fists or weapons. Conflict resolution education includes negotiation, mediation, and consensus decision making, which allow all parties involved to explore peaceful solutions to a conflict. When these problem-solving processes to conflict and strife become a way of life, young people begin to value getting along instead of getting even or getting their way.

Conflict-resolution education programs (Conflict Resolution Education Network, 2002) help support violence-prevention policy by providing skills and processes for solving problems before they escalate to violence. They teach the principles and the skills needed by students to respect others as individuals and group members, as well as responsible and productive intergroup relations in a pluralistic society. Conflict-resolution programs help individual students:

- Develop personal behavior management skills to act responsibly in the school community.
- Accept the consequences of their own behavior.
- Understand the relationship between law, rights, and personal and community responsibility.
- Develop personal relationship-building skills.
- Learn anger-management skills.
- Develop fundamental competencies (self-control, self-respect, empathy, teamwork) needed to make a successful transition into adulthood.

Cohen (2002) states that school-based peer mediation is "one of the most popular and arguably the most effective approach to integrating the practice of conflict resolution into schools." Peer mediation is a form of conflict resolution in which trained student leaders help their peers work together to resolve everyday disputes. He stresses the importance that participation in peer mediation is voluntary, and with the exception of information that is illegal or life threatening, all matters discussed in mediation sessions remain confidential. Student mediators do not make judgments or offer advice. They have no power to force decisions on their peers. However, Cohen points out "because mediation is sensitive to the underlying causes of conflict, the vast majority of peer mediation sessions (85 percent) result in lasting resolutions." Cohen cautions that three conditions must be present for a school-based peer mediation program to be successful. There must be:

- Enough interpersonal conflict to warrant initiating the program: If mediators do not have the opportunity to mediate cases, few of the benefits associated with peer mediation programs will be realized. Every school must decide what constitutes enough conflict. However, experience suggests that if there is not at least one case per week, a peer mediation program might not be very beneficial.
- Administrative support: For peer mediation to succeed, administrators must work aggressively to overcome attitudinal and structural resistance within their schools. In particular, administrators in charge of discipline must be willing to make referrals and support student mediators' efforts.
- Peer mediation coordinator: Like a coach to a team, the peer mediation coordinator oversees all aspects of a peer mediation program. The more resources this school-based adult has in terms of skill, commitment, and time during the school day, the more successful the program is likely to be.

SCHOOL AND COMMUNITY WORKING TOGETHER

School violence is obviously a concern, but Gottfredson (1999) points out that schools also have the potential for preventing violence.

Schools . . . provide regular access to students throughout the developmental years, and perhaps the only consistent access to large numbers of the most crime-prone young children in the early school years; they are staffed with individuals paid to help youth develop as healthy, happy, productive citizens. The community usually supports schools' efforts to socialize youth. Many of the precursors of delinquent behavior are school-related and therefore likely to be amenable to change through school-based intervention.

However, schools cannot work alone. It is often the violence in neighborhoods and communities that finds its way inside school doors. School violence frequently reflects a much broader problem that can be addressed only when everyone—school, home, and community—works together.

The National PTA focused attention on parent involvement and school violence at its June 1999 convention. The three categories ranked as top violence-prevention factors by attendees were parent involvement in schools (42 percent); smaller class size, smaller schools (28 percent); and parenting skills programs on discipline and communication with children (28 percent) (Markell 1999).

Dwyer (1998), focusing attention on the community component, cites the work of Brendtro, Brokenleg, and Van Broken on the issue of belonging in school. He emphasizes that without a support structure from the family or the community, children tend to turn to such substitutes as gang loyalty, cult vulnerability, and the false security of sexually focused relationships. Children without healthy outlets for their emotions feel lonely and rejected, isolated, and unattached. Cooperative and collaborative working relationships among home, school, and community can help guard against these feelings by providing a positive means of self-expression, emotional and spiritual support, and the security of a friendly, trusting, and gregarious network of social interactions.

Even when schools, families, and communities work together, the fact remains that schools are no longer insulated—if they ever were—from negative conditions in the communities around them. The schools' goal is to create learning environments that are safe, secure, intellectually stimulating, and engaging. Thus, schools everywhere—in the most densely to the most sparsely populated communities—are feeling the need to prepare for a variety of situations, including incidents of violence.

REFERENCES

Center for Effective Collaboration and Practice. (1998). *Early warning, timely response: A guide to safe schools*. Washington, D.C.: American Institutes for Research. Retrieved September 9, 2002, from www.cecp.air.org/guide/guidetext.

Center for the Prevention of School Violence. (1999). *School violence: Let's get it out of our system*. Raleigh, N.C.: North Carolina State University. Retrieved March 5, 2002, from www.ncsu.edu/cpsv/ingo%20planning/.

Center for the Prevention of School Violence. (n.d.) *Stats 2000: Selected school violence research findings.* Retrieved March 15, 2002, from www .cpsv.org.

Cohen, R. (2002). *Implementing a peer mediation program.* Retrieved September 9, 2002, from www.acresolution.org/research.nsf/key-print/lib-cohen.

Conflict Resolution Education Network. (2002). *What conflict resolution education offers America's school children.* Retrieved March 11, 2002, from www.crenet.org/What_Is_CR/offers.

Crawford, D., and Bodine, R. (n.d.) *Conflict resolution education guide.* Springfield, Ill.: National Center for Conflict Resolution Education. Retrieved March 11, 2002, from www.nccre.org/guide.

Dwyer, M. D. (1998). *Strengthening community in education: A handbook for change.* Retrieved January 7, 2002, from www.newmaine.com/community/ index.

Gottfredson, D. C. (1999). School-based crime prevention. In L. W. Sherman, and others, *Preventing crime: What works, what doesn't, what's promising.* College Park: University of Maryland, Department of Criminology and Criminal Justice. Retrieved March 11, 2002, from www.ncjrs.org/works/chapter5/.

Lumsden, L. (Ed). (2002). *Trends and issues: School safety.* Eugene: University of Oregon, Clearinghouse on Educational Management. Retrieved March 11, 2002, from eric.uoregon.edu/trends_issues/safety/index.

Markell, G. (1999). Parent involvement, violence prevention tops national PTA priorities. *Our Children, 25,* 1.

National Criminal Justice Reference Service. (2002). *In the spotlight: School safety.* Retrieved September 9, 2002, from www.ncjrs.org/school_safety/ school_safety.html.

National School Public Relations Association. (2002). *Public relations: Information on promoting tolerance after the September 11 terrorist attacks.* Retrieved September 9, 2002, from www.nspra.org/entry.

Opalewski, D., and Robertson, J. C. (1998). *Crisis response planning.* Kalamazoo, Mich.: Balance Group Publishers.

Paine, C., and Sprague, J. (2000). *Crisis prevention and response: Is your school prepared?* Eugene: University of Oregon, Clearinghouse on Educational Management. Retrieved March 11, 2002, from eric.uoregon.edu/ trends_issues/safety/bulletin.

Reno, J. (n.d.) Forward. In D. Crawford and R. Bodine, *Conflict resolution education guide.* Springfield, Ill.: National Center for Conflict Resolution Education. Retrieved September 10, 2002, from www.nccre.org.

Riley, P. L. (2000). *How to establish and maintain safe, orderly, and caring schools.* Raleigh, N.C.: Center for the Prevention of School Violence. Retrieved February 10, 2002, from www.ncsu.edu/cpsv.

Stephens, R. D. (2001). *Safe school planning: The art of the possible.* Retrieved September 10, 2002, from www.nsscl.org/message.

U.S. Departments of Education and Justice. (1999). *Annual report on school safety.* Retrieved September 10, 2002, from www.ed.gov/pubs/AnnSchoolRept98.

U.S. Departments of Education and Justice. (2001). *Annual report on school safety 2000.* Retrieved February 10, 2002, from www.ed.gov/pubs/SchoolSafety/.

WEBSITES FOR MORE INFORMATION AND LINKS TO OTHER RELEVANT SITES

Center for the Prevention of School Violence, www.nscu.edu/cpsv

Center for the Study and Prevention of Violence, www.colorado.edu/scpv

Clearinghouse on Educational Management, eric.uoregon.edu

Trends & Issues: School Safety, eric.uoregon.edu/trends_issues

Conflict Resolution Education Network, www.crenet.org

National Center for Conflict Resolution Education, www.nccre.org

National Criminal Justice Reference Service, www.ncjrs.org

National School Safety Center, www.nssc1.org

U.S. Department of Education, www.ed.gov/pubs/SchoolSafety

Safe and Drug-Free Schools Program, www.ed.gov/offices/OESE/SDFS

Planning and Evaluating a Comprehensive Home, School, and Community Partnership Plan

It is not a matter of luck that some schools have broad community support and successful community involvement programs and some do not. Schorr (1997) points out that successful schools take a broad, long-range view of neighborhood transformation.

> The success of neighborhood schools depends not only on formal and specialized services, it also depends on the creation of informal helping networks, including church and social ties, family support services, youth development programs, mentoring, recreational opportunities, and strong bonds among adults. . . . Instead of focusing on limited problems with circumscribed solutions, [schools] need to take a broader long-range view. . . . The problems of depleted inner-city neighborhoods cannot be overcome by relying on neighborhood resources alone. Effective neighborhood transformation requires that community-based organizations be able to draw on funding, expertise, and influence from outside, and that outsiders be able to draw on the information, expertise, and wisdom that only can come from the neighborhood itself.

As the percentage of households with school-age children continues to decline, the success of a school system's educational efforts is likely to depend directly on its ability to communicate with the *total* community. Its public image is almost certain to affect the community's willingness to provide support. In the past, a home, school, and community partnership program might have succeeded simply by ensuring the community that the schools were doing a good job. Today, an increasingly skeptical public, concerned with both fiscal and academic accountability, demands accurate, credible, and detailed information from the schools it is asked to support.

Our society expects schools to deal not just with formal learning, but with such difficult social issues as child abuse, drug addiction, teen parenthood, AIDS, violence, and guns. Responding to these issues is not made easier by the fact that there is little agreement on what the school's response should be.

The question becomes whether a public school that must serve all students can be both operationally effective and strategically positioned to meet a specific community's needs and expectations. In the context of educational reform, "operational effectiveness" means performing similar activities better than other educational outlets or better than it was done previously. "Strategic positioning" means performing different activities better than other educational outlets or performing similar activities in different ways.

A school cannot do everything for everybody. To build support for a school among the general public, a home, school, and community partnership program must be planned carefully and have in place an evaluation process that allows for adjustments as dictated by changes in the community and the society as a whole. A fragmented approach simply will not work.

THE FOUR TYPES OF PLANNING

Wegner and Jarvi (1999) believe that an organization, regardless of its size or focus, should engage in four types of planning. *Strategic planning* develops an organization's vision and mission, and then its goals and objectives, with an action plan. *Comprehensive planning* builds on the vision to provide specific long- and short-term directions and continuity for present and future organizational development. *Community planning* puts the organization in the context of the total community and involves all sectors of the community. *Internal systems planning* is planning for the operational systems of the organization.

Strategic Planning

In their attempts to reform public education, educators have sought out "best practices" to incorporate them into a specific school or situation. The lesson learned from the failure rate of many such efforts for change is that a best practice cannot be pasted on a school's operation, ignoring the unique expectations and needs of a specific community.

Strategic planning provides direction and meaning to the day-to-day activities of an organization. A strategic plan provides direction to effectively guide professional educators and staff in day-to-day decisions. Romney (1996) explains why strategic planning is essential to any organization that must operate in a changing environment.

> Strategic planning is a practical process for dealing with the ambiguities of the environment. Its purpose is to move the organization from being a pawn of changing events to being a proactive participant, making decisions about, and acting to create, its own future. It requires organizational flexibility to adapt and revise as conditions change and a willingness to move beyond obsolete paradigms.

Romney recommends a six-step planning process, which must be adapted and adjusted to meet the needs of a particular organization. In general, the larger the organization, the more formal the process.

1. Assess the external environment.
2. Assess internal capacity.
3. Develop a vision or mission for the future.
4. Develop the goals and objectives to reach the future.
5. Implement the plan.
6. Measure progress and revise the plan.

The first two steps involve environmental scanning—viewing the organization in the context of its internal and external environments. Internal factors—the organization's culture, its belief systems, its financial resources, the strengths and weaknesses of staff, the interaction of its members, and organizational barriers and strengths—are directly related to *what* the organization can do and *how* it can do it. An internal assessment provides answers to such questions as: Who are we? What do we believe? What can (and cannot) we do? Whom do we serve? How are we seen?

Environmental scanning also looks at the community and the organization's place in its external environment. This assessment seeks answers to such questions as: What is the community like, and how is it changing?

Who else serves the community and the organization's clients? What needs to be done today, and what will need to be done tomorrow?

In its most basic state, the strategic planning process asks the organization's stakeholders to address three basic questions (Wegner and Jarvi, 1999):

1. Where are we now? How do stakeholders best describe the current environment surrounding the organization, as well as the strengths, weaknesses, opportunities, and threats facing it?
2. Where would we like to be? If the world were a perfect place, how would we be likely to describe ourselves ten to fifteen years from now? (This constitutes the organization's vision of itself or its preferred future.)
3. How do we get there? If stakeholders have a good idea of where they are now and what their preferred future looks like, they need to determine their part in developing strategies for moving the organization from its current condition to its preferred future. This part of the plan manifests itself as a set of strategies around which action steps must be designed and performance measured. The strategic plan thus becomes the measure by which success of the organization is judged.

Wegner and Jarvi (1999) emphasize that, beyond the obvious outcomes of the planning process, important additional benefits can be expected because the process itself

- Helps articulate questions that ordinarily would not be addressed about the function and direction of the organization.
- Helps identify constituent groups that have a need to be served and that may otherwise have been overlooked.
- Creates partnerships that may have been formerly overlooked.
- Generates new and constructive ideas from all levels within the organization.
- Helps prioritize resources to ensure efficiency of effort.
- Helps to eliminate programs and services that are no longer viable.
- Encourages ownership and commitment from all stakeholders.
- Creates benchmarks for assessing the performance of the organization itself, as well as of individual managers within the organization.

- Develops tremendous power within the organization as all of its elements focus on commonly held strategies, unleashing formerly unidentified synergism.

Comprehensive Planning

Comprehensive planning is based on the strategic plan. It identifies the specific steps that need to be taken to implement the vision and mission. It is both an inventory of existing conditions and a list of recommendations for future programs and services, acquisition and development of areas and facilities, and administration. It provides specific long- and short-term direction and continuity for both present and future programs, services, and physical resource development. The comprehensive system plan has two distinct but related dimensions—a program/services plan and a physical resources plan—and is the operational blueprint for the administrator, as well as a valuable tool for ongoing decision making (Wegner and Jarvi, 1999).

Community Planning

Community planning implies a commitment to work together. It is a collaborative effort in which representatives of agencies and organizations get together to consider the needs, resources, and objectives of each, and work out plans for integrating each agency and organization into the community as a whole. It may involve social planning or physical resource planning or both. It includes assessing what is happening in legislatures and other regulatory bodies, as well as population shifts and changing social and economic conditions. Community planning has the benefit of helping agencies and organizations understand each other and the direction taken by each, and of mitigating some potential turf issues (Wegner and Jarvi, 1999).

Internal Systems Planning

Internal systems planning is essential for effective operational management. It integrates the various components of an organization: typically, the plans for maintenance, information technology, public relations and marketing, human resources, financial management and budgeting, risk management, law enforcement and security, and evaluation (Wegner and Jarvi, 1999).

THE BASIC STEPS IN PLANNING

Planning is the continuous process of obtaining, organizing, and using information systematically by answering the following questions (Decker and Associates, 1994):

- What is the scope of the planning effort, and who will be involved?
- What outcomes are desired?
- What resources will help the effort, and what restraints will hinder it?
- What specific things must be achieved to reach the goals?
- How many methods or ways are possible to accomplish each specific thing to be done?
- Which method or methods are best?
- Who is going to implement the methods, and when?
- Was the effort successful? If not, what changes need to be made?

The planning process should be viewed as a cycle that revolves through the following steps:

Focus Planning Effort

The basic premise should be that the planning is done *with*, not *for*, the people whose interests are at stake. Everyone needs to understand the following dimensions:

- What will be planned.
- What type of process will be used to plan.
- Who will be involved in, or directly affected by, the planning effort.
- Whether the planning effort is directed at immediate or long-range goals.

Determine Goals and Priorities

Goals, the foundation of the entire planning process, are usually based on the results of a needs-assessment process. Without goals, planning is impossible. Goals are broad, general statements of desired outcomes, but they must not be vague. If a goal is not understood clearly by everyone involved, it may be impossible to gain the support and commitment necessary to achieve it. Objectives are concrete statements of specific, desired outcomes expected as a result of achieving a goal.

Identify Resources and Constraints

In this step, the setting is analyzed to determine, in a general sense, the major resources and constraints for each goal. Resources are those things that will help, support, or have a positive impact on the achievement of a specific goal. Constraints are those things that will hinder, inhibit, or have a negative impact on goal achievement. Some things may be either resources or constraints:

people	material	geography
money	transportation	technology
facilities	structure	culture
time	environment	communications
agencies	laws	institutions

Formulate Objectives

Objectives are formulated by breaking the goal statement into its parts. Each objective should be specific and clear so that everyone involved understands exactly what needs to be accomplished. Objectives are statements of desired outcomes or purposes around which programs and activities are to be developed. Clarity requires that the objectives include a statement of who will benefit from the outcome, and when the outcome is expected to be achieved.

Generate Alternative Methods

The process of generating alternative methods provides an opportunity for creativity. The purpose of this step is to identify as many ways as possible to achieve the stated objectives. Those involved in the idea-generation process should make a conscious effort not to criticize any of the ideas put forth. Only after all of the alternatives have been generated and listed for each objective should they be analyzed and compared.

Analyze and Select Best Methods

Next, decisions must be made on which methods would work best in the program of action. Each alternative should be analyzed carefully using a combination of systematic analysis and sound judgment. Only after the criteria have been agreed upon and their relative weight determined can each alternative be analyzed and a method selected. Some common criteria are cost, convenience, effectiveness, and feasibility.

Develop Program of Action

The program of action has at least four major components: (1) goal statements, (2) objectives, (3) methods, and (4) activities. The program development procedures in the planning process provide answers to the following questions:

- What major activities are necessary to implement the methods selected?
- Who (specific names) is responsible for performing each of the major activities?
- What are the starting and completion dates for each of the major activities?
- What basic resources (people, money, materials, facilities, and so on) are needed to perform each major activity?

Evaluate Process and Results/Outcomes

Process evaluation involves monitoring and reporting on implementation procedures to determine if the methods and activities are performed in the way in which they were designed. Process evaluation should describe the methods for collecting, organizing, and reporting information about the progress of the program of action. It should provide answers to the following questions:

- Who (specific names) will be responsible for monitoring each major activity and for reporting on the progress?
- When (specific dates) will the progress reports be submitted?
- Who (specific names) will be responsible for collecting the progress reports and developing a program status report?
- When (specific dates) will the status reports be available?
- What will be the form of the progress and program status reports?
- Who (specific names) will receive the program status reports?

Results evaluation also can be performed by monitoring and reporting. The description of the procedures to be used for collecting, organizing, and reporting information regarding the outcomes of the program of action should answer the following questions:

- Who (specific names) will be responsible for collecting and reporting information on the achievement of the objectives of the program?
- What indicators will be used to determine the degree to which the objectives have been achieved?
- Will the program of action be modified and continued, or will it be phased out if the objectives are not achieved as stated?
- Who (specific names) will receive reports on the results of the program of action?

Information from the evaluation of both process and results should be used to improve the program, with the cycle beginning again in a continuous process.

FRAMEWORK FOR A COMPREHENSIVE HOME, SCHOOL, AND COMMUNITY PARTNERSHIP PLAN

To be effective, home, school, and community involvement programs should match the needs and shared interests of families, schools, and communities. The National Coalition for Parent Involvement in Education (n.d.) recommends using the following concepts as a framework on which to build specific programs. The coalition emphasizes that a comprehensive and meaningful home, school, and community partnership incorporates each of them in ways that are unique to the school community.

Supporting Communication
Communication is the foundation of effective partnerships. Families and schools should communicate regularly and clearly with each other about information that is important to student success. This includes informing families about standards and how they relate to curriculum, learning objectives, methods of assessment, school programs, discipline

codes, and children's progress. Schools should also form partnerships with community and faith-based organizations to engage families who do not feel comfortable in schools.

Supporting School Activities

Families and community members can support schools and children's learning in many ways. The school environment is critical to making families and other community members feel welcome and needed. Signs at the school door, central office, and classroom should convey a warm greeting and be in languages spoken by the community. A school-based family resource center providing information, links to social services, and opportunities for informal meetings with staff and other families also contributes to a family-friendly atmosphere.

Supporting Student Learning

Families model and support children's education at home. Families can help their children develop good study habits, supervise their homework, monitor television viewing and after-school activities, and supervise bedtimes and school attendance. Teachers can suggest family activities that are coordinated with the curriculum. Community members can serve as tutors and mentors.

Supporting Lifelong Learning

Families and community members can be encouraged to participate in programs that develop their knowledge and skills. To support these learning activities, schools can offer the use of facilities and other resources. Schools can provide staff development in cultural and community values and practices that are common to their students and families.

Promoting Advocacy and Shared Governance

When parents and community members are members of school advisory or site-based management councils, Title I, parent organizations such as PTAs, and other groups, they can advocate for change, help develop family and community involvement and school improvement plans, participate in the development of school policy and governance procedures, and provide community representation and support. Leadership training should be provided for educators, staff, families, and other community members interested in participating in school governance.

Collaborating with Community Agencies and Organizations

Schools support families and students by forming collaborative relationships with public and private agencies that provide family-support services. These relationships may include partnerships with public health and human service agencies, local businesses, institutions of higher education, youth-serving organizations, and religious, civic, and other community-based organizations. Linking families to services and community organizations can strengthen home environments and student learning. These partnerships create shared responsibility for the well-being of children, families, and schools by all members of the community.

EVALUATION: AN OUTCOMES ORIENTATION

A comprehensive home, school, and community partnership plan should be viewed as an integrated whole—each step influencing and being influenced by every other step in the process. Evaluation should, therefore, be a continuous process throughout the development of the plan. New information or changes at any point in the process may prompt reevaluation of the preceding steps and a rethinking of the organization's future. The final, formal evaluation step can then be seen as a fine-tuning of the plan to fit the realities of actual day-to-day implementation.

Schorr (1997) points out that evaluation methods have been changing since the mid-1980s because of the public's desire for proof of results. She argues that "traditional evaluation models have been ineffectual in helping to understand which aspects of a program are having a desired effect and which components are weak and ineffective" and explains why theory-based evaluation is superior to statistical analysis alone:

> Most traditional evaluation studies lack a strong conceptual and theoretical framework that would explain how and why a social intervention might achieve a desired outcome. Theory-based evaluation provides what statistical analysis alone cannot furnish: conceptual specification of underlying causal mechanisms through which a program is thought to operate. By combining outcome measures with an understanding of the process that produced the outcomes . . . theory-based evaluation can shed light both on the extent of impact and on how the change occurred. . . . These innovative

approaches are not only guided by a strong conceptual and theoretical base; they also employ multiple research techniques, including both quantitative and qualitative methods, to capture and document the full complexity of the social intervention.

An outcomes orientation encourages planners to think about the results they are trying to achieve rather than the procedures they are following. Outcomes accountability requires clarity about goals, and focuses everyone's attention on why they are doing what they are doing. Schorr emphasizes that this approach is essential when local agencies are given greater discretion in interventions. It also allows "communities to be more deliberate in support of shared purposes" and "illuminates whether investments are adequate to achieve expected results."

There are, Schorr acknowledges, some legitimate fears about outcomes accountability:

- Programs may be distorted—what gets done is what is most easily measured or what has the most rapid payoff.
- Even effective programs will seem to accomplish less than they actually do, especially if rapid results are expected.
- In complex, interactive strategies that are the most promising, responsibility for both progress and failure cannot be ascribed accurately to any one agency.
- Determinants of outcomes are often outside the control of those being held accountable.
- Outcomes accountability could become a screen behind which protections for the vulnerable are destroyed—for example, it could lead to the abandonment of the input and process regulations that now restrict the arbitrary exercise of frontline discretion by a powerful institution against powerless clients.

Schorr finds that most of these fears are countered when planning starts with the following premises:

- The goals are ambitious and the outcomes measurable. Ambitious goals can become a framework within which outcome measures can be selected for purposes of accountability, with the understanding that only some aspects of these goals can be measured currently with available data and with outcome measures around which it is possible to gain broad agreement.

- The outcomes are easy to understand and persuasive to skeptics. Outcomes measures must be consistent with common sense and be broadly compelling, not just to experts and those who already support the program.
- The outcomes authentically reflect the purposes to be achieved. The challenge is to devise measures that come as close as possible to reflecting what ought to get done.
- A distinction is maintained between outcomes and processes. A failure to distinguish between process measures describing what is going on and outcome measures describing what is being accomplished will result in confusion between means and ends, and planners will lose sight of what is actually happening to people as a result of the activity.
- Outcomes are placed in a broader accountability context. Even at its best, outcomes-based accountability may not always capture the full effects of some excellent interventions.

Schorr adds a reminder: "In efforts to select the right outcomes, no one should be under the illusion that any one set of outcomes or outcome measures will be perfect. They will have to be refined always, sometimes renegotiated, and evolve continuously."

OUTCOMES AND ACCOUNTABILITY IN HOME, SCHOOL, AND COMMUNITY PARTNERSHIPS

Almost everyone—educators as well as the American public—agree that improved academic success for all children cannot be achieved if outcomes that are prerequisites to learning, such as improved health, appropriate behavior, and a stable home environment, are ignored. The incentive to create home, school, and community partnerships is to improve and enhance many nonacademic supports to learning. However, not all partnership initiatives are created equally. Gardner (2001) points out that

At its inception, every [home, school, and community] partnership must reach a consensus on the relative importance of non-educational outcomes. . . . When there is consensus that the [partnership's] focus on non-academic outcomes should either be co-equal or proportional to academic outcomes, then relative importance of classroom performance and interventions aimed at the external causes of classroom achievement gaps must be negotiated. In that discussion, schools are correct to emphasize the academic outcomes, but the school's partners are also correct to emphasize how their efforts can make a major contribution to academic performance and other goals in the lives of the students and their [families]. An overarching concern must be identifying where overlapping goals can form the "glue" that cements the partnership. . . . At this point, the partners must establish accountability by negotiations toward a consensus on what outcomes should determine success and what levels of attainment indicate a project should be replicated. . . . Partners can then determine what outcomes indicators will be used as fair measure of progress and how data will be collected and reported.

Gardner suggests conceptualizing the relationships between the types of outcomes sought by most home, school, and community partnership programs as three concentric circles. The *innermost circle* represents the core, school-based outcomes: achievement (test scores), attendance, and school graduation rates. The *middle circle* still represents achievement-related outcomes, but is no longer restricted to what happens in the classroom, involving situations such as family involvement, help with homework, reading to children, and family engagement with teachers to respond to student problems in the classroom. The *outer-most circle* represents community building and youth development and includes such outcomes as the school's success in attracting community volunteers, improved human-services delivery in the community, and effects of a program to improve school readiness.

Gardner points out that circles also suggest the range of options home, school, and community partnerships may pursue, and adds that "Circumstances—such as strong or strained relations with families and the community—will dictate the extent to which the outer circles of outcomes can be goals of the partnership; academic achievement may be all the partnership can handle."

Many factors in today's educational environment, including passage of the No Child Left Behind Act of 2001, focus attention on accountability. When examining home, school, and community partnerships,

Gardner explains, "Accountability issues are driven by (a) the types of agencies and their appropriate goals, (b) the collaborative's capacity to evolve from lower to higher stages of cooperation, and (c) the willingness of partners to negotiate shared outcomes concerning academic achievement as opposed to other goals."

Gardner differentiates four different kinds of partners. Each has a different approach to working with and in schools and a particular set of funding sources, and therefore different forms of accountability.

1. Public city, county, and regional agencies: An example is a child-protective services agency. These agencies receive institutionalized, recurring funding. They are accountable to legislatures, resulting in a compliance mentality that emphasizes rules for spending money.
2. Major nonprofit agencies: Examples are Boys and Girls Clubs or children's hospitals. These agencies rely on the United Way, contracts with public agencies, and, sometimes, fee income. Some of them have developed in-depth outcomes measures.
3. Community-based agencies: These agencies are funded more informally than the nonprofits. They range widely in accountability, from those that have used outcomes to a larger group that still measures success based on the number of clients contacted.
4. Organizations that represent families: Frequently this type of partner has no formal budget and, typically, no explicit outcomes framework.

Gardner points out that accountability issues are also affected by the stage of collaboration.

A four-part approach to the stages of collaboration distinguishes between the initial stages of *information exchange* and *joint projects*, and the third and fourth stages of *changing the rules* and *changing the system*. As long as it is working at the level of a project, a [partnership] can get along without emphasizing accountability. When the collaborative begins to change the rule of service—because of changes in its shared outcome or as it attempts to scale up the operation—accountability issues become more important. That is because changing the rules should not be done for convenience but to achieve different or better outcomes than the old rules permit.

When the collaborative is working on changing the rules and moving from the project level of collaborative operations to going to scale, both client and systems outcomes matter. Assessing the relations among the partners may be as important as assessing the impact on students and families. Tracking the efforts made by [home, school, and community] partnerships to change the rules, enabling agencies to work together more effectively, can help ensure that "fixing the kids" does not always become the sole focus, with "fixing the institutions" being ignored.

SOME TECHNIQUES AND TOOLS IN EVALUATION

A variety of techniques and tools are available to evaluate home, school, and community partnership programs. One technique is an audit. Audits are sometimes completed by outside experts and consultants with broad experience and knowledge of comprehensive school–community relations efforts. An audit should pinpoint both strengths and weaknesses, uncover needs, and give a rationale for greater effort in school–community relations.

The National School Public Relations Association (1999) recommends doing a communications audit, described as a compilation of the school's or school district's needs, policies, capabilities, activities, and programs. An audit assesses the effectiveness and credibility of current publications and other communications and marketing activities. It involves a review of public relations/communications policies and examines budgets, current plans, and staffing patterns. It looks at demographic data, long-range plans, and past surveys of family, staff, and community attitudes and reviews coverage by the local newspaper, radio, and television media. NSPRA recommends using focus groups of eight to ten people representing citizens, parents, businesspeople, administrators, teachers, support staff, and other key audiences whose support is needed to improve communications in the district or the community.

NSPRA suggests using five major steps in a comprehensive communications audit:

1. Make the decision to do it. Nothing is more important in building trust and support between your organization and the public you

serve than the quality of your communications effort. Are you addressing the community's concerns? Are you communicating effectively? Does your staff understand and support what you are trying to do?

2. Analyze the current program. It is important to review your existing policies, publications, strategies, media relationships— every aspect of your internal and external communications effort.

3. Listen to your audiences. The core of the audit is focus groups that are representative of your internal and external audiences. They can generate more useful information than most surveys because a trained facilitator can probe the feelings behind their opinions. The number and composition of focus groups may vary depending on the main purpose of a particular aspect of the audit.

4. Develop constructive recommendations for improving your communications program. Based on an analysis of your current program and the input from the focus groups, make recommendations for improvement.

5. Get implementation assistance when appropriate. Once the decision is made to take steps to improve or update aspects of your public relations/communications programs, it may be necessary to examine sample materials and policies. Colleagues who have successfully dealt with similar situations can be contacted and experts can be consulted.

Beyond monitoring communications efforts, the National Committee for Citizens in Education (1993) developed a process for assessing a school's progress toward increasing family involvement. The process, known as *Taking Stock,* is a systematic way of looking at a school's relationship with families. The designers stress that the process is not an evaluation by outsiders to be used against the school, but a family-friendly way for a school to identify its strengths and weaknesses from families' perspectives. The process uses a survey form resembling a report card. Families are asked to grade each item on a scale of 1 to 4, with 4 being excellent. When the report cards are returned, the average

Table 9.1.   Taking Stock

Taking Stock: Family Report Card

School _____

	Grade	Final Grade
(Grade each of the following on a scale of 1 to 4, with 4 being excellent. Calculate the average for each category.)		
Reaching out to families		
1. Communicating often and openly with families.	_____	
2. Reaching all cultures and language groups.	_____	
3. Reaching working and single parents.	_____	
4. Extra efforts to reach all families.	_____	_____
Welcoming families to the school building		
5. School's welcome to families.	_____	
6. Open and available school and staff.	_____	
7. Encouraging volunteers.	_____	
8. Active and strong PTA/PTO.	_____	
9. Major PTA/PTO activities.	_____	
10. Reaching out to the community.	_____	_____
Developing strong relationships		
11. Teachers communicate with parents.	_____	
12. Parent–teacher partnership.	_____	
13. Parent–principal relationship.	_____	
14. Parents involved in decision making.	_____	
15. School's parent-involvement policy.	_____	_____
Helping parents understand the curriculum		
16. Information about the curriculum.	_____	
17. Goals for student achievement.	_____	
18. Information on student performance.	_____	_____
Helping parents be more effective		
19. School supports parents.	_____	
20. School links to community services.	_____	

A	3.2 to 4.0	Great job. Keep up the good work!
B	2.6 to 3.1	Good work. A little more will put you on top.
C	2.0 to 2.5	Solid beginning. Time for some next steps.
U	1.0 to 1.9	Needs improvement. Let's get to work!

for each category is calculated, giving the school a final grade in each section. Table 9.1 is an example.

How Customer Friendly Is Your School? (Chambers, 1998) is a survey that focuses on a visitor's or telephoner's first impressions. It asks yes or no questions about the school environment and telephone services to find out how people perceive the school. Table 9.2 is an example.

Table 9.2. How Customer Friendly Is Your School?

HOW CUSTOMER FRIENDLY IS YOUR SCHOOL?
(Answer each question "yes" or "no.")

Environment

Grounds:
____ Are the grounds attractively landscaped?
____ Are they clean and well maintained?
____ Is there adequate visitor parking?
____ Is there easy access from visitor parking to the main entrance?

Entrance:
____ Is the main entry clearly marked (including directions for visitor parking)?
____ Do entry signs welcome visitors and give directions to the main office?
____ Does the main entrance set a good tone for the school?
____ Does it feel warm and welcoming?
____ Is it clean and in good repair?
____ Does it highlight student, teacher, and school accomplishments (pictures, awards, student projects, artwork, etc.)?
____ Does it provide a positive image?
____ Is it free of unpleasant noises or unfriendly written rules or directions?

Interior:
____ Are halls and rooms clean well decorated, and in good repair?
____ Are rooms and common areas such as the library clearly marked?
____ Are students' work and accomplishments highlighted on the walls or in display cases?
____ Is the lighting bright and the temperature comfortable?
____ Are announcement and bell systems set at a comfortable decibel level?

Main Office:
____ Can the sign for the main office be clearly seen from a distance?
____ Can office personnel easily see visitors when they enter?
____ Is the decor of the office inviting?
____ Are desks and other areas in view of visitors kept organized and clean?
____ Is there a nameplate identifying the person responsible for greeting visitors?

Main Office (continued):
____ Do office personnel greet visitors within a few seconds of their entry, letting them know they will be right with them if they cannot help them immediately?
____ Are all office personnel welcoming and helpful?
____ Is there a comfortable place for visitors to sit while waiting for appointments?
____ Is the noise level comfortable and the area free of unpleasant odors?
____ Do office staff avoid personal conversations in public areas?

Telephone Etiquette
____ Are all employees—not just secretaries—informed about proper etiquette for answering calls and taking messages?
____ Do they answer by immediately identifying the school or department and themselves?
____ Do they answer in a pleasant tone of voice, making callers feel they are happy to be of assistance?
____ Are they helpful to callers? When unable to answer a question, do they try to find the answer themselves to avoid routing the call to another person?

Automated Answering Services and Your Voice Mail
____ Is the automated answering service easy to understand and follow, giving the caller an option to speak to a person if desired?
____ Does it give office hours and let callers know when school is not in session?
____ Does it provide callers with directions to the school?

The Coalition for Community Schools offers a community school-assessment tool that contains three checklists intended to help school and community leaders create or strengthen community–school partnerships: the first checklist helps assess the development of the community–school partnership; the second helps take inventory of existing programs and services in or connected to a school that supports children, youth, families, and other community residents; and the third helps catalog the funding sources that support these programs and services. Blank and Langford (2000) explain the rationale for the three checklists:

> To be effective, partnerships need to engage in a thoughtful process to define a vision and clear goals. Partnerships need to have effective governance and management structures to ensure that programs operate efficiently and the partnership is responsive to community needs. Community school partnerships also need to draw from a broad range of perspectives and expertise—from inside the school as well as from other organizations and individuals within the community. Finally, community school partnerships need to connect, coordinate, and leverage resources from a variety of sources to support and continue their work.

The first checklist, *Community School Partnership Assessment* (Coalition for Community Schools, n.d.), focuses on the *process* of bringing partners together and working to achieve desired results. It is designed to help partnerships focus on, assess, and improve the quality of their collaborative efforts. The checklist is a series of statements. Respondents are directed to rank the statements on a scale of 1 (disagree) to 5 (agree).

The statements are:

- Our partnership has developed a clear vision.
- Our partnership has collaboratively identified the result we want to achieve for children, youth, families, and our community.
- Our partnership has successfully engaged a broad base of partners from a range of individuals and organizations representing the school and the community.
- Our partnership has developed strategies for coordinating and linking the array of supports and opportunities for children, youth, families, and community members that are available at or connected to the school.

- Our partnership has established a clear organizational structure.
- Our partnership has agreed on the roles that individual partners will play and ensured that all partners understand and accept the responsibilities of those roles.
- All partners involved in our community school have an understanding of who the other partners are, what organizations they come from, and what those organizations do.
- Our partnership regularly communicates with all partners to keep them informed about its work.
- Our partnership engages in activities to create awareness about and increase support for the work of the partnership.
- Our partnership has identified and mobilized resources (financial and others) from partner organizations and other entities throughout the community.

Some other planning and evaluation resources related specifically to home, school, community relations are *School, Family, and Community: Techniques and Models for Successful Collaboration,* edited by Michael J. Dietz; *Everybody's House the Schoolhouse: Best Techniques for Connecting Home, School, and Community,* by Carolyn Warner (with Marilyn Curry); and *Learning from Others: Good Programs and Successful Campaigns,* by Chrissie Bamber, Nancy Berla, and Anne T. Henderson.

ACHIEVING A COMMON PURPOSE

In her examination of programs and interventions, Schorr (1997) identifies what she calls the "Seven Attributes of Highly Effective Programs." Successful programs, she says (1) are comprehensive, flexible, responsive, and persevering; (2) see children in the context of their families; (3) deal with families as parts of neighborhoods and communities; (4) have a long-term, preventive orientation, a clear mission, and continue to evolve over time; (5) are well managed by competent and committed individuals with clearly identifiable skills; (6) have staffs that are trained and supported to provide high-quality, responsive services; and (7) operate in a setting that encourages practitioners to build strong relationships based on mutual trust and respect.

In addition, Schorr describes eight strategies used by successful programs:

1. Recognize the Seven Attributes of Highly Effective Programs and create environments that will support them.
2. Distinguish between essentials that can be replicated from other programs and components that must be developed or adapted locally.
3. Find ways to surmount obstacles to fundamental change, so that the attributes of successful demonstrations can become the norms of mainstream systems. Do not limit innovation to program changes. Find new ways to balance bureaucratic protections against the imperative of accomplishing public purposes.
4. In undertaking major initiatives, make sure that funders, managers, frontline staff, and program participants agree on valued outcomes. Make sure that all stakeholders understand how the initiative's activities and investments are related to outcomes, so that they will be able to use results to judge success.
5. Take a broader view. Give up on searching for a single intervention that will be a one-time fix, and forget about selecting among economic development, public safety, community building, education reform, or service reform in an effort to find a single, most-promising way to intervene. Try to carve out a manageable piece of the problem, but look for opportunities to have an impact broader than a circumscribed solution to a circumscribed problem.
6. Take a long view. Forget about getting results overnight, and be prepared to build for the future.
7. Recognize that intensity and critical mass may be crucial. Create the synergy that can bring about real change and tip a neighborhood toward becoming functional.
8. Forget about choosing between bottom-up and top-down approaches. Effective neighborhood transformation requires that community-based organizations be able to draw on funding, expertise, and influence from outside, and that outsiders be able to draw on the information, expertise, and wisdom that can come only from the neighborhood itself.

THE PRESSING NEED FOR DOCUMENTATION

Wang (2001) points out that over the past decade, a wide variety
of home, school, and community partnerships have been created to improve educational and social outcomes for children and families by
connecting collaborative services with school-reform efforts. However,
one of the most serious problems confronting collaboratives is the general lack of evidence about the effects of these partnerships. Wang
explains that

> The urgency of placing a sharp focus on this complex but essential task
> of documenting outcomes of school/community/family partnerships is
> emanating from a variety of forces shaping current school reform initia-
> tives:
> - Advocates of standards-based education reform and accountability
>   recognize that students learn both in and outside of school and that
>   communities have a responsibility for students' academic success
>   and to ensure all students are ready to learn.
> - Emergent brain research findings are creating even more clarity
>   about the effect of early childhood development on later school and
>   life successes.
> - The sporadic, but nationally chilling episodes of violence in school
>   have brought home the understanding that students' "connected-
>   ness" inside and outside of school walls is everyone's concern.
> - The federal devolution of reforms in the welfare and workforces
>   development systems have served to heighten the awareness of
>   local partnership participants of their critical role in fostering eco-
>   nomic self-sufficiency for poor families.
>
> These forces are among the most important reasons why more school
> and community leaders and parents are pushing harder for the develop-
> ment of partnerships. But a major question still remains: What difference
> do they make?

REFERENCES

Bamber, C., Berla, N., and Henderson, A. T. (1996). *Learning from others:
Good programs and successful campaigns*. Washington, D.C.: Center for
Law and Education, with the Academy for Educational Development.

Blank, M. J., and Langford, B. H. (2000). *Strengthening partnerships: Community school assessment checklist.* Washington, D.C.: Institute for Educational Leadership.

Coalition for Community Schools. (n.d.) *Strengthening partnerships: Community school assessment checklist.* Retrieved March 25, 2002 from www. communityschools.org.

Chambers, L. (1998). How customer friendly is your school? *Educational Leadership,* 56, 2.

Decker, L. E., and Associates. (1994). *Home-school-community relations: Trainers manual and study guide.* Charlottesville, Va.: Mid-Atlantic Center for Community Education.

Dietz, M. J. (1997). *School, family, and community: Techniques for successful collaboration.* Gaithersburg, Md.: Aspen Publishers.

Gardner, S. (2001). Outcomes and accountability in school-community partnerships. *The CEIC Review,* 10, 1.

National Coalition for Parent Involvement in Education. (n.d.). *Developing family and school partnerships: Guidelines for schools and school districts.* (n.d.). Fairfax, Va.: National Coalition for Parent Involvement in Education.

National Committee for Citizens in Education. (1993). *Taking stock.* Washington, D.C.: National Committee for Citizens in Education.

National School Public Relations Association. (1999). *Communications audit.* Retrieved March 15, 2002, from www.nspra.org/main_audit.htm.

Romney, V. (1996). *Strategic planning and needs assessment.* Fairfax, Va.: National Community Education Association.

Schorr, L. B. (1997). *Common purpose: Strengthening families and neighborhoods to rebuild America.* New York: Anchor Books, Doubleday.

Wang, M. C. (2001). Pathways to school/community/family partnership results: Measures of success and student learning. *The CEIC Review,* 10, 1.

Warner, C. (with Curry, M.). (1997). *Everybody's house the schoolhouse: Best techniques for connecting home, school, and community.* Thousand Oaks, Calif.: Corwin Press.

Wegner, D., and Jarvi, C. K. (1999). Planning for strategic management. In B. vander Smissen and M. Moichichik (Eds.), *Management of park and recreation agencies.* Ashburn, Va.: National Park and Recreation Association.

CHAPTER 10

Making Friends Before You Need Them

Former President Lyndon Johnson is credited with having said, "The best time to make friends is before you need them." Today's educational leaders would do well to follow his advice. Meek (1999) emphasizes the importance of this advice in the context of contrasting the current educational environment with what are sometimes called "the good old days."

> Only a few years ago, teachers and administrators could count on a fair amount of community support for schools or at least on broad passive acceptance of their efforts. . . . Schools closely reflected the traditions and priorities of their local community. In many communities, even when parents could afford the tuition for private or parochial education, public schools enrolled the majority of students. . . . Whether private, public, or parochial schools were the choice, however, most families expected to stay put, the curriculum was relatively unchanging, and teachers typically taught for years, often in the same classroom. School affairs were predictable, uneventful, even downright dull. . . .
>
> Today, schools operate in a demanding policy climate—one in which national, state, and local policymakers advocate new programs, demand results, and scrutinize endless amounts of data to see whether schools are performing acceptably. The importance of schools in the economic development of both the nation and the local community, along with the potential of schools to contribute to the quality of life in a locality, has become increasingly clear. . . .
>
> In addition, schools currently face a rather long list of expectations and needs generated by families. . . . Indeed, as clients, today's parents are demanding consumers—they know what they want, they have high

standards for service, and they may complain loudly if they don't find services up to standard. Parents are accustomed to moving from place to place, often selecting housing based on the reputation of neighborhood schools. . . .

In addition, as voucher or choice provisions increase, many more parents may have the option of sending their children to schools outside the immediate neighborhoods. . . .

Schools themselves have changed, too. Today's public schools possess a number of attributes and offer a variety of services and programs unheard of when today's parents were growing up. . . . What's more, the curriculum is no longer the predictable entity it was in the past. New research findings and new concepts of how students learn, professional associations, religious conservatives, textbook and software publishers, as well as the demands of policymakers and business leaders contemplating the role of the United States in the global marketplace all have influenced today's curriculum frameworks. What's more, today's schools serve all students, including those who might have, in an earlier era, quietly vanished from school to work on farms or in factories.

In short, profound changes have occurred in U.S. schools. School programs are different from those of the past. Parental needs and expectations have grown more complex and challenging. The environment in which schools operate reflects an often critical attitude, with intense competition for tax dollars at a time when the majority of the public has no children in school. Under such circumstances, educators face a new imperative: we must [effectively communicate] so as to inform, listen to, and learn from our various publics. . . . [We must] make friends before we need them.

WOOING THE PUBLIC

The influence of the family and the community on what happens inside school walls has been well documented by many research studies. Rich (1998) counsels that what happens inside the school also affects the community. Educators, she suggests, must find ways—or take the time—to fulfill the public's need for a new set of R's: respect, reassurance, and recognition. These three R's can improve children's achievement and woo the public at the same time. Respect, reassurance, and recognition, like the old three R's of reading, 'riting, and 'rithmetic, are intimately connected with academic achievement, especially when the goal is building a sense of investment for everyone in the community.

Rich explains that educators who want the public to care about local schools must develop school and district plans that

Build Respect

- Set educational responsibilities for the family. Send messages and establish climates that communicate the ideas that families are important partners in the educational process and that every family has strengths that can be mobilized on behalf of children.
- Make school schedules convenient for families. Overcoming the problems caused by conflicting schedules of working parents and teachers may mean changing the time and place of parent–teacher conferences or restructuring teacher time.
- Undertake collaborative efforts to reach families. A network of agencies, community groups, businesses, and media can help provide a variety of supports, including mentoring and apprenticeships.
- Use school for community needs. By increasing the use of school facilities to serve community needs, schools can position themselves to be more than just suppliers of services. They can be facilitators of learning for the community.

Supply Reassurance

- Provide practical information families need. Research confirms families' readiness to learn more about how to help their children. They want to know how to help before there are problems. Materials are already written and are readily available from a variety of sources.
- Offer a realistic picture of what school can accomplish. Build public awareness of the many roles and services the school provides, its basic strengths, and the challenges and problems encountered by families and schools today. Create a strong understanding of what even the best schools cannot do.
- Encourage family involvement at all levels of schooling and at every age. School efforts focusing on parent–child communication

can allay the fear of teens that no one cares about them and that their schooling lacks meaning.

- Provide an active role for fathers. Find ways to encourage fathers to be involved directly at home and at school. Use messages that support the image of men as caregivers, not just providers.
- Provide training and information for teachers. Part of a new and enhanced role for teachers is integrating what is learned outside the classroom with what is learned inside. This involves working with adults as well as children.

Provide Recognition

- Start early, before children come to school. Provide information to parents about their educational role, starting with a child's birth. Education for successful schooling can begin with in-hospital programs sponsored by schools.
- Establish connections with family day care. Schools can offer training about education for daycare providers through a variety of media, from print to local cable channels.
- Create helpful roles for the private sector. Provide businesses with information on how they can support family–school relationships. Businesses can contribute more than volunteers for classrooms. They can provide employees with time off for parent–teacher conferences and offer information and support that reduces stress and work–home conflict.
- Let people know they are appreciated. It is important that every person involved with the school is recognized and feels valued. Recognition is especially vital to parents. Share news about what has been accomplished. Ensure that both school and family accomplishments are widely shared through a variety of media and at local civic and community group meetings. The accomplishments of schools, students, and families are community accomplishments. If they are presented in that light, everyone will share in this sense of success.

Purkey and Stanley (1995) reflect a similar theme in what they call "invitational education," the practice of creating a school environment that helps people realize their potential in all areas of human activity.

The purpose is "to make learning, teaching, leading, and living an exciting, satisfying and enriching experience for everyone in and around schools." The five propositions of invitational education are:

1. Education should be a cooperative activity.
2. Process is as important as product.
3. People are able, valuable, and responsible and should be treated accordingly.
4. People possess untapped potential in all areas of worthwhile human endeavor.
5. Potential can be realized best through programs and processes designed to invite development, participated in by people who intentionally unite with others.

TAPPING THE POTENTIAL

A national survey by the League of Women Voters, *Working Together: Community Involvement in America* (Duskin, 1999), concluded that the growing pressures of juggling the multiple tasks and responsibilities of contemporary life are reflected in a new form of involvement. The emerging trend is for community engagement to be localized and personalized and channeled through individual and group-based activities rather than through established organizations. "One of the key factors in whether people are going to get involved nowadays is whether they feel they are going to be able to make a difference."

People seem to be channeling their energy in more personal ways. As Duskin points out, "There is a growing tendency to want to connect personal responsibility and individual freedom. They [the participants in the study] see the community as the place to do this." The study also found that not everyone limits the concept of community to geography. Shared values and experience often play a role in what, for participants, makes up a community.

The study found that the barriers that keep people from community involvement are attitudinal or structural. The attitudinal barrier is the belief that one person cannot make a difference in solving problems. The stronger the belief that the person can make a difference, the more likely his or her involvement in community activities. The biggest structural barrier is time. Involvement that requires a regular time commitment or requires big blocks of time discourages participation. Providing *flexibility* and *choice* in terms of both time and tasks is a major way to overcome attitudinal and structural barriers.

SUCCESSFUL HOME, SCHOOL, AND COMMUNITY PARTNERSHIP INITIATIVES

Flaxman, Schwartz, Weiler, and Lahey (1998) stress that the most successful education reform initiates are collaborations between families and schools that are situated within the context of the surrounding community. "Since schools alone cannot solve the problems imported into them from society, some projects reach beyond the schools; they draw upon the power of community institutions, such as churches and civic groups, to improve schools and aspects of life in the community that impact education." The authors outline general characteristics that these collaboratives share (1998):

- They view the school and community as part of a social ecology that is interdependent and must be understood as a whole in order to identify problems and develop solutions.
- They build relationships based on common concerns and mutual self-interest to foster increased involvement; create resources such as trust, information channels, and shared norms among people; and promote constructive action for change.
- They acknowledge the role of power, or *the ability to act* in a school–community relationship in order to help families and educators recognize the self-interests of different groups and individuals in a particular education bureaucracy and the relative power that each has over educational policy and practices, and then to constructively influence these various groups to make decisions beneficial to students in their schools.
- They foster the collaborative leadership of principals, with the goals of creating an environment in which teachers and families feel safe enough to take risks, and even to fail, in an effort to create positive change; and of enabling principals to share the responsibilities of

leadership with teachers, parents, and community members who have been identified as leaders.

• They develop and train parents and educators as leaders so they can build networks of relationships and motivate and recruit people to accomplish a task and develop the skills needed to reform education in the community and resolve conflicts.

• They monitor and evaluate progress, track the impact of reform efforts on outcomes, and ensure accountability for educational improvement.

SUMMING UP

Making friends before you need them requires proactive educational leaders. Strengthening connections requires reaching out to families and community members and achieving an accurate understanding of the kind of family, school, and community collaboration needed to achieve the goal of academic success for all children.

Too often, school communications are reactive, involving some kind of crisis: a student is failing, a weather emergency looms, a classroom is affected by an environmental hazard, a parent faction or community group is unhappy about part of the curriculum or a particular program. These kinds of communications precipitated by such emergencies frequently have negative repercussions, both short- and long-term.

If educators want family and community support, they must ask for it, regularly and often. The key to whether support is forthcoming is the way people are asked; the more personal the approach, the more likely it is to elicit the desired response. When messages were tested in the League of Women Voters' study (Duskin), those that got the best response spoke directly to the stake people have in their communities and the tangible difference their involvement could make. The two types of invitations that were the most persuasive were those that emphasized personal responsibility and those that conveyed a *can do* message. One particularly effective message was: "There is no better way to demonstrate good values to a child than to show him or her what it's like to make a difference in that child's particular community."

The Annenberg Institute of School Reform's newsletter (1999) describes today's public educational leadership as the "art of pushing from behind":

> While [school leaders] are still key conveners and facilitators of the work of school improvement, they must also invite a new corps of school and community leaders to the forefront in building a collective vision for the work. Leadership isn't pulling people along anymore: it's about orchestrating ideas, people, visions, potential, and organizations into a cohesive program for educational improvement. The most effective and inclusive styles of educational leadership today combine both bottom-up and top-down approaches. School and district leaders must share power and delegate key decision-making authority to representative teams of teachers, parents, business leaders, senior citizens, and others. The multiple interests and expectations that these stakeholder teams bring to the table are crucial to building a common vision for their community's education system. A sustained, inclusive dialogue identifies priorities, targets strengths, and insures that even the softest voice is heard.

Engaging families and communities in public education is the pathway to educational success. However, in *Facing the Hard Facts in Education Reform,* Barton (2001) believes that some problems are not being addressed or have been addressed insufficiently, in the current education debate. He explains that

> [He has] attempted to glean from many efforts and information sources those avenues to improve student achievement that are not being traveled—or at least not being given the emphasis they deserve—in the current education reform movement. In conclusion, he leaves the following thoughts.
> - Standards-based reform is in danger of becoming simply a testing movement. Testing itself is not the treatment, but a way of finding out whether new content standards, rigorous curriculum, and teacher preparation are producing results. In a full standards-based reform effort, testing is just one important component.
> - If there is no order in the classroom there will be no learning. While widespread attention has been given to murders at school, disruptive student behaviors have not been the focus of attention. Research shows that such behaviors do, in fact, adversely affect student

achievement.

- While educational improvement sits at the top of opinion polls, families, student peers, and society send weak signals to students that high achievement is important. More than two out of five parents think extracurricular activities are as important as academic studies; students fear that they will be less socially popular if they work hard in school; employers of high school graduates do not ask to see school transcripts; and many colleges have such low standards for admission that they routinely provide remedial courses.
- The nation's focus has been largely on education policy and schools. But a *learning* policy that encompasses preschool development and draws on the resources of family and community is necessary to raise achievement. Research clearly shows that, in addition to school factors, family factors are important to learning. We need to better track sources of incentive for educational achievement and learning, whether in school or out.
- The great promise of computers is not near to being realized. While hardware is becoming widely available, we are not yet putting educational content into these machines and we must invest in the preparation of the teacher to perform the miracles these machines may well be capable of.

In identifying these areas where he believes too little attention has been paid, Barton adds that

[He does] not suggest that we lessen our effort in implementing the standards-based reform agenda; it makes good and common sense to make instruction rigorous, set high standards, and develop quality standardized tests, the validity of which has been established for the purposes they are used. The quality of teacher preparation has drawn national attention, and important policy approaches are still being debated. However, drastic changes and considerable resources are needed, and there is little indication that the nation is prepared to do what needs to be done.

Calling attention to Barton's report, Gitomer (2001), senior vice president of the Statistics and Research Educational Testing Service, emphatically states:

Facing the Hard Facts in Education Reform is a synthesis of a decade of work and illuminates some very critical issues involved in transforming American education, issues that are not at the center of the current educational debate and developing legislation. If we pay attention to Barton's claims, we will make progress on issues that open up opportunities for all students. If we only focus on the test scores, and not on the alignment of educational policies and practices that influences those scores, we do nothing more than blame those who have not benefited from the system.

REFERENCES

Annenberg Institute for School Reform. (1999). *Public Engagement Today,* 2. Retrieved March 7, 2002, from www.annenberginstitute.org/publications/pe/news2pl.html.

Barton, P. E. (2001). *Facing the hard facts in education reform: A policy information perspective.* Princeton, N.J.: Educational Testing Service.

Duskin, M. (1999). Community activism: An untapped reservoir," *National Voter,* 49, 1.

Flaxman, E., Schwartz, W., Weiler, J., and Lahey M. (1998). *Trends and issues in urban education.* Springfield, Va.: ERIC Clearinghouse on Urban Education. Retrieved April 3, 2002, from eric-web.tc.columbia.edu/monographs/ti20.

Gitomer, D. H. (2001). Preface. In P. E. Barton, *Facing the hard facts in education reform: A policy information perspective.* Princeton, N.J.: Educational Testing Service.

Meek, A. (1999). *Communicating with the public: A guide for school leaders.* Association for Supervision and Curriculum Development. Retrieved September 10, 2002, from www.ascd.org/readingroom/books/meek99toc.html.

Purkey, W. W., and Stanley, P. H. (1995). Invite school success: A treasury of 1001 ideas. *Journal of Educational Relations,* 16, 4.

Rich, D. (1998). Respect, reassurance, recognition. *Journal of Educational Relations,* 19, 3.

Association and Organization Contact Information

The following are the addresses, websites, and phone numbers for active associations and organizations cited in this publication.

Organization	Address	City/State/Zip	Website/URL	Phone
A-Plus Communications	2300 Clarendon Blvd., Suite 1102	Arlington, VA 22201	www.aplusworld.com	703/528-7100
Afterschool Alliance	PO Box 65166	Washington, DC 20035	www.afterschoolalliance.org	202/296-9378
Alliance for Parental Involvement in Education	PO Box 59	East Chatham, NY 12060	www.croton.com/allpie	518/392-6900
America's Promise	909 No. Washington St., Suite 400	Alexandria, VA 22314	www.americaspromise.org	703/684-4500
American Association of Retired Persons	601 E St. NW	Washington, DC 20049	www.aarp.org	800/424-3418
American Association of School Administrators	1801 North Moore St.	Arlington, VA 22209	www.aasa.org	703/528-0070
American Federation of Teachers	555 New Jersey Ave. NW	Washington, DC 20001	www.aft.org	202/879-4400
American Institutes for Research	1000 Thomas Jefferson St. NW	Washington, DC 20007	www.air-dc.org	202/342-5000
Annenberg Institute for School Reform	Brown University, Box 1985	Providence, RI 02912	www.annenberginstitute.org	401/863-7990
Annie E. Casey Foundation	701 St. Paul St.	Baltimore, MD 21202	www.aecf.org	410/547-6600
Asset-Based Community Development Institute	Institute of Policy Research Northwestern University/ 2040 Sheridan Rd.	Evanston, IL 60208	www.nwu.edu/IPR	847/491-8711
Ass'n for Supervision & Curriculum Development	1703 North Beauregard St.	Alexandria, VA 22311	www.ascd.org	703/578-9600 800/933-2723
Association for Volunteer Administration	PO Box 32902	Richmond, VA 23294	www.avaintl.org	804/346-2266

Organization	Address	City, State Zip	Website	Phone
Benton Foundation	1800 K St. NW, 2nd Floor	Washington, DC 20006	www.benton.org	202/638-5770
Carnegie Corporation of New York	437 Madison Ave.	New York, NY 10022	www.carnegie.org	212/371-3200
Center for Civic Education	5146 Douglas Fir Rd.	Calabasas, CA 91302	www.civiced.org	818/591-9321
Center for Democracy & Citizenship	Humphrey Inst. of Public Affairs 301 19th Ave. South	Minneapolis, MN 55455	www.hhh.umn.edu	612/625-0142
Center for Education Reform	100 Connecticut Ave. NW, Suite 204	Washington, DC 20036	www.edreform.com	800/521-2118
Center for Effective Collaboration and Practice	American Institute of Research 1000 Thomas Jefferson St. NW, Suite 400	Washington, DC 20007	www.air-dc.org/cecp	202/944-5400 888/457-1551
Center for Law and Education	1875 Connecticut Ave. NW, Suite 510	Washington DC 20009	www.cleweb.org	202/986-3000
Center for the Improvement of Child Caring	11331 Ventura Blvd. Suite 103	Studio City, CA 91604	www.ciccparenting.org	818/980-0903
Center for the Prevention of School Violence	North Carolina State University 313 Chapanoke Rd., Suite 140	Raleigh, NC 27603	www.ncsu.edu/cpsv	919/773-2846 800/299-6054
Charles S. Mott Foundation	1200 Mott Foundation Building 503 S. Saginaw St.	Flint, MI 48502	www.mott.org	810/238-5651
Child Trends	4301 Connecticut Ave. NW, Suite 100	Washington, DC 20008	www.childtrends.org	202/362-5580
Children, Youth, and Family Consortium	University of Minnesota, McNamara Center, 270A, 200 Oak St. SE	Minneapolis, MN 55455	www.cyfc.umn.edu	612/625-7849
Children's Defense Fund	25 E St. NW	Washington, DC 20001	www.childrensdefense.org	202/628-8787

Organization	Address	City/State/Zip	Website/URL	Phone
Civic Practices Network	Center for Human Resources Brandeis University, 60 Turner St.	Waltham, MA 02154	www.cpn.org	617/736-4890
Close-up Foundation	44 Canal Center Plaza	Alexandria, VA 22314	www.closeup.org	800/256-7387
Coalition for Community Schools	Inst. for Educational Leadership 1001 Connecticut Ave. NW, Suite 310	Washington, DC 20036	www.communityschools.org	202/822-8405
Colorado Parent Information and Resource Center	1445 Market St., Suite 350	Denver, CO 80202	www.cpirc.org	303/820-5624
Comer School Development Program	55 College St.	New Haven, CT 06510	info.med.yale.edu/corner	203/737-1020
Communitarian Network	2130 H St. NW, Suite 703	Washington, DC 20052	www.gwu.edu/~ccps	202/994-7997
Communities in Schools	277 S. Washington St., Suite 210	Alexandria, VA 22314	www.cisnet.org	703/519-8999 800/247-4543
Community Education at Florida Atlantic University	FAU/COE, Bldg.47, Room 260 777 Glades Rd.	Boca Raton, FL 33431	www.leadership.fau.edu	561/297-3599
Community Leadership Association	200 S. Meridian St., Suite 250	Indianapolis, IN 46225	www.communityleadership.org	317/637-7408
Community Tool Box	University of Kansas Health & Community Development	Lawrence, KS 66045	ctb.lsi.ukans.edu	785/864-0533
Connect for Kids/ Benton Foundation	950 18th St. NW	Washington, DC 20006	www.connectforkids.org	202/638-5770
Corporation for National and Community Service	Learn and Service America 1201 New York Ave. NW	Washington, DC 20525	www.cns.gov	202/606-5000

Organization	Address	City/State/Zip	Website	Phone
David & Lucile Packard Foundation	300 Second St., Suite 200	Los Altos, CA 94022	www.packfound.org www.futureofchildren.org	650/948-7658
Do Something	423 West 55th St., 8th Floor	New York, NY 10019	www.dosomething.org	212/523-1175
Education Commission of the States	707 17th St., #2700	Denver, CO 80202	www.ecs.org	303/299-3600
Education Week	6935 Arlington Rd. Suite 100	Bethesda, MD 20814	www.edweek.org	301/280-3100 800/346-1834
Educational Development Center	55 Chapel St.	Newton, MA 02458	www.edc.org	617/969-7100
Energize, Inc. . . . Leaders of Volunteers	5450 Wissahickon Ave.	Philadelphia, PA 19144	www.energizeinc.com	215/438-8342
Families and Work Institute	267 Fifth Ave., 2th Floor	New York, NY 10016	www.familiesandwork.org	212/465-2044
Family and Advocates Partnership for Education	Pacer Center 8161 Normandale Blvd.	Minneapolis, MN 55437	www.fape.org	888/248-0822
Family Friendly Schools	13080 Brookmead Dr.	Manassas, VA 20112	www.familyfriendlyschools.org	800/658-6082
Family Support America	20 N. Wacker Dr., Suite 1100	Chicago, IL 60606	www.familysupportamerica.org	312/338-0900
First Day Foundation	PO Box 10	Bennington, VT 05201	www.firstday.org	802/447-9625
George Lucas Educational Foundation	Learn and Live PO Box 3494	San Rafael, CA 94912	www.glef.org	415/507-0399
Harvard Family Research Project	Longfellow Hall Appian Way	Cambridge, MA 02138	gseweb.harvard.edu/~hfrp/	617/495-9108
Home & School Institute	Mega Skills Education Ctr. 1500 Massachusetts Ave., NW	Washington, DC 20005	www.MegaSkillsHSI.org	202/466-3633
Innovation Center for Community and Youth Development	7100 Connecticut Ave.	Chevy Chase, MD 20915	www.theinnovationcenter.org	301/961-2837

Organization	Address	City/State/Zip	Website/URL	Phone
Institute for Educational Leadership	1001 Connecticut Ave. NW, Suite 310	Washington, DC 20036	www.iel.org	202/822-8405
Institute for Public Relations	University of Florida Box 118400	Gainesville, FL 32611	www.instituteforpr.com	352/392-0280
Institute for Responsive Education	Northeastern University 21 Lake Hall	Boston, MA 02115	www.responsiveeducation.org	617/373-2595
Kettering Foundation	200 Commons Road	Dayton, OH 45459	www.kettering.org	937/434-7300
League of Women Voters	1730 M St. NW, Suite 1000	Washington, DC 20036	www.lwv.org	202/429-1965
Learning First Alliance	1001 Connecticut Ave. NW, Suite 335	Washington, DC 20036	www.learningfirst.org	202/299-5220
Learning Network/ Family Education	20 Park Plaza, 12th Floor	Boston, MA 02116	www.learningnetwork.com	800/323-4776
National Association of Community Action Agencies	1100 17th St. NW, Suite 500	Washington, DC 20036	www.nacaa.org	202/265-7546
National Association for the Education of Young Children	1509 16th St. NW	Washington, DC 20036	www.naeyc.org	202/232-8777 800/424-2460
National Association of Elementary School Principals	1615 Duke St.	Alexandria, VA 22314	www.naesp.org	703/684-3345 800/386-2377
National Association of Partners in Education	901 North Pitt St., Suite 320	Alexandria, VA 22314	www.napehq.org	703/836-4880
National Association of Secondary School Principals	1904 Association Dr.	Reston, VA 20191	www.nassp.org	703/860-0200
National Center for Community Education	1017 Avon St.	Flint, MI 48503	www.nccenet.org	810/238-0463
National Center for Conflict Resolution Education	Illinois Bar Center 424 S. 2nd St.	Springfield, IL 62701	www.nccre.org	217/523-7056

Organization	Address	City, State ZIP	Website	Phone
National Center for Family Literacy	325 West Main St., Suite 200	Louisville, KY 40202	www.famlit.org	502/584-1133
National Center for Fathering	PO Box 413888	Kansas City, MO 64141	www.fathers.com	800/593-3237
National Center for Schools and Communities	Fordham University 33 W. 60th St., 8th Floor	New York, NY 10023		212/636-6617
National Center for Strategic Nonprofit Planning and Community Leadership	2000 L St. NW, Suite 815	Washington, DC 20036	www.npcl.org	202/822-6725
National Child Care Information Center	243 Church St. NW, 2nd Floor	Vienna, VA 22180	nccic.org	800/616-2242
National Civic League	1445 Market St., #300	Denver, CO 80202	www.ncl.org	303/571-4343
National Coalition for Parent Involvement in Education	3929 Old Lee Highway, Suite 91-A	Fairfax, VA 22030	www.ncpie.org	703/359-8973
National Community Building Network	1624 Franklin St. Suite 100	Oakland, CA 94612	www.ncbn.org	510/663-6226
National Community Education Association	3929 Old Lee Highway #91-A	Fairfax, VA 22030	www.ncea.com	703/359-8973
National Criminal Justice Reference Service	Box 6000 2277, Research Blvd.	Rockville, MD 20849	www.ncjrs.org	301/519-5063 800/851-3420
National Dropout Prevention Center	Clemson University 209 Martin St.	Clemson, SC 29631	www.dropoutprevention.org	864/656-2599
National Education Association	1201 16th St. NW	Washington, DC 20036	www.nea.org	202/833-4000
National Fatherhood Initiative	101 Lake Forest Blvd., Suite 360	Gaithersburg, MD 20877	www.fatherhood.org	301/948-0599
National Head Start Association	1651 Prince St.	Alexandria, VA 22314	www.nhsa.org	703/739-0875

Organization	Address	City/State/Zip	Website/URL Phone
National Information Center for Children and Youth with with Disabilities	Academy for Educational Development PO Box 1492	Washington, DC 20013	www.nichcy.org	800/695-0285 202/884-8200
National Institute on Out of School Time	Center for Research on Women Wellesley College 106 Central St.	Wellesley, MA 02181	www.niost.org	781/283-2547
National Mentoring Partnerships	1600 Duke St., Suite 300	Alexandria, VA 22314	www.mentoring.org	703/224-2200
National Middle School Association	4151 Executive Parkway Suite 300	Westerville, OH 43081	www.nmsa.org	800/528-6672
National Network for Collaboration	ND Univ Extension, 219 FLC PO Box 5016	Fargo, ND 58105	crs.uvm.edu/nnco	701/231-7253
National Network of Partnership Schools	3003 N. Charles St., Suite 200	Baltimore, MD 21218	scov.csos.jhu.edu/p2000	410/516-8800
National Parent Information Network	Teachers College Columbia University 525 W. 120th Street	New York, NY 10027	www.npin.org eric-web.t.c. columbia.edu	800/601-4868
ERIC				
National PTA	330 N. Wabash Ave., Suite 2100	Chicago, IL 60611	www.pta.org	312/670-6782
National Recreation & Park Association	22377 Belmont Ridge Rd.	Ashburn, VA 20148	www.nrpa.org	703/858-0784
National Resource Center for Youth Development	University of Oklahoma 4502 E. 41 St., Bldg. 4W	Tulsa, OK 74135	www.nrcys.ou.edu	918/660-3700
National School Boards	1680 Duke Street	Alexandria, VA 22314	www.nsba.org	703/838-6722

Organization	Address	City, State ZIP	Website	Phone
Association				
National School Public Relations Association	15948 Derwood Road	Rockville, MD 20855	www.nspra.org	301/519-0496
National School Safety Center	141 Duesenberg Dr., Suite 11	Westlake Village, CA 91362	www.nssc1.org	805/373-9977
National School-Age Care Alliance	1137 Washington St.	Boston, MA 02124	www.nsaca.org	617/298-5012
National Service Learning Clearinghouse	ETR Associates PO Box 1830	Santa Cruz, CA 95061	www.servicelearning.org	866/245-7378
National Study of School Evaluation	1699 E. Woodfield Rd. Suite 406	Schaumburg, IL 60173	www.nsse.org	847/995-9080
National Youth Leadership Council	1667 Snelling Ave., North	St. Paul, MN 55108	www.nylc.org	651/631-2955
National Youth Development Information Center	1319 F St., NW Suite 601	Washington, DC 20004	www.nydic.org	877/693-4248
National Urban League	120 Wall Street	New York, NY 10005	www.nul.org	212/558-5300
Parental Assistance Coordination Center	8601 Georgia Avenue Suite 601	Silver Springs, MD 20910	www.pacc-pirc.net	888/385-7222
Parent Institute	PO Box 7474	Fairfax Station, VA 22039	www.par-inst.com	703/323-9170
Parents for Public Schools	1520 North State St.	Jackson, MS 39202	www.parents4publicschools.com	800/880/1222
Parents as Teachers National Center	10176 Corporate Square Dr. Suite 230	St. Louis, MO 63132	www.patnc.org	314/432-4330
Partnership for Family Involvement in Education	400 Maryland Ave. SW	Washington, D.C. 20202	pfie.ed.gov	800/872-5327
Phi Delta Kappa International	408 N. Union St., PO Box 789	Bloomington, IN 47402	www.pdkintl.org	800/766-1156 812/339-1156
Public Agenda ONLINE	6 East 39th St.	New York, NY 10016	www.publicagenda.com	212/686-6610

Organization	Address	City/State/Zip	Website/URL	Phone
Public Education Network	601 13th St. NW	Washington, DC 20005	www.publiceducation.org	202/628-7460
Public Relations Society of America	33 Irving Place	New York, NY 10003	www.prsa.org	212/995-2230
Reading Is Fundamental	1825 Connecticut Ave., NW Suite 400	Washington, DC 20009	www.rif.org	800/590-0041
School-Age Notes	PO Box 40205	Nashville, TN 37204	www.schoolagenotes.com	615/279-0700
School Public Relations Journal	Scarecrow Press 15200 NBN Way	Blue Ridge Summit, PA 17214	www.scarecroweducation.com	800/273-2223
Search Institute	615 First Ave., NE, Suite 125	Minneapolis, MN 55413	www.search-institute.org	612/376-8955 800/888-7828
Study Circles Resource Center	697 Pomfret St., Box 203	Pomfret, CT 06258	www.studycircles.org	860/928-2616
Together We Can Initiative	Inst. for Educational Leadership 1001 Connecticut Ave. NW, Suite 310	Washington, DC 20036	www.togetherwecan.org	202/822-8405
U.S. Department of Education	400 Maryland Ave. SW	Washington, DC 20202	www.ed.gov	800/872-5327
Youth Service America	1101 15th St. NW, Suite 200	Washington, DC 20005	www.ysa.org	202/296-2992
Youth Today	1200 17th St. NW, 4th Floor	Washington, DC 20036	www.youthtoday.org	202/785-0764

Websites by Major Focus or Content Area

After-School/Child Care

Afterschool Alliance	www.afterschoolalliance.org
Afterschool.gov Federal Support to Communities	www.afterschool.gov
Center for the Improvement of Child Caring	www.ciccparenting.org
National Child Care Information Center	nccic.org
National Institute on Out of School Time	www.niost.org
National School-Age Care Alliance	www.nsaca.org
School-Age Notes	www.schoolagenotes.com

Community Development and Organizing

Asset-Based Community Development Institute	www.nwu.edu/IPR
Community Leadership Association	www.communityleadership.org
Community Tool Box	ctb.lsi.ukans.edu
National Association of Community Action Agencies	www.nacaa.org

National Center for Strategic
Nonprofit Planning and
    Community Leadership   www.npcl.org

National Community
    Building Network   www.ncbn.org

Community Education/Community Schools

Coalition for Community Schools   www.communityschools.org

Community Education at Florida   www.leadership.fau.edu/
    Atlantic University

National Center for
    Community Education   www.nccenet.org

National Community
    Education Association   www.ncea.com

Foundations

Annie E. Casey Foundation   www.aecf.org

Benton Foundation   www.benton.org

Carnegie Corporation
    of New York   www.carnegie.org

Charles S. Mott Foundation   www.mott.org

Close Up Foundation   www.closeup.org

Connect for Kids/Benton
    Foundation   www.connectforkids.org

David & Lucile Packard   www.packfound.org
    Foundation   www.futureofchildren.org

George Lucas Educational
    Foundation   www.glef.org

Kettering Foundation   www.kettering.org

National Associations

American Association of
    School Administrators   www.aasa.org

American Federation of Teachers	www.aft.org
Aspira Association	www.aspira.org
Association for Supervision & Curriculum Development	www.ascd.org
National Association for the Education of Young Children	www.naeyc.org
National Association of Elementary School Principals	www.naesp.org
National Association of Secondary School Principals	www.nassp.org
National Education Association	www.nea.org
National Middle School Association	www.nmsa.org
National Recreation & Park Association	www.nrpa.org
National School Boards Association	www.nsba.org

National Centers or Organizations

AARP Grandparent Information Center	www.aarp.org
American Institutes for Research	www.air-dc.org
Child Trends	www.childtrends.org
Children's Defense Fund	www.childrensdefense.org
Communitarian Network	www.gwu.edu/~ccps
Education Week	www.edweek.org
Education Commission of the States	www.ecs.org
Educational Development Center	www.edc.org
Educational Resource Information Center (ERIC)	www.askeric.org
Institute for Educational Leadership	www.iel.org

League of Women Voters	www.lwv.org
Learning First Alliance	www.learningfirst.org
National Center for Conflict Resolution Education	www.nccre.org
National Head Start Association	www.nhsa.org
National Information Center for Children and Youth with Disabilities	www.nichcy.org
National Study of School Evaluation	www.nsse.org
National Urban League	www.nul.org
Phi Delta Kappa International	www.pdkintl.org
Public Education Network	www.publiceducation.org
Public Agenda ONLINE	www.publicagenda.com
Reading Is Fundamental	www.rif.org
Study Circles Resource Center	www.studycircles.org

Parent/Family Involvement

Alliance for Parental Involvement in Education	www.croton.com/allpie
Center for Law and Education	www.cleweb.org
Colorado Parent Information and Resource Center	www.cpirc.org
Family Friendly Schools	www.familyfriendlyschools.org
First Day Foundation	www.firstday.org
Home & School Institute	www.MegaSkillsHSI.org
Institute for Responsive Education	www.responsiveeducation.org
National Center for Fathering	www.fathers.com
National Coalition for Parent Involvement in Education	www.ncpie.org
National Fatherhood Initiative	www.fatherhood.org
National Parent Information Network ERIC	www.npin.org

National PTA   www.pta.org

Parent Institute   www.par-inst.com

Parental Assistance
   Coordination Center   www.pacc-pirc.net

Parents as Teachers
   National Center   www.patnc.org

Parents for Public Schools   www.parents4publicschools.com

Partnerships and Collaboration

Center for Effective Collaborative
   and Practice   www.air-dc.org/cecp

Communities in Schools   www.cisnet.org

Families and Advocates
   Partnership for Education www.fape.org

National Association of
   Partnership in Education   www.napehq.org

National Network
   for Collaboration   crs.uvm.edu/nnco

National Network of
   Partnership Schools   scov.csos.jhu.edu/p2000

Partnership for Family
   Involvement in Education   pfie.ed.gov

Together We Can Initiative   www.togetherwecan.org

Public Relations and Communications

A-Plus Communications   www.aplusworld.com

Institute for Public Relations   www.instituteforpr.com

National School Public
   Relations Association   www.nspra.org

Public Relations Society
   of America   www.prsa.org

School Public Relations Journal www.scarecroweducation.com

School Safety and Crisis Management

Center for the Prevention of
    School Violence   www.ncsu.edu/cpsv

National Criminal Justice
    Reference Service   www.ncjrs.org

National School Safety Center   www.nssc1.org

School Reform

Annenberg Institute for
    School Reform   www.annenberginstitute.org

Center for Education Reform   www.edreform.com

Comer School Development
    Program   info.med.yale.edu/comer

School of the 21st Century   www.yale.edu/bushcenter/21C

Service Learning and Citizenship

Center for Civic Education   www.civiced.org

Center for Democracy
    & Citizenship   www.publicwork.org

Civic Practices Network   www.cpn.org

Corporation for National
    and Community Service   www.cns.gov

National Civic League   www.ncl.org

National Dropout
    Prevention Center   www.dropoutprevention.org

National Service
    Learning Clearinghouse   www.servicelearning.org

National Youth Leadership
    Council   www.nylc.org

Youth Service America   www.ysa.org

Volunteers

Association for Volunteer Administration	www.avaintl.org
Energize, Inc . . . Leaders of Volunteers	www.energizeinc.com
National Mentoring Partnership	www.mentoring.org
Youth Serve America	www.servenet.org

Youth/Family Organizations

America's Promise	www.americaspromise.org
Children, Youth, and Family Consortium	www.cyfc.umn.edu
Communities in Schools	www.cisnet.org
Do Something	www.dosomething.org
Families and Work Institute	www.familiesandwork.org
Family Support America	www.familysupportamerica.org
Harvard Family Research Project	gseweb.harvard.edu/~hfrp/
Innovation Center for Community and Youth Development	www.theinnovationcenter.org
Learning Network/Family Education	www.learningnetwork.com
National Center for Family Literacy	www.famlit.org
National Resource Center for Youth Development	www.nrcys.ou.edu
National Youth Development Information Center	www.nydic.org
Search Institute	www.search-institute.org
Youth Today	www.youthtoday.org

Index

AASA. *See* American Association of School Administrators

advisory committees and task forces, 127–129, 200

after-school program(s), 47, 115, 124–127

American Association of School Administrators (AASA), 36, 53, 55, 133, 147, 165

America's Promise, 33–35, 138

Annenberg Institute for School Reform, 107, 258

Annie E. Casey Foundation, 20–22, 24, 30, 42

Ascher, C., Fruchter, N.; & Berne R., 196

Bagin, D., 154

Bagin, D., Gallagher, D., and Kindred, I., 155

Bamber, C., Berla, N., & Henderson, A. T., 247

Barton, P. E., 258–259

Belenardo, S. J., 11

Benson, P. L., & Walker, G., 134

Berg, J. H., & Hall, G. E., 181

Blank, M. A., & Kershaw, C., 108

Blank, M. J., & Langford, B. H., 246

Bolman, L. G., & Deal, T. E., 195–196

Broder, D. S., 132

Bruner, C., 139

Carnegie Foundation, 19, 24, 36, 48

Carroll, S. R., & Carroll, D., 156, 158–159

CDF. *See* Children's Defense Fund

Center for Effective Collaboration and Practice, 210, 216

Center for Law and Education, 77, 107

Center for Leadership Studies, 188

Center for the Prevention of School Violence, 207, 212–213, 220

Charles Stewart Mott Foundation, 46–47, 115

Children's Aid Society, 125, 127

Children's Defense Fund (CDF), 19–20, 24

citizen politics. *See* politics

Clinton, W. J., 45, 181

Coalition for Community Schools, 246

Cohen, R., 222–223
collaborative leadership, 109–112, 256; qualities and skills of collaborative leaders, 109–111
collaborative relationships: barriers to developing, 117–118; characteristics of effective/ successful, 115–116, 256–257; establishing/developing, 112–113, 116–117, 139–140; factors increasing chances for success, 113–115
communication: barriers to, 153; components of, 152; skills and processes, 200–201; strategies related to, 6, 59–60, 70, 114, 235. *See also* technology; electronic communication; and marketing communications
communications audit, 242–243
community: building a sense of community in school, 11–12; definition of, 9–11; healthy communities, 13–15; reconceptualizing the role of schools in relation to, 36–40, 49
community building, 28–32, 40, 240
community education, 40–42
community engagement, vii, 109, 141, 255. *See also* family involvement
Community of Promise, 34
community organizing, 187. *See also* grassroots activism
community politics. *See* politics
community power structure, 182, 189, 194–195, 203
community school, 40, 42–43
conflict: dealing with criticism, 201–203; sources of conflict, 196–197;

conflict prevention/resolution: conflict resolution education, 220–223; finding common ground, 198–200; school-based peer mediation, 222–223; school and community working together, 223–224
continuum of parent and community involvement partnerships, 120–121
Cortes, E., Jr., 182–183, 198
crisis management, plan for 218–220

Davies, D., 102, 104
Decker, L. E., & Associates, 124
Decker L. E., & Decker, V. A., 15, 128
demographics and socioeconomic variables, 12, 15–17; *Kids Count* findings, 20–24; status of children and families, 17–20
Dietz, M. J., 247
Donlevy, J. G., Hilliard, A., & Donley, T. R., 172
Dryfoos, J. G., 40, 44
Duskin, M. S., 255
Dwyer, M. D., 3, 10–11, 13, 224

education reform, 27, 53, 105, 256, 258
Education Week, 48, 55, 141
Elementary and Secondary Education Act, vi, 54
Epstein, J. L., 58–59, 88, 104
evaluation: need for documentation, 249; outcomes and accountability, 238–242; outcomes (results) orientation, 235, 237–239; techniques and tools of, 242–247;

theory-based vs. traditional, 237–238
external public, 150, 156

family involvement: barriers to, 79–80, 255–256; overcoming barriers, 80–87; benefits of, 55–58; involving the hard-to-reach, 83–87; models for, 58, 63–66; preparing educators for, 87–93; Title I provisions for, 77–79. *See also* National PTA Standards for Parent/Family Involvement Programs
family resource centers, 76–77
Fashola, O. S., 126
Finders, M., & Lewis, C., 80
Flaxman, E., 44
Flaxman, E., Schwartz, W., Weiler, J., & Lahey M., 256
full-service schools, 44–45, 138–139
Funkhouser, J. E., & Gonzales, M. R., 68–69, 80, 83

Gardner, S., 239–241
Giles, H. C., 108, 112
Gitomer, D. H., 259
Gottfredson, D. C., 223
grassroots activism, 103, 105–107. *See also* community organizing

Harkavy, I., & Blank, M., v–vi, 42, 54
Hart, J. K., 99
Harvard Family Research Project, 68, 87–88, 93, 106, 161
Haugen, J., 83
Henderson, A. T., & Berla, N., 56, 67
Hersey, P., & Natemeyer, W. E., 188

Hiemstra. R., 195, 199
Hodgkinson, H., 16
home, school, and community partnerships: characteristics of successful partnerships, 69–70, 247–248, 256–257; creating successful partnerships, 102–105; framework for comprehensive plan, 4–6, 235–237; goals of, 122; implementation of policies for, 72–73; policies for, 71–72, 192–194
home visits, 75–76
Houston, D., 36, 53
Houston, P., and Bryant, A., 176

IBM, 170
Inger, M., 83–84, 123
Institute for Public Relations, 172
internal public, 154–155, 157
issues and trends affecting education and schools, v, 15–17, 35, 127, 196–198, 208, 228, 258–260
issues management, 208

Katzenbach, J. R., & Smith, D. K., 111
Keedy, J. L., & Björk, L. G., 181, 183, 196–197
Kettering Foundation, 14, 27–28, 185
key communicators, 168–170
Kids Count, 20–23, 86
Kingsley, G. T., McNeely, J. B., & Gibson, J. O., 30
Kowalski, T. J., & Wiedmer, T., 176
Kretzmann, J. P., & McKnight, J. L., 28–29

League of Women Voters survey, 140, 255, 257

Ledell, M., 200

Ledell, M., & Arnsparger, A., 202

Lindblom, C. D., 190

Litrenta, L. E., 176

Lyday, W. J., Winecoff, H. L., & Hiott, B. C., 135

Manning, M. L., & Baruth, L. G., 84

marketing communications, 158–160

Marx, G., 201–202

Martinson, D., 150

Mathews, D., 14, 28

Mattessich, P. W., & Monsey, B. R., 113

Meek, A., 251

Melaville, A., 122

Melaville, A., & Blank, M., 118

Millennium Communications Group, 200

Moles, O. D., & D'Angelo. D., 58

Moore, L., 68

Mullen, M., 165

Murphy, J., 181

NAESP. *See* National Association of Elementary Schools Principals

NAPE. *See* National Association of Partners in Education

National Assembly of Health and Human Service Organizations, 115

National Association of Elementary Schools Principals (NAESP), 108, 124–125, 127

National Association of Partners in Education (NAPE), 116

National Center for Education Statistics, 85–86, 137

National Center for Fair and Open Testing, 54

National Coalition for Parent Involvement in Education (NCPIE), 59, 71–72, 187, 192, 235

National Commission on Service-Learning, 137–138

National Committee for Citizens in Education, 107, 243

National Criminal Justice Reference Service, 207

National Education Association, 132–133, 177

National Opinion Research Center, 99

National PTA, 59, 73, 133, 177, 224

National PTA Standards for Parent/Family Involvement Programs, 59–63, 101

National School Public Relations Association (NSPRA), 150–151, 154, 174, 217–218, 242

National School-to-Work Learning Center, 131

National Standards for Parent/Family Involvement Programs, 59–63, 101–102

National Youth Leadership Council, 134

NCPIE. *See* National Coalition for Parent Involvement in Education

Neff, M., 10

Network for Good, 122

news media, working with, 164–168

Nicoll, W. G., 76, 86

No Child Left Behind Act, v, 47, 54, 240

Norton, M. S., 154
NSPRA. *See* National School Public
    Relations Association

Opalewski, D., & Robertson, J. C.,
    219
Ordovensky, P., & Marx, G.,
    165–166, 168
outside-inside marketing, 158. *See
    also* school image

Paine, C., & Sprague, J., 218
Parent Institute, 171
parent-teacher conferences, 73–75
parenting styles in relation to school
    success, 76–77
Parson, S. R., 113, 140
partnership continuum, 118–119
Partnership for Family Involvement
    in Education, 47, 93, 106
Phi Delta Kappa, 79, 154, 177
Phi Delta Kappa/Gallup Poll, 55,
    100, 148, 164
planning: basic steps of, 232–235;
    community planning, 228, 231;
    comprehensive planning, 228,
    231; internal systems planning,
    228, 231; related to
    environmental scanning, 229–
    230; strategic planning, 228–231
policymaking, in a political
    context,189–190
political subcultures and interest
    groups, 190–192,198
politics: and academic success,
    203–204; in education, 181–183;
    citizen politics, 183–185;
    community politics, 185–186; in
    social marketing, 160–162. *See
    also* community

organizing; and grassroots
    activism
power, types of, 188–189. *See also*
    community power structure
principals'/school administrators'
    role: in politics, 181–182; in
    public relations, 155; in working
    with the community, 107–109;
    needed political skills for,
    195–196; suggested changes to
    engage in cooperative
    relationships, 3
principles for corporate involvement,
    133–134
Project Public Life, 183, 185
public confidence in schools,154,
    164–165
Public Education Network, 141
public relations. *See* school public
    relations
Purkey, W. W., & Stanley, P. H., 254

Regional Educational Laboratory
    Network, 7
Reno, J., 221
Rich, D., 252
Riley, P. L., 209, 213
Romney, V. 229
Rotenberg, R. L., 14

Sarason, S. B., 79–80
school business partnerships,
    129–134. *See also* principles for
    corporate involvement
school image 156–158, 227. *See also*
    outside-inside marketing
School of Promise, 34–35
school public relations: definition of,
    149–150; developing a
    comprehensive program for, 155,

173–174; need for, 151; staffing for, 174–176; tools of. *See* key communicators; marketing communications; news media; social marketing; and technology

school safety: and discipline, 216; and tolerance, 217–218; characteristics of safe school, 208–212, 214,–215; planned response to crisis, 218–220; planning for, 212–213; scope of school crime and violence, 208–210, 220–221

Schorr, L. B., vi, 227, 237–239, 247–248

Search Institute, 32–33

Sensiper, S., 161

service learning, 134–138

social marketing, 160–164

Stahl, L., vii

Stehle, V., 123

Stephens, R. D. 208.

Swap, S. M., 58, 63, 67, 70

TALK systems. *See* technology, audio

technology: audio, 171–172; electronic communication, 170, 172–173; machine translation, 170–171

testing, emphasis on, vii, 54–55, 100, 187, 258, 260; and standards-based reform, 258–259

Timberman, L., 130

Timpane, P. M., 36, 48, 107

Twenty-first (21st) Century Community Learning Centers, 42, 45–48, 138

U.S. Department of Education, 7, 45–48, 69, 86, 106, 127, 132, 208; Office of Educational Research and Improvement, 46, 69; Office of Special Education Programs; 93;

Office of Vocational and Adult Education, 131

U.S. Department of Health and Human Services, 86

U.S. Department of Housing and Urban Development, 30

U.S. Department of Justice, 47, 208

volunteer programs, 122–124

Vondra, J., 198

Wang, M. C., 249

Warner, C., 247

Wegner, D., and Jarvi, C. K., 228, 230

Weinreich, N. K., 160–162

Wherry, J. H. , 58

WhiteClark, R., and Decker, L. E., 83, 86

Withrow, F., 112

Yantis, J., 154–155

About the Authors

Larry E. Decker is the Charles Stewart Mott Professor, an Eminent Scholar Chair in Community Education, at Florida Atlantic University, Boca Raton. Formerly, he was director of the Mid-Atlantic Center for Community Education, professor of educational leadership, and associate dean at the Curry School of Education, University of Virginia. He earned his Ph.D. at Michigan State University. A leading spokesperson for the community education/community school movement, he is the author of numerous publications that address educational reform and strengthening the collaboration of home, school, and community for educational success.

Virginia A. Decker is managing editor of Community Collaborators, Boca Raton, Florida. Formerly, she was the facilitator of the National Community Education Computer Network, an international teleconferencing system, a research assistant with the Bureau of Business and Economic Research at the University of Oregon, and an instructor at Lane Community College in Eugene, Oregon. She earned her MBA from the University of Oregon. She has coauthored a number of publications on grant seeking, family and community involvement, and educational planning and reform.

Breinigsville, PA USA
11 August 2010
243386BV00001B/7/P